CW01240224

The Honesty Box

The Honesty Box

The diary of a broken marriage,
a mental health crisis and a large marrow

LUCY BRAZIER

BLOOMSBURY PUBLISHING
LONDON · OXFORD · NEW YORK · NEW DELHI · SYDNEY

BLOOMSBURY PUBLISHING
Bloomsbury Publishing Plc
50 Bedford Square, London, WC1B 3DP, UK
Bloomsbury Publishing Ireland Limited,
29 Earlsfort Terrace, Dublin 2, Ireland

BLOOMSBURY, BLOOMSBURY PUBLISHING and the Diana logo are trademarks of Bloomsbury Publishing Plc

First published in Great Britain 2025

Copyright © Lucy Brazier, 2025

Lucy Brazier is identified as the author of this work in accordance with the Copyright, Designs and Patents Act 1988

Some names have been changed and small liberties taken with inconsequential elements of the timeline.

All rights reserved. No part of this publication may be: i) reproduced or transmitted in any form, electronic or mechanical, including photocopying, recording or by means of any information storage or retrieval system without prior permission in writing from the publishers; or ii) used or reproduced in any way for the training, development or operation of artificial intelligence (AI) technologies, including generative AI technologies. The rights holders expressly reserve this publication from the text and data mining exception as per Article 4(3) of the Digital Single Market Directive (EU) 2019/790

Bloomsbury Publishing Plc does not have any control over, or responsibility for, any third-party websites referred to in this book. All internet addresses given in this book were correct at the time of going to press. The author and publisher regret any inconvenience caused if addresses have changed or sites have ceased to exist, but can accept no responsibility for any such changes

A catalogue record for this book is available from the British Library

ISBN: HB: 978-1-5266-7295-7; eBook: 978-1-5266-7296-4; ePDF: 978-1-5266-7301-5

2 4 6 8 10 9 7 5 3 1

Typeset by Newgen KnowledgeWorks Pvt. Ltd., Chennai, India
Printed and bound in Great Britain by CPI Group (UK) Ltd, Croydon CR0 4YY

MIX
Paper | Supporting
responsible forestry
FSC® C171272

To find out more about our authors and books visit www.bloomsbury.com and sign up for our newsletters.

For product safety related questions contact productsafety@bloomsbury.com

To Rafferty, Hebe and Jesse, always

PROLOGUE

It is the week before Christmas. I am way behind on everything I was hoping to have done by now and it is almost too late. Most of my work emails elicit festive out-of-office responses, and last-minute gifts I look at online are promising delivery in January. The schools have just broken up, which means three teenagers at home, roaming the kitchen in search of food, so I put unmissable yellow Post-it notes on packets of biscuits in the larder and cheese in the fridge that scream 'NOT FOR NOW!'

I do love Christmas. I have even written books about it, although that doesn't mean I am an expert. I just hold an indefatigable and genuine child-like awe for the spirit of the season. People tell me that this is unusual at my age. They gravitate towards me in the hope that it will rub off on them, but it isn't infectious. If it was, my husband, Steve, would be full of festive joy too and he isn't. He hates Christmas. As he tells everyone.

The last twenty or so Decembers since we have been together have looked the same. As I feel the excitement grow, and watch the wonder and delight on our children's faces, Steve slips deeper and deeper out of reach into a murky melancholy. This isn't the only time of year it happens – he has been dealing with depression throughout his adult life – but it feels so much worse against the backdrop of sparkling fairy lights, incessant festive tunes and a million gurning Santas. He brushes his teeth like normal, he makes the children's packed lunches like normal and he goes to work like normal. Yet his taut thread of reality continually vibrates, like a fly hitting a spider's web. His insides are chewing at him. While others around him may sense it but say nothing, I am enveloped by it. It threatens to scorch the joy out of my celebratory mood.

Each year I hope it will be different, as the children grow up, as we find a structure to the holiday that he can cope with and as we do less socially. I had the idea of giving him jobs to distract him from the heavy weight of his mood. Make the mincemeat! Wrap the presents! Come up with a new trifle recipe! Hand-decorate Christmas cards! He takes each one on with the intensity and respect of someone who has been tasked to build Big Ben out of matchsticks or restructure the NHS. As he buries himself further in every assignment, my frustration builds and so does my list of chores, which I move through faster and faster, always disappearing through a door or up the steep stairs holding a basket of laundry while on an eternal hunt for the Sellotape.

What Steve produces is always beautiful, delicious and a tiny work of triumph. I am envious of his creative ability and how he finds solace in these single-minded endeavours. If only I could spend time focusing on one thing, I think. If only I wasn't rushing around having to do so much to compensate for his painstaking perfectionism, I say to myself, I could have created something lovely too. But this isn't true. My middle name is 'slapdash', and my superpower is to multi-task. If I think a job is worth doing… I give it to Steve.

PROLOGUE

On this particular evening, we are getting ready to go to an annual Christmas party thrown by people we know. Acquaintances sounds too formal, but they aren't friends either. It has been looming: a hurdle I am supposed to jump in full make-up, fashionable clothes and undetectable Botox. I don't do any of those things. I only wear lipstick for work meetings, my dress sense was sartorially cool twenty-five years ago, and I am bemused by the rise in 'tweakments'. I try not to judge, even though a small voice inside me squeaks 'Whatever happened to the sisterhood?!' but maybe I am the fool because I look ten years older than those ten years older than me.

I stand in front of the mirror, the bed piled high with potential outfits I have discarded. This is part of the routine before every social event we go to, as is the rising panic I feel about how Steve will behave. He finds them impossible to navigate unless we are with close friends. Recently, I have thought we should stop going to things together because I can't cope with the knot in my stomach. I am not a helicopter mother so how have I become a helicopter wife? Besides, I am bone-tired. Maybe this is a low-level flu bug, and I should have an early night.

'I think I've got a low-level flu bug. Perhaps we shouldn't go out?' I look at Steve across the room as he buttons his shirt. He doesn't respond. 'Also, I've put on weight. Nothing fits. I look ridiculous and my hair's frizzy. I'm a walking advert for menopausal women everywhere.'

He looks up. 'I think you're beautiful,' he says, and he means it.

PROLOGUE

Most of the party is happening in the cavernous hallway of the house. Our consummate hosts live in an imposing, stately place with a grand front door, adorned with a fat wreath of foraged hedgerow and pheasant feathers, leading into a galleried hall with a blazing open fire. Everything is festively generous, from the platters of oysters to the champagne glasses being constantly refilled. Towering foliage arrangements flank the sweeping staircase, and a hand-carved wooden nativity scene plays out on top of the grand piano. The heightened atmosphere reminds me of theatre press nights in my previous career as a talent agent, when I had to keep my wits about me, ready to work the room or rescue a client from an awkward situation.

Steve has been offered a glass of red wine by our host, which he accepts until he sees the label.

'Oh, I don't like Rioja. Have you got anything else?' he asks.

I cringe at what I perceive as bad manners.

Our host smiles benignly in front of a table stacked with many bottles of the same wine. 'What do you like, then?' he asks, unruffled and charming, and I imagine him mentally crossing us off next year's invitation list.

'I really like Burgundy,' Steve says.

Our host disappears while I tell Steve there is a nicer, politer way to say the same thing. Or just to take the bloody wine that is offered.

He is nonplussed. 'But I don't like it, so why would I drink it? I can only have one drink because I am driving, so I want it to be what I want.'

He looks at me as if I am the one with the issue. He is only ever himself in these situations, which means bald honesty, whereas I am a pathological people-pleaser, who will resort to social fibbery for fear of upsetting anyone. It is too late to debate, because our host has returned with what is clearly a very expensive bottle of Burgundy.

'Oh, that's more like it,' Steve says happily, and I move away.

I skirt around a group of men who converse through the tedious medium of sexual innuendo, avoid the judgemental 'mean girl' gang and find myself wedged into a conversation with a few women I like but don't know very well. They are reminiscing about their school days, one after the other telling funny stories about pony clubs, clinging to parents' legs as they are abandoned for a new term and abseiling out of windows after dark to dig out cigarette packets hidden in plant pots. I realise they all went to boarding school and that I have nothing to add to this conversation.

Please, God, let nobody ask me.

'So where did you board, Lucy?' one of them turns to me.

I am tempted to lie, to avoid the awkwardness that is about to descend, but there is no easy escape from this question. 'Me? I didn't board. I went to a massive state comprehensive on the outskirts of London. But I read a lot of Enid Blyton and was desperate for a tuck box with my initials on it.'

I mean that sincerely, but it sounds defensive, maybe even sarcastic. They laugh politely and then someone changes the subject. I sidle off in search of Steve.

I can see him standing in the far corner talking to someone. Or at them. I can't tell whether he is stuck in the chat, or the other person is. Maybe I need to save them both. In socially stressful situations, Steve can have two settings – silent or constant – and little awareness of how to manage either. Once he has fixated on a subject, he is off, revelling in a bit of random info-dumping with mixed results. I know some people avoid him. I imagine their heart sinks if they are sat next to him at dinner. He gave up big drinking a long time ago because that just made things worse, making him loud, belligerent and prone to getting into pointless arguments. Alcohol and drugs do not agree with him.

Before each social event, I give him a little pep talk, even though I tell myself not to. I can't fight the terrible urge to issue helpful instruction. 'Just remember, when you've been talking about something for a bit, pause and then swing the question around to the other person,' I say in a sing-songy 'it couldn't be easier' tone. How have I become this controlling?

He always seems exasperated. 'That's the problem, I don't know how to pause. My brain doesn't seem to compute things in the way yours does.'

I think, but don't say, that maybe he should just try a bit harder.

Tonight, I don't get to Steve because someone has thrust a wooden board of canapes at me. It is a local chef I know who has been hired to cater for the evening. He pushes the wobbly stacks of oily bruschetta into my face, so I take one to avoid wearing it in my hair. He has the pallor of sweaty cheese. His jaw moves as if he is trying to dislocate it, and his dilated pupils sparkle with the reflection of the candles. For a moment, I am worried he is going to pass out and I wonder if I will try to catch him or just watch him topple into other guests. He starts to talk, and I am not sure if he is speaking gibberish or if I am suddenly very drunk, so I chew and nod thoughtfully.

A woman interrupts us and tells me she heard I used to be a theatrical agent and how her teenage daughter wants to be an actress.

'Her godfather promised to get her an agent for her thirteenth birthday, but it didn't happen so I was wondering if you could get her one?' She looks at me hopefully.

It is during moments like these when I wish I had never mentioned my past life.

'It doesn't really work like that.' I try to sound kind. 'You can't just get someone an agent...'

I begin to explain how it does work, but it is not what she wants to hear so the people-pleaser in me suggests her daughter meets a casting director pal of mine who is often looking for good child actors. I am instantly cross with myself for doing this.

By now I am standing close to the fire and feel faint from the heat, the too-tight, black velvet blazer I found in a charity shop that has begun to give off a whiff of mothballs, and the effort of polite conversation with strangers. I need to find a quick way to cool down, so I escape outside. Parked in the drive is an old Land Rover – not the farming type, but the sort that effortlessly implies wealth with its tweed upholstery and leather piping – and I lie over the bonnet, resting my cheek in relief on the cold, unforgiving metal.

I know I should go back in to find Steve, but I can't face it so instead I text him and hope the phone vibrates in his pocket. I suddenly miss him. A few minutes later, he comes out and helps me off the car.

'I used to like parties,' I say sadly, and he squeezes my hand.

'Well, you won't have to go to this one again.' He smiles, ruefully. 'Everyone in there probably thinks I'm a dick – they couldn't get away from me fast enough. And if you feel I was rude about his Rioja, then we won't be invited back anyway.'

*

I don't know if it is the effort of the party or the proximity of the date to actual Christmas that triggers a slippery decline in Steve, but it is more rapid than usual. He hugs the corners of rooms, scowling and unapproachable. I can't get close to him to help, so instead I put all my efforts into distracting the children from their father. They know, I know they know, but none of us talk very much about it because there isn't much to say. They have grown up with this and don't take it to heart as they wait patiently for him to resurface.

I cry on the twenty-third of December every year. This is a bit of a family tradition. My dad's mother used to do the same when he was small, and she had just worked a long Christmas shift at a fancy Knightsbridge florist. I don't cry very often. I think I would be happier if I could cry more, but I can't. Unless I am rewatching the film *Truly, Madly, Deeply* and get to the part where the ghost of Alan Rickman recites Pablo Neruda's poem in Spanish to Juliet Stevenson, who then translates it back in English. It gets me every single time.

I am overwhelmed with the amount of effort it has taken to get everything ready, and I still have to pack Christmas into a car and drive it over to my brother Rob's house. Mostly, I am up to here with a husband who has now gone from monosyllabic to raging. At some point before we leave the house, I throw myself on the bed and have a little sob, as is customary, and nobody mentions it.

We arrive at Rob and my sister-in-law Ali's warm, loving and festively inviting house in a state of tension that combines relief, excitement and the darkening clouds of Storm Steve, as his December mood reaches its conclusion. Usually, within the hour, but with enough time for me to have downed my first gin, Steve will blow and have a shout about something seemingly trivial. One, or several of us, will pull him up on his behaviour. It is the culmination of weeks of jangling nerves, and I am sorry that we bring this to Rob and Ali's home, but they always make room for it. We are held up by them and their almost grown-up kids, Jacob, Emilia and Kitty, who my three adore – less like cousins and more like six siblings when they are together.

Steve is also reassured by their unconditional love for him, and sinks into it. He opens their fridge to find his favourite brand of oat milk, tucks into packets of ready salted crisps (the only ones he eats), drinks the alcohol-free beer he likes and slices through a big bowl of lemons for his morning drink ritual. What he isn't aware of is that every year, when Rob books the Italian restaurant for Christmas Eve, Rob asks them if they would make mushroom risotto, a dish that has been off the menu for several years now but is one of Steve's soothing touchstones. He doesn't know that they make it specially for him.

Steve always rallies just in time for Christmas Day. At the point where the rest of us start to lose patience, he appears to step back into himself (or out of himself) and becomes the life and soul until the final notes of 'Auld Lang Syne' fade away and he faces desolate January.

For someone so curious and inspired by the world around him, I wonder how he can often be so intent on hiding from it. This cycle of behaviour is exhausting for Steve, but it is not just happening to him. It is impacting me on a regular basis and, as much as we try to protect them from it, it must be affecting our kids too. It is like being on a slow-moving rollercoaster surrounded by dull scenery, unsurprised as we painfully trundle to the lows, and mistrustful as we climb to the highs.

When we first got together, I was seduced by Steve's humour and intelligence, his sensitivity and big heart, with occasional foreboding glimpses of something jagged. I knew he was complicated and I wasn't, so this felt like a good match. Then followed the whirlwind years of babies, relocation and career changes, which morphed into money worries, tiredness and lack of fun, the easy breezy times being gnawed at until we were left clinging to each other on a tiny patch of solid ground.

I am still here in this relationship, but for how much longer? I can't imagine going through another year together like the one we have just had. I have been stuck in the miserable rut of Steve's mental health – but I can escape, he can't. I used to not want to leave him behind. Now, I feel as if I am about to be entombed in his pyramid, and the thought occurs to me that I should run for my life.

January

The time for old knits and porridge. A month with a terrible reputation. The moment when everything you put off in December turns up to heckle you. I usually welcome the bleak midwinter after the jazz-hands production of Christmas, but this time around it is harder to love these days wrapped in darkness and frugality. It is an effort to heave myself out with the dog, into the drabness of it all, so the recent discovery of a track from the end of the village across the fields revitalises my early-morning walk.

Margot, our golden retriever, trots ahead past a skeletal crab-apple tree still clinging to its mummified fruits and the cheering blossom of winter honeysuckle, which I stick my nose in for a hit of intense fragrance. We splash through vast puddles, fracturing the reflection of the gunmetal sky, and squelch across the waterlogged fields.

One of my village neighbours, Keith, is out on his quad bike, the wheels skidding along the track, churning the sludge of soil and fallen leaves. He is whistling for Darren, his exuberant Irish setter, who runs up to me and jumps, landing two substantial paws in a high five on my chest, before lovingly nose-bumping me and bounding away again. I wipe dog saliva off my glasses and ignore the mud-smeared paw prints on my coat.

When I am furthest away from the house, I realise there is a hole in my welly and I limp all the way home with a soggy sock and a dog who has rolled in the gagging stink of fox poo. So far, so January.

I have given up on New Year's resolutions – or 'intentions' as they like to be known these days – because God forbid there should be any pressure to commit. I have tried all the traditional pledges in the past, such as Dry January (I tend to postpone this to February as it is a shorter month), Veganuary (I did this once, but everyone near me hated me almost as much as I hated myself), Couch to 5K (don't ask), a household screen amnesty (I am the worst offender) and the earnest vow to be in the moment (I keep forgetting). Nothing sticks. So this year, I am going to take a slightly different approach and add something rather than abstain. I am setting up an honesty box outside my garden gate.

The honesty box is both a national treasure and a global movement. I have always had a thing about them, and my obsession was further fuelled when we left London and moved to Dorset seventeen years ago. These tiny beacons of trust, selling home-grown and handmade produce, stand as proud signposts of an abundant garden and productive kitchen. Each honesty box shines brighter against the backdrop of a deepening cost-of-living crisis and an untethered world, governed by some with questionable moral compasses. Of course, these simple transaction stores won't solve any of the big issues, but they are powerful symbols of a generous, hopeful humanity and could be a way of making the smallest difference, one marrow at a time. I know my honesty box won't save the world, but it may just save my sanity and possibly my marriage. For now, at least.

JANUARY

Setting up my own honesty box had been Steve's idea. We were on Dartmoor for a family walk the previous September. I had blackmailed Raff (eldest and enjoys the position), Hebe (middle child, only girl, curator of the messiest bedroom) and Jesse (youngest, most mature) with a rucksack of sausage rolls, Thermos flasks and a cross-my-heart promise of a tearoom, but they were still wary after the time a four-mile stroll turned into an eight-mile hike through a bog.

Initial harrumphing was replaced with early autumn light filtering through the beech trees, whooping on fraying rope swings, foolhardy river games and hot-chocolate moustaches. Margot, the dog, was in muddy ecstasy. Steve refused to use the OS app on his phone and spent much of the time wrestling with a paper map while simultaneously saying he didn't really need it because he had a natural sense of direction. This meant accidental and long-winded diversions down narrow lanes, through tiny villages and past sprawling farms.

I stopped at every honesty box we found. There were always eggs. I picked a dozen from a stack on a garden wall, where the seller had drawn little hens and ducks on the boxes to illustrate which eggs were which. Then I bought rosy windfall apples from the large wicker basket perched on a chair by a front gate. There were two signs. One in childish scrawl tied to the handle read: *10p each. Ella's poket mony fund.* On the other, chalked on a blackboard propped against the chair leg, was written: *Thieves, please don't steal 2 little girls pocket money! Thanks.*

I overpaid, and poked apples into every corner of my rucksack.

In the next village, there was an old bookcase propped against a wall, unsteady with homemade preserves, indicating an enviable harvest of summer berries and a glut in the veg patch. After much deliberation, I popped a jar of blackcurrant jam in one pocket and a spicy runner bean pickle in the other, as there was no room left in my rucksack and I was worried about the eggs surviving a slip-slide down the steep hill.

Then we came across the ramshackle barn housing the unmanned second-hand bookshop in aid of the Air Ambulance. I moved the apples into the children's hoods in preparation.

When we eventually arrived back at the village where we had parked the car, the tearoom was full, apart from a table in the corner. We squeezed around it and waited impatiently for the nice lady to tell us we were too late to order. She took one look at our desperate faces and gave in, coming back with a couple of pots of tea and 'whatever I've got left, but don't get your hopes up' – a wedge of Victoria sponge cake oozing raspberry jam, two sticky squares of cherry-flecked flapjack and the trimmed, overcooked edges from the chocolate-brownie tray. As I was attempting to cut everything into fifths, the café door pinged and a man walked in, cradling an enormous marrow in his arms like a baby.

'Look what I just found down the road in an honesty box,' he said to his friend, who was sitting at the next table to ours.

The children, knowing what was coming next, sunk as low in their seats as their apple-heavy hoods would allow.

'Excuse me,' I said, smiling nicely, 'were there any more and can you tell me *exactly* where you found it?'

Nobody spoke as we trawled around the village on the hunt for the marrow. Even Margot took on a martyred plod. I thought I had pushed my luck too far and would have to return to the car defeated, when we turned a corner and there it was, alone on a table on the grass verge, waiting for me. For just 50p, I had a vastly overgrown courgette that would feed five of us the following day. I attempted to take a photo of everyone holding the prize aloft, which didn't go down well, so instead I got a shot of Steve standing next to the marrow, looking bemused.

'If you love honesty boxes so much,' Steve said as we headed back to the car, 'then why don't you set up one of your own?'

*

Steve and I are sitting opposite each other at the kitchen table, avoiding eye contact. The Christmas holiday is over, and we have just waved the kids off on the school bus. Steve's mood has taken a predictable swan dive and yet it also feels different this time around. Maybe it is because I feel different; my reserves of hope are hollow after years of optimistic plunder, and I am beginning to drift away from my marriage mooring. Change is charging towards us as our family dynamic will shift irrevocably when Raff goes to university later in the year and I am already dreading that moment, not just because of his absence but because this is the beginning of the goodbyes. Next it will be Hebe, followed by Jesse. Leaving Steve and me, probably like this, sitting opposite each other at a kitchen table that will be too big, in a house that will be too quiet.

I am usually the first to speak in these situations, but I stop myself, and so we sit in silence for several long minutes. Through the window, I can see our right-side neighbour's magnolia tree is in hopeful bud, and I pray it won't get hijacked by a vicious frost. Eventually Steve starts talking.

'I have tried everything over the years.' He begins to count on his fingers. 'Cognitive behavioural therapy, antidepressants, psychotherapy, group therapy, EMDR therapy for PTSD. You name it, I have done it. I have given up booze, taken up yoga, cut out dairy and avoided processed meat. I have worked so hard, for so long, at trying to find some answers, but I still hate myself.' His eyes brim with tears. 'I won't blame you if you want to leave me. I want to leave me. You've been so patient, so great throughout, and I don't want you to waste any more time in this marriage…'

I don't reach for the usual platitudes or reassurances. We have diligently searched for clarity for over twenty years, and I have run out of meaningful words and ideas. And Steve is wrong: I don't think I have always been that patient or great. I have stumbled through our life together, sometimes thinking more about how his behaviour affects me than how it hurts him. Maybe I am part of the problem and have somehow exacerbated rather than soothed his pain.

'Whatever happens with us,' I say, 'you need to get answers for you. We have to find a way through this for your quality of life and the relationship you have with our children. It's not about our future together, it's about your survival.'

We both agree, and then more silence while we acknowledge that this is a place we have not been in before. A point of mutual separation. It feels like stepping off a crowded bus you were desperate to leave,

JANUARY

only to find yourself standing on an unfamiliar street full of strangers, with no idea where you are going next. What if I get off too soon? No sudden moves, I decide, for both our sakes.

'Let's go back to the GP and have this conversation again,' I suggest because I want to be constructive and this is all I can think of. Secretly, I don't hold out much hope and I don't think Steve does either, but we don't say this out loud. Now is not the time to stare directly into the abyss, we have dealt with enough for today, so I try to think of something to distract us both. 'Anyway, we can't break up yet because I need help with my honesty box. There are some raised beds that need sorting.'

The garden has always been Steve's refuge, and this could be the ideal project for us to tackle together.

'And for the dog,' he says. 'She doesn't like change.'

Neither of us mention the children because that is too huge and painful to contemplate.

Later, I hear on the radio that today is known as Divorce Day, the first working day of the new year, when many couples throw in the towel. Steve is at the office, ensconced in solving people's architectural problems and I text him, telling him about the date and saying we can't be such a cliched statistic, so we need to hang on until tomorrow at least. He responds with a long line of laughing-until-they-cry emojis.

*

These fledgling days struggle to lift themselves out of the fog. It is difficult to imagine the veg patch punctuated by sunshine-yellow courgette flowers, a turret of rambling, climbing beans or wigwams tilting under the weight of sweet peas. I wait for a morning that is lighter than the rest, a watery sun half-heartedly pushing through the gloom, to tug at the weeds and spread a few bags of compost onto the raised beds. I spend longer with my hands wrapped around a mug of tea than I do with them in the soil. I am just playing at gardening. Mostly I am at the kitchen table with a notepad, a pile of helpful books and a box of half-opened seed packets. This is the bit I am quite good at.

The produce I want to grow is based on several key factors. Firstly, we are on a tight budget, so we need to grow most things from seed. Secondly, we must all like them, which in fairness is most vegetables (except please, please, hands clasped together in prayer, mime retching, please *not* parsnips, begs Jesse). Thirdly, the plants need to be easy to nurture and prolific, meaning we can feed our family as well as stock the honesty box and, if any of them become a glut (be still my greedy heart), they can be effortlessly transformed into preserves. I am not including fruit because my track record with berries is woeful, and any triumphs will be eaten straight from the stem by the grower (me), hopefully before the scavengers (birds, dog, teenagers).

I make my selection, ignoring the fact that it requires double the space and more money than we actually have, and write a list that I can run through with Steve.

1. *Courgettes – green, yellow and striped*
   They won't fit in the raised beds so we need to find a suitable space where we can pile manure. I wonder if it would be too drastic to dig up the grass. Probably yes, because sometimes it doubles as the world's smallest football pitch.

2. *Beans – all of them*
   I always plant runners because they were my nan's favourite and I love them, broad beans as they crop early, and Borlottis (which failed us last year, or we failed them, so will give it another go).

3. *Lettuce – mixed leaves including rocket*
   I want heat, freshness, bold colour and to avoid anything with the texture and taste of old lace. Unlikely I will offer this in my honesty box, although I may sell any spare plug plants if I run out of room.

4. *Herbs*
   If we plant *one* thing, let it be *all* the herbs, keeping as many as possible in pots by the kitchen door. I make a note to prune the enormous rosemary bush out the front and be nicer to the tiny bay tree. The parsley, thyme, mint, marjoram and sage are established now, and I want to add basil, coriander, oregano, tarragon, ginger rosemary, lovage and both summer and winter savoury so they aren't lonely. I am not sure we should bother with dill, although I will try again with chervil for the third year running, but this is its last chance. The lemon verbena is looking sickly so if it doesn't bounce back I need to replace it, as it is unbeatable for herbal tea.

5. *Kale*
   This is a diligent, eternally producing leaf favoured by Steve, which always saves me when I am low on other vegetables. Roasted in the oven or

shredded and sauteed in butter and garlic, this adds much needed green to many dishes including pasta and as a soup topping.

6. *Rainbow Chard*
   Just like kale, this keeps going through the year and looks pretty in the veg patch and on the plate.

7. *Cime di rapa*
   Very much a TBC. I have eaten this bitter Italian turnip-related leaf but never grown it. Should I be planting something I can't pronounce?

8. *Radish*
   Unbeatable, easy to grow, great for successional sowing and the best snack with butter and flaky sea salt. I can't imagine having more than we will eat, so will need to sow a row of seed every week to increase supply.

9. *Peas*
   They very rarely make it to the kitchen. Am I growing them just for me? Rhetorical.

10. *Sweet Peas*
    These cut-and-come-again beauties can easily provide for the kitchen table, to give as gifts and sell in the honesty box. Also, the scented variety disguises the smell of damp dog. Win-win.

11. *Sunflowers*
    I have become a big fan of these after years of scoffing at them. I am planting a wide range, not just the traditional yellow, but the heritage mix of reds and whites.

JANUARY

12. *Squash/pumpkins/gourds*
    Again, this raises a question over space, so we need to consider our options, but I love the idea of some autumn garden glory, delicious soups and a Halloween decoration.

13. *Carrots*
    I am undecided. Steve always plants these. I enjoy seeing their vibrant green fronds in the veg patch, but we never seem to grow enough to make it worthwhile.

14. *Fennel*
    Tempted but, as with carrots, we need to consider space versus yield.

15. *Beetroot*
    Steve's favourite, so yes.

What we are not going to plant this year are potatoes (we didn't get a good crop last time), sweetcorn (requires a large grid of soil), swede (alone in my fondness, although I may tuck a couple behind the shed) and asparagus (my patience can't be stretched over three years while I wait for them to grow). I run through the list with Steve, who approves the plan but immediately starts a campaign for reinstating potatoes. I can sense he has a flicker of optimism for the growing year ahead, a place for him to escape.

This is the only challenge I think we are both ready for in our year of reckoning. We have given ourselves twelve months to plant, grow, harvest and stock our honesty box, but what is left unsaid is whether our marriage can stay the course. Will our relationship survive long enough to see the broad beans flower or the pumpkins ripen? Rhetorical.

*

I am relying on a lot of googling and social media stalking for honesty box knowledge. They may seem like a limited rural pursuit but there is a vast network of boxes, tables and sheds, stretching out from the tip of Cornwall through the southwest and beyond, to Wales, Suffolk, Norfolk, the Hebrides and Shetland. The tradition also spreads far beyond these shores and meanders across rural Sweden, driving through upstate New York, lost in Japan, pulling up on the Australian roadside or hidden in Croatia. Whether it is a farm stand, ceramics stall, book exchange, bakery, curry fridge or 'cut your own' flower meadow, they share a universal language of honesty that must not be dismissed as an eccentric pastime.

During my rabbit-hole research, I discover a gang of community fruit and veg stands in New Zealand. They use their Facebook feed as a noticeboard, posting details of honesty stands, giving a rundown of their produce, when and where they have dropped off a glut, and share recipes they swear by. At this time of year, I can only dream of the sort of seasonal produce that the New Zealanders are nonchalantly listing. Even in the height of summer here, we will struggle to offer the same variety and amount. There are vegetables I have never even heard of before, such as Kamo kamo, a Maori squash that looks like it has courgette ancestors. In their latest post, one stand is full of tomato plants, courgettes, free-range eggs, plums, melons, avocados, beans and chillies. Somebody has included a small stack of books they

JANUARY

no longer want – *The Lonely Planet Guide to Spain*, a parenting manual titled *Of Course I Love You… NOW GO TO YOUR ROOM*, and a book on health and healing. I would grab all of those.

Inspired by the global stories, I take the first tentative steps into my project of curiosity and hope. Not with ingredients I have grown myself yet, but with a tray of knobbly Seville oranges, their skins tough and gnarly. There is a small window of availability for these sour fruits. Impossibly bitter to eat raw, they transform through the alchemy of preserving to make the best marmalade.

The Seville season seems early this year. The local farm shop has been piling them up next to discounted Christmas treats for several days. Along with a tray of the oranges, I can't resist a bag of pink grapefruits too. Citrus to cut through the dank greyness. As I squeeze, de-pip, thinly chop and soak the fruit, I listen to a podcast about how to fail and learn from things going wrong. The broadcaster, Alex Jones, is talking about her husband's struggle with depression, her feelings of powerlessness and the inability to really understand what he was going through. She admits to wondering why he couldn't just 'pull himself together'. This is such a taboo statement and so familiar to me, I stop what I am doing and listen intently, relieved that someone else, someone successful and well known, is voicing my own inadequate reactions.

The kitchen is filled with the tangy fug of boiling orange peel and the rhythmic drip of rain trickling through a gap in the gutter. I had been deliberating where and how to set up the honesty store, but the current weather reminds me that we need a water tight backup.

I want to show my intent (resolve?) for what is to come. After the rain, I put the still-warm jars out on the back step and prop up a hand-chalked sign on a jagged piece of roof slate advertising *Seville Orange Marmalade and Pink Grapefruit Curd. Donations welcome.*

Begin.

*

I have sold out of marmalade and curd, but what appeared to be a success was actually a few friends dashing over after seeing a post I put on Instagram. Several more messaged me to ask if I would courier them to London, Kent and, in one instance, Australia. I think they are missing the point of the honesty box. I am not sure a single jar was bought by a random passer-by.

*

I can tell from the way Steve slept that he is at the bottom of a dark, inhospitable well. I feel like the matron of a school dormitory, pinging open blinds, letting the rare winter sun into the room which illuminates the dust and despair. I have a towering pile of clothes on the chair which I need to put away, but instead I just take things off the top. Or I wear the same old denim dungarees on repeat, which I vowed I would never leave the house in before revising the rule to only if I am going to the supermarket, petrol station, a dog walk or school pick-up, although I have never been 'out out' in them. Yet. Hebe says I look like a cartoon character who spends eternity in one outfit.

'How did you sleep?' I know Steve is now awake, but he doesn't respond. He is resisting the new day and fighting to stay submerged in the duvet and oblivion.

JANUARY

I stand looking at him. I don't have time to get back into bed, stroke his hair, cajole him into the morning. I have a busy day ahead, starting with getting the kids on the school bus with their packed lunches. I am not sure we have any bread, so I am mentally planning a pasta salad. 'Not good.' I answer for him, saying this as a statement rather than a question.

'I'm sorry,' he says into the pillow, 'it's got its claws into me.'

'Perhaps taking the dog out will help clear the cobwebs?' I know this is a terrible response, but I can't find anything else to say. I try. I scrabble around for something reassuring, but my brain is a blank other than a loud voice that shouts, 'Get out of bed!' At least I manage not to say that.

Downstairs, as I scrape together enough leftovers for three packed lunches, Zoe Ball is being cheery on R2 and the shouty voice in my head changes tone to a wheedling, 'You can't carry on like this. Just imagine living in a tiny cottage somewhere with the freedom to wake up without this unpredictability. Just a calm, little life. That's what you need.'

Steve walks into the kitchen and sits down to pull on his walking boots, the trusted pair he has had since his late teens that have been resoled and mended many times over. Then he pulls on his orange bobble hat, another reassuring mainstay in his wardrobe.

'I'm sorry,' he says again.

'Don't apologise.' I go over and put my arms around him. Margot barks impatiently at this display of affection and delay in getting out of the house. 'You were late back from the office last night. Was that because you were working, or did you just slump?'

'Some work. And then I slumped.' He looks defeated and goes out of the back door.

I watch him walk down the lane, weighed down by an invisible load, until he turns the corner, Margot bouncing happily ahead of him.

*

A parcel wrapped in sturdy brown paper arrives. It is the first of my seed orders. I leave it to one side while I put a pot of coffee on the stove. I am zipped tightly into my coat for most of the morning. Both fires are lit – the log burner in the kitchen blasts the heat out through the back doorway, and the open fire in the sitting room whips it straight up the chimney.

City people are not prepared for country living in winter, surviving all the weather with nowhere to go, other than your own kitchen or someone else's. Nor do they have the right clothes. Living in London, I never owned an appropriate coat. It was only when I moved to Dorset that I realised I needed to be protected from driving rain, an easterly and something called a wind chill factor. I still haven't got it right. It takes three types of coat to survive a winter here, and invariably I will go out in the wrong one.

I have been known to sleep in one of my coats when we run out of oil, which is more frequently than a responsible, middle-aged mother of three dependants should admit. We never run out in June. It is always just before or just after Christmas. This is immediately followed by Steve making a plaintive call to the sympathetic lady at the fuel company, who does her best to get us on the delivery list within the week. It is getting harder to afford a full tank of oil too, so thermals are the thing. They make great underlayers for long walks, pull-ons after sea swims (yes, I am one of those people) and toasty, warm pyjamas. In the olden days, you would be sewn into your starchy undergarments from the first frost in October, and be cut out of them on the first of June. This now makes complete sense, verging on a practice that I may soon adopt.

In cities and big towns, you can escape January in large department stores, cinemas with wine bars, museum exhibitions and brisk marches through elegant parks to favourite cafés. It is an expensive way to drag yourself through the month, but not as costly as ski trips and exotic beach holidays. In Dorset, there is a simpler approach. You walk in the woods, on the beach, along a cliff (but not too close to the edge because we have regular landslips), to someone's house, or around the market.

Bridport market in the winter is a shadow of its summer self, but it pulses through the coldest months in a small, vital way like an arterial vein. Held every Wednesday and Saturday, it starts the year with stalwart market traders, who vigorously stamp their feet on the spot until Easter and the fair-weather arrival of additional stalls, tourists and the ice-cream seller on his bike. I have been in love with this market since I moved here, and it has never disappointed me. I often find something I didn't know I needed – and always something that I do.

The stalls start at the top of South Street, on the side of the road that doesn't get the sun until midday. What begins with the regular stallholders in their official pitches with their usual wares becomes more of an eclectic and surprising line-up once you get past the record shop with a life-size David Bowie waxwork, and the museum famous for its real stuffed tiger in a glass case. Do you need a set of fish knives with bone handles, a pair of dented brass doorknobs or keys the size of your palm, for mysterious doors they will never be reunited with? How about a roll of apple-green garden netting, a tower of chipped terracotta plant pots or a hoe with bright red paint peeling off the handle? Maybe you fancy a set of vintage Kilner jars for preserving your lemons, a heavy, orange 1980s Le Creuset dish or a brown teapot with its own knitted tea cosy? Whether you are looking for a bargain, a find or a practical solution to a problem, join me and we can fight over the enormous pile of yellowing textiles that smell of damp attics and decaying rodents. Actually don't, because I can get very competitive over an old pillowcase.

In January, I have no shopping list. If the weather is shocking, the market is pitiful, but on a bright, blue-skied, frosty morning there are little surprises worth turning up for. I am there on one of those days and bump into a local friend. She is weighed down by a baby in a sling, which she hugs with satisfaction, like a rotund belly full of Sunday roast. The tip of the tiny girl's nose is pink from the cold, and I resist the urge to squidge her dumpling cheeks. This woman, with her three children under the age of five, reminds me of me over a decade ago, full of love, bewilderment and daily defeat. Her two little boys are wearing matching boiler suits and wellies and are up to their armpits in a large tub of old toy cars, in search of tractors. The stallholder looks on anxiously as they are rummaging on the kerb next to the main road, but their mother just shrugs.

'I've told them not to be dicks and go into the road,' she says.

JANUARY

I nod in agreement as we both watch them proudly, not being dicks.

Soulshine Café is at the far end of the street. Even in winter there is a queue before it opens. I join it, behind the early magpie shoppers clutching bags bulging with treasures that I have already missed out on. The queue shuffles past cinnamon-and-orange buns tied in doughy knots, cricket ball-sized Scotch eggs with a spicy mayonnaise dip, seeded rye bread the weight and shape of a house brick, and a wheel of frittata, fat with potatoes, peppers and herbs and slathered with a roast garlic mayonnaise topping. I manage to resist it all and order a takeaway coffee and a warm sourdough loaf which, tucked under my arm, doubles as a hot water bottle as I head back up the road.

The Egg Lady is snug in her van, and I almost miss the sign on her table, propped against the polystyrene trays of eggs: *Broad Bean seedlings available end of January. Will be hardy!*

I make a mental note to check back at the end of the month. These will be our first plants of the year.

*

The snowdrops are out. They have sprung from nowhere – these delicate commas of pure white, scattered along the verge, heads bowed in chattering groups. Their resilience at this time of year always amazes me, and they lift my tired winter heart. Not so, the number of migrating toads splattered on the tarmac, innards trailing like a biblical warning, all thwarted as they point towards the village pond.

*

My neighbour Sheila, who lives on our left, walks past as I am hacking into the cemented soil in the flower bed in the front garden. I have propped my phone up against a bin and am half-listening to a podcast about how to know if you are perimenopausal. A large pile of tulip bulbs sits next to me. I know I am almost too late to plant these out, but a girl must hope (and not waste the thirty quid they cost).

'If they're tulip bulbs, you're too late,' Sheila says, pulling her hood tight against the biting winter cold. 'They won't sprout now.'

'Probably,' I say, struggling to stand up (achey joints, menopausal tick), 'but I've spent the last three months walking around a box of them in the kitchen, so I figured they weren't going to do any better there.'

Sheila changes tack. 'Is it true you're starting an honesty box in the village?' she asks, and I am aware this conversation could go either way.

'Yes!' I say enthusiastically. 'Our nearest shop is a ten-minute drive so I thought it might come in useful for the village. And we get walkers coming through here too...'

'Right,' she says, brow furrowed. 'So what sort of thing will you be stocking?'

'Well, I'm hoping to fill it with stuff I have grown in the garden, as well as things I will make in the kitchen. And if anyone has extras of anything to donate or fancies making a few jars of...'

'Will you sell tinned tomatoes? They are always useful.' Sheila looks hopeful.

'That's not quite the point of the honesty box. It's less of a general store and more of a resource to share gluts.' I can sense Sheila's disappointment.

'I see,' she says, unconvinced, 'but how about a milk delivery to the honesty box? Save someone having to get in their car for a pint of milk.'

'Worth considering.' I have decided not to argue.

'And eggs? You need to get chickens. You should have a proper think about what you are doing. It sounds a bit vague to me.' And with a wave, Sheila stomps off, her old Labrador grumbling at her heels.

I am not getting hens again. Nobody helps clean the coop, they are a siren call to rats, and I haven't got the stomach for picking up decapitated birds once the fox has found a way through the impenetrable fence. And no ducks either, after we made the mistake of giving our old hen, Dorothy, a clutch of what I thought were chicken eggs to sit on when she was broody. They turned into ducks, who terrorised all other animals and children so we gave them away, except for the malicious ringleader who couldn't be trusted anywhere. We cooked him for Christmas lunch instead. That was a defining moment, six years after moving to the country, when I felt I had taken a step unfathomable to the old me. Especially the vegetarian old me.

Sheila is right. Even though there is an egg honesty box nearby, it would be good for me to have eggs in my honesty box too, but there is no reason why I should be the provider of them. I speak to my friends at Haye Farm, at the far end of the village. They produce industrial amounts of organic eggs from their hen colony and sell them locally, as well as providing them for the kitchens of their other family business, Petersham Nurseries. On slow weeks, they are happy to sell me a tray of eggs.

Just wait till I tell Sheila. I am going to say that I have asked them to lend me a cow too so she can have a go at milking it.

*

Steve and I have formed a truce of kindness. Both of us are temporarily immobilised by the idea of breaking up coupled with the realisation of a whole new year ahead to make exactly the same mistakes again. We talk only about whether to scramble or boil the eggs, when we should order more logs and if we should plant potatoes again this year (me, still very much no, and him, yes because he has a potato-growing bag and he hates to see it go to waste).

He has made an appointment with the GP.

One evening, I take a large glass of red wine and my phone up to our bedroom and sit on the floor with my back against the lukewarm radiator, which is inefficiently drying a line of mismatched socks. It is as if I am sixteen again and hiding away for secret conversations. I call Thea. She and her husband Adam have been friends of mine for thirty years, since we all worked together as talent agents. They are close to Steve too, and we are godparents to each other's firstborns.

I can offload to Thea without feeling disloyal, knowing that she is just as likely to stand up for Steve as she would for me, and as I do for Adam. Fairness at all times. I update her on recent revelations and how we have exhausted all the options. We are looking down the barrel of separation, swiftly followed by divorce, a house sale, even less money than we have now and devastated children. I take a massive gulp of wine.

JANUARY

'Hang on,' she says, and I can hear her scrabbling around. 'Right, here it is. I have a list of questions to ask so try to answer them as honestly as you can. Do not overthink this.'

Ten minutes later and the quiz is finished, and I can tell I have scored pretty highly, but am not sure what for. 'This is from a book a friend gave me, about the ADHD effect on marriage. From everything you have just said, it sounds like Steve might have ADHD? I am going to send it to you, so have a read and let me know what you think. Adam and I have been reading it, and a lot resonates with us both. We're wondering if Adam might be neurodivergent too.'

For the first time in a long time, I feel the tiniest glimmer of possibility – and something else: recognition. ADHD, of course. The assumption has always been that trauma and difficult early adult years led to Steve's depressive behaviour. What if everyone has been looking in the wrong place? What if his history has kept the full truth hidden, he has been misdiagnosed or perhaps these things have become entangled together? Suddenly, the thought of ADHD seems startlingly obvious, and I feel incredibly stupid.

*

The book arrives, and I hide it.

*

As we are getting into bed a couple of nights later, I mention the conversation I had with Thea, but am careful what I say because I don't want Steve to think I have blabbed. Which of course I have. I tell him about the quiz and whip the book out from its hiding place. He says nothing. It is not a disgruntled nothing or a furious nothing; it is a disengaged nothing. A few days later, I realise the book is missing from my bedside table, but I don't say anything and wait for Steve to talk, which doesn't take long.

'That book,' he says. 'I have just finished reading it. It's me. This is exactly how I feel. They are writing about me!' There is a tone of wonderment and relief in his voice. 'So, what do we do now?'

February

One of the local farmers has instructed the parish council to tell us we need to cut our hedge. Or he will cut it for us. But either way, the hedge needs to be cut because 'it may get tangled in the booms of the sprayer' as he clanks up the lane, and this is 'likely to cost thousands'. He says we have until the end of the month to do it ourselves, or else he will and it won't be pretty, meaning the hedge not us. I think.

'What I object to, Nigel,' I say to my neighbour, the parish council member who has been tasked with delivering the ultimatum, 'is that he drives past here several times a day so he could have just stopped and mentioned it to us. Why bring it up at a public parish meeting like he expects us to cause trouble?'

'I don't know. Maybe it's because you're from London and he thinks you won't understand? Anyway, he thought he should make it official.' Nigel shifts uncomfortably in his squeaky-clean wellies and checks his watch.

This is a constant refrain that has followed us around for the almost two decades we haven't been Londoners. It feels like a muddy slur on our rural respect and how hard we have worked to fit in to this environment. After all this time, there is still a vague divide between the born-and-bred of the village and the rest of us, which isn't aggressive or unwelcoming, but it is there. They and the generations before them are embedded in this place, and we are temporary visitors who do not know the names of the fields or what to do with an escaped cow.

Left up to me, I would take the lazy path of least resistance and let the farmer butcher the hedge in his tea break. Instead, Steve's eyes light up at the thought of another project.

He is impatiently counting down to his GP appointment. He is ready to deliver our homespun verdict of ADHD, be fast-tracked through the system for diagnosis and then be furnished with the appropriate medication. He has been reading about how the pills can help with concentration and mood regulation, two things he has always struggled with. I try to manage his expectations, but I am also sure we have hit on something.

In the meantime, Steve jumps on any opportunity to keep busy, so he decides to embark on laying the hedge. This is a simple yet terrifying process of hacking into branches, forcing them over each other at right angles and attempting to plait them together. I say 'simple', but it is also an ancient country craft that takes years to learn and perfect. In fairness, we have tried to get a professional on the job. A master hedgelayer, Malcolm, lives at the other end of the village but he has just had an operation so is out of action. It was his encouragement and the promise to wander up and give a bit of early direction that bolstered Steve's confidence.

'You'll be wanting to keep 'im to your left,' Malcolm says, leaning heavily on one crutch while he uses the other to point at the branch he is referring to. 'Remember you need a perpendicular lay, and push each down as you go. Cut into the branch no more than two-thirds of the way. There 'e goes, easy does it.'

Steve has the glint in his eye that suggests he has found a new hobby, and I can see him cataloguing all the shiny kit he will need for it.

'Malcolm, should I get myself some protective gauntlets?'

'Malcolm, should I get my own bill hook?'

'Malcolm, should I go on a hedgelaying course?'

'No, you should just bloody well get on with it,' Malcolm says, before limping off down the road as the farmer in question comes clanking around the corner in his old Land Rover, the pipe clenched between his teeth making a beard of smoky puffs. The farmer notes Malcolm, he clocks Steve swinging an axe, he catches sight of the children suspended from various sections of the raised hedge, and then he sees me. He gives a curt nod as he drives past, but I swear I see him chuckling in the rear-view mirror.

'Daft city folk, thinking they can lay a hedge,' I imagine him saying to his wife that night as she takes a handsome forerib of beef out of the Aga.

It is bloodied, back-breaking work with the constant danger that someone will leave an eyeball behind on a protruding stick. Steve has all the kids involved – although I draw the line at any that aren't related to us – and I come to terms with the likelihood that one of them may be missing a finger by the time the hedge is finished. I build and tend the bonfires, strip the hazel offcuts to use as pea-stick supports in the veg patch and keep the workforce fed on an hourly basis. We spot the first of the primroses. Everyone gives them a wide berth until Margot, with her enormous paws, bounds through, splatting everything in her wake.

As the hedge is tamed, the wide strip of soil underneath is exposed, becoming just the right length and width for the courgette plants. This solves the problem of where to put them and gives me an excuse to go inside and make a phone call to score more well-rotted manure. The kitchen is warm and impossible to leave, so I bake a quick batch of biscuits under the pretence of keeping spirits up. Mine, mainly. The nutty, malty smell of toasted oats encourages me to make more, some as a thank you to Malcolm, and the rest for the honesty box. A stack of warm cookies mists the glass of the jar as I leave them outside on the wall. They get snapped up by villagers labouring in their gardens like us, donations left in the jam jar.

I bring up the crumbly biscuits with a pot of tea, and we stand back to survey the woven beauty in all its erratic, patched glory, ignoring the large golden retriever-sized hole halfway along. It screams amateur, but what a sense of achievement.

'I reckon I could do this for a living,' Steve says dreamily, and the rest of us back away.

*

Propped up on the tall mantelpiece in the kitchen is an old sepia picture of our house, taken in 1910 when it was still the village forge. It shows the bearded blacksmith, Joshua Loveridge, in flat cap, braces and a tattered apron, with his hand resting reassuringly on the muzzle of a blinkered horse next to him. His young nephew and apprentice, Ernest, is holding up the horse's front hoof, a hammer dangling from his other hand. Both men look straight ahead of them instead of at the camera, caught awkwardly in an everyday moment. Shortly after this photo was taken, Ernest was sent to fight in the First World War and I imagine him in the trenches, dreaming of the village he left behind. He never came home. After the Second World War, the low-slung building was cobbled together into a solid two-storey home by a determined and desperate father of nine children, and it hasn't changed much since then. It looks like a house a child would draw: square with a front door in the middle, windows either side and a smoking chimney at each end of the slate roof. The painted render has faded to the softest pink, and the splintering sills of the rickety wooden windows give up in heavy weather, springing startling leaks that we rush to mop at ineffectually with old towels. The ground floor is sixteenth century with the sturdy stone structure dug directly into the soil, but the first floor is constructed with cavity walls that have been insulated with post-war rubbish and big dreams for a different future. There used to be a breeze-block wall painted the same colour as the house, which divided the narrow front garden from the access to the neighbouring field, but someone reversed into it, and we came home one day to a pile of rubble blocking the front door.

Inside, the black and red terracotta floor tiles keep the house cool in summer, create small puddles of condensation in autumn and freeze the soles of our feet in winter. Every room downstairs has them – the long narrow sitting room, tiny loo and big kitchen. Up steep stairs are four small light-filled bedrooms and a bathroom. It isn't an easy house to live in. We aren't quite pulling water from a well, mangling the laundry and cooking over a sooty fire, but we aren't basking in comfort either.

When we first moved in, a friend popped over to see the house. She burst into tears. 'It's awful,' she said, unable to contain her horror. 'You can't stay here. It's like something from the Dark Ages.'

This place isn't big enough to defeat us, but somehow it has. It has fought back over every improvement we have tried to make, as if it is determined to transform back into its previous life of thatched roof, dirt floors and a horse tethered out the front. It mutters when a builder's van parks outside, the chainsaw shudders into action or a pile of paint charts is spread out on the table. It doesn't want kitchen suppers, walls the colour of dead trout, decking for sundowners or phone chargers trailing out of every socket. It is unsurprising that the internet often stops for no detectable reason, and we have had many engineers out to try and solve it.

What this building longs for is white heat, clanging irons and the humid compost-breath of a horse on icy mornings. Luckily for the old forge, we don't have any money so, other than the occasional flurry of crucial maintenance, it rests easy. We live within it, both grateful for its secure, safe sanctuary and wishful that it was something better.

The garden, on the other hand, is a modest treat. Albeit a steady climb from the small courtyard, up a set of stone steps to three grassy levels and then beyond to the cabin, which has been a mix of glamping (read basic) retreat, teenage hangout and a space for me to work. From here, there is a small, gravelled section leading through to the biggest part of the garden with raised beds, a triffid-like gunnera, the bonfire patch, compost heap and a constant crop of nettles edging the footprint of the old greenhouse.

FEBRUARY

We inherited the greenhouse with the cottage, but it was a death trap. Dagger-sized pieces of glass would hurtle down without warning, until Steve made me admit defeat and we spent a sad weekend dismantling it. Instead, we use the stone and timber lean-to that butts up wearily against the back of the house, with its clear, plastic corrugated roof amplifying the sound of the softest raindrops. It may be a dumping ground but, as well as wellies of every size (with the occasional toad nesting in them), single football boots, skateboards, log stack and recycling bins, it is the perfect little spot for seed growing. There is a small work surface and a sink, and we have power again, after a recent leak into an exposed socket blew the electrics in the house.

I spend a happy afternoon in the lean-to, planting rainbow chard seeds in plastic fruit punnets we have saved and the sweet peas in loo roll tubes, filled with soil and tightly sandwiched together in a tray. They sit on the kitchen windowsill before we start a monotonous game of moving them around from house to lean-to and back again as the temperature drops and climbs. I have been looking at heated propagators, but right now any amount of money feels like too much for a novice to spend and I don't have the space for it. I would rather buy a few more seedlings, like the broad beans I have picked up from Bridport Market. They are strong little plants, but it is too early to risk putting them straight into the veg bed. They perch on the top shelf in the lean-to, valiantly reaching towards the light filtering through the corrugated plastic.

I am not a methodical, patient or natural gardener so I have just had to accept I will make mistakes – otherwise, I would never do it in the first place. Gardening has crept up on me over the years, along with dodgy Achilles and going to bed early. When I hit fifty, Steve gave me a copper trowel and fork, which, if I am being completely honest, was not top of my list because I was ogling a Bella Freud jumper, but it was insightful recognition of my growing interest. In our life together, Steve has always been the gardener and I have been the chef, although Steve is a better cook than me. He is better at everything, when he can focus, and by that I don't mean hyper-focus, which is almost as hard to deal with as not focusing at all, because when he is wholly committed to something he can forget everything else around him. Being in the garden is a sanctuary for him. I think that is why he sometimes finds it uncomfortable to see me in it. He watches me make a mess, summarise instructions rather than follow them and bodge my way through the veg patch. It must be infuriating. He stands in the middle of the garden issuing orders, fists clenched by his sides, face turned up towards the sky, frustration vibrating through him as I hum my way around.

'A bean is part of the legume family and known for putting nitrogen into the soil, so remember not to plant beans back in the patch they were in last year. Something else can benefit from that goodness.' He continues for some time, imparting information until he has exhausted everything he knows on the subject. My actions seem to cause him real discomfort. This behaviour is beginning to make sense to me.

When he speaks in statements, I used to think it stemmed from a deep-rooted insecurity to prove his worth, but since January I am working on reframing this, which is challenging after over twenty years and when my instinct is to be annoyed at being told what to do.

FEBRUARY

Be kind, I think.
I am too tired for that, I say defensively back to myself.
But I need to rethink everything I ever thought about this man, I rebuke myself.
Yes, I respond, but not today. I cannot do this today.
Instead, I just flick the V's at him behind his back, and it is amazing how much better it makes me feel.

*

I text my friend Pam, who lives in Saratoga, three hours upstate from Manhattan. She is a food writer in her mid-sixties and swears like a marine.

Pam, quick question. Do you have any honesty boxes in your State? X

Her response is quick. *What the fuck are they?*

She doesn't do kisses. Then, five minutes later. *Do you mean Honor Stands? We have those in the summer. Local farms put out piles of peaches and sweetcorn. I love them! And somewhere else stacks firewood out front. Why?*

Peaches straight from the tree! Fresh cobs of sweetcorn! Chopped firewood! OK, maybe not the last one, I have quite a lot of that already.

I am setting one up here. Amazed at the global network of them. Keep me updated. Send photos! Xxx

*

It is too early to know if our honesty box endeavour will be enough to keep us communicating with each other, but the fact we are still waiting for the GP appointment doesn't make me feel hopeful of Steve's and my future together, and we start conversations about trial separations that we don't finish.

I am acutely aware that we share the blame for our marriage breakdown. I want to say equally, but I don't really believe that. I am looking at a 70/30 split right now, with me being the least culpable, but then I am hardly the best judge. I speak to Rob, and he listens with all the empathy and old-soul wisdom that makes him seem like the big brother, rather than it being the other way around.

'You need to stop talking about divorce when you have a big bust-up,' Rob counsels. 'It isn't helping Steve's issues with insecurity. You need to find a way through this.'

Well, yes, and also no. While Rob is right because he often is and not in an irritating way, we have already done a lot of work trying to find answers, and we don't seem to be any further forward. When do we acknowledge it is too late? Our marriage is turning to ash around us.

In the past, Steve and I had blazing rows about his attitude, which may have been triggered by a social situation (see earlier Rioja faux pas), punctuality (lack of), admin (specifically the avoidance of official letters) or money (impulsive spending). I never once bundled all these things together and thought they might stem from the same source. I put it down to him being tired, rude, deluded, scared, ill-equipped or stubborn, depending on what had happened. And sometimes, of course, it wasn't his fault, it was mine. And oftentimes, it was born of a situation where he was being truthful, and I was taking the socially acceptable route of pretence (again, I refer you back to the Rioja). Both of us in valid positions, but Steve couldn't decipher when to switch between the two effectively and stuck to his default setting of uncomfortable honesty, which caused no end of trouble between us. In hindsight, this was a big clue for what was to come.

Steve's social skills have been an issue for me, almost a deal-breaker at times. After years of working in a stridently confident, charm-laden industry of darlings, I fell in love with someone who could be awkward, spiky and unafraid to speak the truth. Then I inadvertently set about trying to change him. I became his unwanted translator, who would jump in to explain what he really meant or jokingly admonish him for his lack of sensitivity, while eye-rolling conspiratorially at whoever was there. I thought I was making it easier for everyone, but I only succeeded in confusing or angering Steve and tying myself in emotional knots. I ended up making things worse.

I stopped confiding in him too. Not about everything, but I would pick and choose what to share because he was unable to store the information in his brain, in the box marked 'secret'. He would know not to repeat it to others, but as time went on he might forget and think it was general knowledge, so it would filter out and he would be perplexed by how upset I was. He never did this with anything personally private. It was the silly stuff – maybe my irritation with a neighbour, which he would then think he could fix. I wanted to be able to offload on him so I wouldn't have to deal with it further, not expect him to inflate it. He could not understand why you wouldn't say what you meant.

His bluntness has been a huge bone of contention. As has my inclination towards worrying about the other person in any situation, rather than myself. It has become an issue for me, a debilitation in fact, and I have spent years finding ways to address it. If someone stands on my foot, I say sorry for being in the way. If there is a scratch on my car, I assume I did it. If someone is angry with me, I find it easier to put myself in their shoes than my own. Steve and I can be poles apart in the way we approach or consider things, and we talk about being irrevocably incompatible. Perhaps he needs someone less cheerfully deferential and confrontation avoidant, I suggest, and he says maybe I need someone calm and laidback who is able to regulate their mood. Yet, without Steve's influence, his ability to be totally himself, a measure against my own reactions and to show me how this is possible, I am in danger of laying not just my coat in a puddle for someone to step on, but my whole self.

The good news is that Steve finally gets an appointment with the mental-health team at the local surgery. The bad news, they tell him, is that there is a two-year (and the rest) waiting list for an ADHD assessment. The professional he speaks to sounds sceptical that this is a queue he should even be allowed to join. There has been a lot of chat about it in the media, she says, as if Steve had been idling around town, spotted a shiny neurodivergent bandwagon and decided to jump on it. She thinks recent press about the condition has been unhelpful in some cases, and she reminds Steve that he is not a psychiatrist and therefore can't diagnose himself. 'This is the problem with the internet,' she sighs.

While Steve is waiting for the huge NHS cogs to turn, she advises signing him up for a course of cognitive behavioural therapy. This is like suggesting Lewis

FEBRUARY

Hamilton takes driving lessons, or David Hockney tries painting by numbers. Steve lists all of the past therapy he has had, including a month-long stint in a secure unit, which was the result of a terrifying period of depression and self-harm before we got together. He says that if he is sent back to square one, he is not sure he will still be here by Christmas. He says he is desperate, and she encouragingly repeats the benefits of CBT and suggests he does more exercise. Preferably in the fresh air.

In the first instance, this comes as a massive disappointment. Steve has pinned all his hopes on a different reaction. I have been reading about the flaws in the system and how self-diagnosis can be ignored and am feeling more galvanised than him, probably because it isn't happening to me. We talk about the options. Steve borrows some money from his mum and googles private psychiatrists. We consider the minefield of finding someone this way as he picks through a plethora of clinics offering answers. He knows which qualifications to look for and chooses a psychiatrist who has his own practice and ticks all the review and qualification boxes.

'He's like me,' Steve says enthusiastically. 'A one-man band. He isn't part of a big corporate set-up designed to fleece me. Anyway, the main reason I chose him is because he has a kind face in his photograph.'

The psychiatrist sends a stack of questionnaires that cover every period of Steve's life. The childhood section is the hardest to answer as those years are shrouded in the mists of time and trauma, so the responses are vague. Too vague, it turns out, for the psychiatrist to go any further. He reads through the returned forms and tells Steve he can't take him on without a clear overview of his early life. As frustrating as this is, it reassures me that the psychiatrist is not just taking the money and throwing out a diagnosis in return. To Steve, this is another brick wall, but he has fire in his belly and spends Sunday afternoon in the attic rooting out his old school reports. Reading them again is more painful than he expected, his cheeks red with the shame and indignation of a small boy who has been misunderstood and labelled unruly and hopeless.

'It reminds me of a school swimming lesson. Being in a line of children who single-filed out of the changing room and were instructed to wait at the shallow end. I remember the water being glassy clear. If I close my eyes I am back there, seven years old, in my trunks.' Steve shuts his eyes tightly to demonstrate and continues the story. 'Fearsome Mrs Pocklington was in charge that day. I don't know where she was in that moment, but I know she wasn't near me so there was nothing and nobody to save me from myself. One minute I was standing with my back to the wall, the next I had launched myself into the water. I am not sure I could even swim. I surfaced to find her at the side of the pool shouting at me to get out. I was sent back to the changing room, past the line of wide-eyed children, dripping with water and humiliation.'

He opens his eyes. This is not the first time I have heard this, but he usually tells it as a funny story, hiding from the way the stomach-churning memory still taunts him.

Steve painstakingly highlights and annotates relevant sections from his reports and emails them over to the psychiatrist.

> *... he must take care to plan his time wisely and so meet deadlines.*

... too many times however, he is content to allow himself to be distracted.

... has settled down after a shaky start – silly behaviour manifested itself in the playground.

... written work is very careless and Steven even makes mistakes when copying from the blackboard.

... immature behaviour... finds it difficult to concentrate.

... and yet he has a quick mind, but fails to commit to writing an accurate and exhaustive interpretation of his knowledge.

... works with interest but seems incapable of prolonged periods of concentration.

... his termly work is nothing to be proud of.

Stephen (sic) tries to be the comedian in the class but fails miserably ... I hope in future he will attend lessons in a more work-orientated frame of mind.

... but if he can conquer distracting and being distracted he should do well.

The following morning, he calls the practice to check they have received his email and whether this is enough to confirm an appointment. He apologises for his impatience, and the psychiatrist's PA tells him not to worry, she is used to it, it comes with the territory of someone looking for answers. The school reports do the trick, and we laugh about the speed at which the psychiatrist changes his mind after reading them, and then we stop laughing because of what it means. It has been a disconcerting process for Steve and yet he also feels a strange reassurance in seeing how his old teachers' comments have unwittingly pinpointed his

ADHD without possibly even knowing what it was in the early seventies. It would be another twenty years before the word 'neurodiversity' appeared in a piece by the American writer, Harvey Blume.

Steve has timed the Zoom psychiatric appointment for Friday when he knows he will be at work on his own. He shares an office in town with Anna and Dan, friends and village neighbours of ours, who have their own unrelated companies. Neither of them will be there at the end of the day, so he can have complete privacy and a better internet connection than we have at home.

The assessment takes a couple of hours and goes into Steve's complicated mental-health history, as well as his behaviour and outlook on life. When he gets back, I open a bottle of wine and he recounts as many of the questions as he can remember, miming the psychiatrist's thoughtful face and pacing the kitchen, his speech fast and frantic, unable to quieten the adrenaline that pinballs around his system as he goes off on tangents. I need to get to the nub of it all.

'Did he give you any indication of where he thought you were diagnosis-wise?' I can feel my impatience rearing up, and I try to drown it in Pinot Noir. When you want answers, you sort of want them immediately.

'He didn't. He was just very calm and respectful and said he would come back to me within a week.' Steve shrugs. 'So that's that then. I guess we just wait.'

Sure enough, less than a week later, the psychiatrist's report is emailed over. Steve has a confirmed diagnosis, scoring 98 per cent on the 'most likely to have ADHD chart'. It feels strange to celebrate this, but we do. After a lifetime of trying to work out who he is, Steve has been given a response, a framework for the future. This is making sense of the tumult of exhaustion and self-loathing he has carried with him for over fifty years. It is momentous.

'I knew you were!' I say in an annoyingly smug way.

'I knew I was!'

Steve is jubilant. Patterns of behaviour, people and situations flash before his eyes, broken things from his past that are beginning to make sense now that he can shine this bright new light on them. We don't talk about what this means for us because Steve needs to digest this news, but it feels like a positive step. OK, maybe more of a shuffle. Or a lean. But a sort of progress.

He has another appointment with the private psychiatrist to discuss medication that he has asked for, and then waits for the prescription to arrive in the post. As soon as it comes, he rushes around to the pharmacy and returns, chest puffed out with wonder and pride as he shows me the little blue pill that he thinks may be the answer to everything. We are in new territory.

*

After a winter break, the egg honesty box up the lane is back in business, and Gerry, who rents a field in the village and appears to be half-man half-tractor because he is always driving around on one, has built a wooden structure I am envious of. He is offering logs for sale and is promising vegetables from his allotment later in the year. I don't know if I have inspired this, but I hope my own set-up will be a welcome addition and may encourage other neighbours to do the same or donate their gluts to me so that I can do it for them. The more the merrier. I still miss the honesty café and bakery at the top of the lane, which was set up in the decommissioned petrol station. A severe fire, which needed seven fire engines, made one family temporarily homeless and obstructed several businesses. The building spent months in darkness, water puddling on the lino, everything covered in a sticky coating of smoky dust and a sharp, acrid smell that followed you home.

This café was a large part of my daily life. As well as the sociable eggy bread stacks with kids and neighbours, I would go in a lot on my own. Just me and my laptop. And my phone, which Clive, the proprietor, would take off me to save me from myself. It was a good place to write, and it meant I was handily available for testing his latest recipes, such as duck fat chips, salted caramel doughnuts and the monumental but short-lived salt beef sandwich.

Clive was an award-winning advertising executive back in the day and a part-time enfant terrible. He and I sometimes talked about what we used to be, mainly where we used to go. We wasted a lot of time trying to remember the names of long-dead Soho restaurants and bars. He once gave me the draft of a manifesto he had written about village economics and the part his café played in it – he wanted to publish it as a book. I sent him an email with the reasons why I thought it wasn't ready. He went ahead and printed the book, entitled *Different*, with a belly band around each copy that had my email transcribed in full on it (without my permission, but that's Clive the Renegade).

Lucy Brazier, my best critic, said of it, 'Right, I have had a proper look at this. It's a great idea, a breath of fresh air and quintessentially you. If you want any feedback on it, it feels a little confused – part manifesto, part inspiration, part CV. It needs an editorial eye to put it in a sort of order and, I know you disagree with me but, a few stand-out recipes. The text needs a little tidy because there are a few mistakes. It works for the bakery, but I don't think it works as a publication for sale yet. Just my opinion so feel free to ignore! Xxx.' She is bang on. It is very random and confused, but the book had to be produced, warts and all. I'm happy, Clive.

PS. Contains language that some people might be offended by

The *Telegraph* once asked if Clive could in fact be Britain's grumpiest chef after a (positive) brush with a visiting journalist. ITV got in touch to see if he wanted to go on telly and prove that he was or wasn't grumpy, but quite rightly he turned them down. He divided his customer base with his gruff, funny, uncompromising attitude and his potty mouth, sporting a messy apron and a fierce passion for the local community. Some people went in every day; others went once and refused to return.

He also modelled his business on honesty. There were no orders written, bills presented or magic memory. You simply went to the till at the end and told them what you had. Or you popped cash into the pot or tapped your bank card on the machine. Trust in a commercial space is intoxicating, and it created a particular magic at Clive's place.

News and sirens travel fast in the country. As soon as I heard about the fire, I messaged Clive to check he was OK. I knew he would be standing in the wreckage, mind racing with a plan B. The man is a human defibrillator.

A text pinged straight back. *I'm fine, but your office is fucked.*

*

'I spoke to my client Julian today.'

Steve is toasting cumin seeds in the heavy cast iron frying pan that could double as a weapon in case of intruders. He is cooking supper so I can finish a small copywriting job I have virtually begged for. It is getting late, and I was hoping he would heat up last night's bolognese, stick some mash on top and call it cottage pie, but he is making a curry from scratch. I don't want to moan because I know how much enjoyment he gets from immersive culinary activities, but everyone is starving and if I eat too late, I will flop into bed feeling bloated with terrible indigestion. I want him to finish his story so I can tell him to hurry up with the meal.

'He isn't happy about a planning regulation, so I had to explain the reasons why we couldn't just ignore it and what our options are. Anyway, I think I went on too long. When we said goodbye, he thought he had put the phone down, but he hadn't, and I overheard him talking about me.'

I am now fully engaged with the conversation.

'He said to someone that I wouldn't shut up, telling him things he didn't need to know and that I was frustrating. It was a bit of a rant, so I put the phone down.' Steve is very matter-of-fact about it. 'I mean, he's not wrong, I know I talk too much, but I also wanted him to have all the information. I am a terrible communicator.'

I know Julian. He is a nice person, and he has a point. Sometimes when Steve speaks, I want to say 'too many words! Use fewer!' but there is something about Steve's acceptance of his client's behaviour and his ability to try and understand his part in it that is different to past responses. He is calm, a little quizzical about it all, as if he is stuck on a crossword clue. In the absence of his usual rage, I experience some on his behalf along with a fierce jolt of loyalty.

'Fire him,' I say, like a drunk Alan Sugar. 'Fire his sorry arse because you do not need to work for people like that.'

Steve laughs, which is also a departure from his usual behaviour and is good to see. 'No, I emailed him saying I had overheard what he said, and I apologised for banging on, but I was trying to furnish him with all the facts, and I am not always good at knowing how much information is too much. I know I can overcomplicate things.'

I am speechless at this new approach.

'Anyway, he replied saying how sorry he was and sometimes he behaves like a twat. And I thought, I know how that feels because I can be a twat too.'

I decide not to complain about the time the curry is taking.

March

At first light, I am waiting in the beach car park for my friend Ros to turn up. The fingernail moon hovers behind me, waiting to hand over to the rising sun, which blurs the space where sky and sea meet. Ros arrives in a duvet-style coat that she found in a charity shop and turned out to be Prada. I will never not be jealous of that.

She looks a lot like me – greying hair pulled back into a bun, glasses – but thinner. She instructs me not to hug her because she spent the weekend nursing a grandchild with a stinking cold and she is convinced she is coming down with it. Instead, we do an interpretive hello dance that also acts as a Wim Hof-style warm-up because we are being whipped by a bitter easterly. The sand cracks with frost as I slop across in my old sheepskin slippers to the sea wall, where piles of clothes are neatly folded next to smart Thermos flasks and plump hot water bottles. Several swimmers have already beaten us to it, and I can see brightly coloured caps bobbing in the swell, their laughter carried to shore on the froth-tipped waves.

We wade in purposefully, telling each other this is just what we do and no need to make such a fuss about it for goodness' sake. The shock of cold reaches my soft middle as Ros counts to three for our synchronised flop into the water. We paddle furiously with flailing limbs. I am a splutterer and a shrieker, relying on a string of salty expletives and puffing exhalations until my body finds its rhythm in the water. My brain is paused – all thoughts, fears and to-do lists are suspended as we stretch out into the glittering path cast by the sun on the water and discuss the possibility of getting our noses pierced. Today is the first day of spring.

Every morning, there is something different about our swim. Swaggering sunrises of orange, coral and pink mirrored in glassy, calm seas. Or weighty, gunmetal clouds, hanging over shouty surf. Sometimes the gig rowers are in before us, heading towards the sun. Occasionally, there is a fancy yacht or historic tall ship bobbing around beyond the harbour mouth.

On land, the seagulls are an aggressive nuisance, but when we are in the water they dip and arc gracefully above, screeching to each other across our heads. This is one of the reasons I keep coming back in the early light. The anticipation of what it will be like gets me up while the house is still sleeping, dashing straight down to the beach to join a growing group of people braving the ocean. It is a strong start to the day and sometimes my only tangible achievement.

Ros and I dip throughout the year, in all conditions, including the month we were plagued by small jellyfish that gave electric nettle-like stings. When it is calm, we repeatedly praise the sea for good behaviour; when it is choppy, we face the waves as if going into battle, striding forth before they send us reeling and giddy back to the shore. We have come out to rounds of applause from passers-by. A tourist stopped us to take our photo while we stood awkwardly looking past her at our towels and, in the depths of winter, a craggy fisherman stated gravely, 'You need your heads testing.'

'You never regret a swim,' sea dippers always say, 'unless you meet a shark,' I like to respond cheerily, but mostly I just say that in my head. I have inadvertently caught a sprat in my cleavage, mistaken jellyfish tentacles for seaweed, spotted several seals and avoided an aggressive dolphin. I don't wear my glasses in the water, so one whiff of wildlife bigger than me and I head straight back to shore. Other swimmers evangelise about the 'privilege of sharing the water with these magnificent beasts', while I remember the man, front-crawling along the swim line in his sleek wetsuit, who was upended by a confused dolphin looking for his mate and had to be rescued by a fishing boat. I don't want to put anyone off though.

The truth is, I have always been scared of the water. I am a terrible swimmer with no technique – I can't front crawl, jump in or dive, and I hate putting my head under. Childhood swimming lessons were a certain type of agony so, once my parents were satisfied that if I fell off a boat I wouldn't drown, I stopped going. Plus, we never got onto boats unless you count the ferry from Dover to Calais. Had I fallen overboard then, they would have been more concerned about me ruining the family camping trip than my jerky breast stroke.

So I don't get in the sea to swim. There are other reasons like the old classic, cold water therapy, which I can vouch for, although it annoys everyone else who doesn't do it and would prefer that I didn't go on about it. As well as how it makes me feel (which is great, but shush), the second reason I got in the water was as a cure for homesickness.

After almost a decade in Dorset, I still pined for London and my old life, so I turned the thought around. Rather than listing all the things I could do in the city that I couldn't do in the country, I thought about what London couldn't give me. One of those glaringly obvious answers was the sea. I trudged down to Lyme Bay, stripped off against the backdrop of the iconic Jurassic coastline with its impressive curve of cliffs, and walked into the English Channel.

It felt amazing so I kept going back. Here was something I couldn't do if I moved back to the city. Here was something that made the endorphins speed breathlessly through my system, whooping with joy. Here was something that challenged me just enough. This was before wild swimming was the razzling dazzle of a social media phenomenon it is now. I didn't – and I still don't – have any special kit. Just my trusty M&S swimmers, an old towel, a hot drink in a flask, layers of moth-eaten woollens and my funny, clever pal, Ros.

On the way home, with a hot water bottle stuffed up my coat, I drive past a woodland dell and spot the first shoots of wild garlic. This is a magnificent moment after what is an unappetising few weeks, referred to as the 'hungry gap' in the veg-growing community. I screech to a halt and reverse the car into a hedge. It is still early, before the school bus will need to squeeze past me, or dog walkers will think I have crashed.

Wild garlic grows in clumps in damp, shady spots, their bright green leaves splaying out first, before the starburst white flowers begin to appear a couple of weeks later. If in doubt when picking the leaves, the scent will tell you – a fresher, greener smell than the garlic bulb. I pick a handful at a time since they don't keep for long, and I take a few leaves from different plants in line with the forager's code of conduct, even though this place is carpeted with the pungent foliage.

I use wild garlic daily until we are absolutely pig-sick of it and are happy to see the back of it for another year. So it is shredded and stirred through scrambled eggs, poked into focaccia, blitzed with toasted nuts and parmesan for pesto, chucked into all soups and added to salad for some zingy heat. The early leaves are the best for cooking – I keep a bunch in a glass of water, which helps them to stay fresh. The kitchen smells happily of garlic, as does our breath.

Without fail, the recipe I return to every year is for my wild garlic-and-cheese scones. When I post a picture of them on Instagram, I am deluged with messages from friends and followers who live in wild garlic-free zones. I feel bad. I can see how infuriating it is to scroll through food accounts full of bragging foragers. My suggestion of replacing wild garlic with sautéed leeks, spring onions or chives receives a lacklustre response. So I make wild garlic salt and send little jars out to friends who can't get hold of it. And I share the recipe on social media, along with a rallying cry to those who are lucky to roll around in acres of the plant.

'Make wild garlic salt and spread the love!' I proclaim.

This isn't exactly an honesty box approach but it feels related in some powerfully expansive way.

*

My friend Maddie, one of the first people I met when I moved to Dorset, is an excellent gardener with a clear plan, whereas I am still a flibbertigibbet who is always a month behind where I should be. She keeps me updated with regular texts saying *My courgette seeds are in* and *Don't forget to net your strawberry plants* and *Do you want any climbing bean plugs?* Whenever Maddie has an excess of anything, I put my hand up for it. She also has an ingenious way of planting seeds in sections of old guttering filled with soil and has made one up for me. It is waiting snugly in her greenhouse: kale sprouting in one end, while runner beans grow at the other.

It is a relief not to be responsible for them right now as I am spring cleaning the lean-to at the back of the house. This is a dirty job, and halfway through I regret ever starting it because there is nowhere else to store all the stuff we have. As I am moving things, I spot a desiccated object in the corner of a box, and I know instantly what this is. The last time I saw one of these was in London many years ago, when I was working for the actress and jolly good egg, Kate Winslet.

I was wading through a pile of her fan mail and came across a shoe box with holes poked in the top. Inside was what I assumed had been a mouse stretched out on a bed of straw. Luckily for me – unluckily for it – it was dead, and had been for some time, but not before it had been posted from America to London. A transatlantic gift of a small mummified pet. I didn't tell Kate. She was busy filming in Mexico, surviving the sinking of the *Titanic*, so she had enough on her plate.

I put almost everything back in the lean-to, albeit neater and cleaner. Now there are no cobwebs, the concrete floor has been swept, the sink scrubbed of dirt, and the work surface is empty because I am turning it into my makeshift honesty store. This feels like a temporary solution because I am not sure how many passers-by would venture into what appears to be someone's house. And one of the kitchen windows looks through to it, which makes me feel as if I am spying on customers, or they can catch me eating the kids' chocolate straight from the fridge. But for now, I have set myself the challenge of opening it on Mothering Sunday for village purposes, with the theme of breakfast so that local children can scoot up and do some shopping.

Stocking the store has been the most fun I have had for months: a bit like playing shops as a child. In the absence of any homegrown produce, Steve has decided to bake a few loaves to offer. Our neighbour Dan, founder of the local brewery, offers me a case of apple juice to sell when I tell him my plan. I invest in more eggs from the farm too. This is an outlay that subverts the traditional honesty box structure, but I am keen to try things out. I am not in it to make a profit right now.

I have a few precious jars of Seville Orange Marmalade left over, but I decide not to part with them and make a batch using blood oranges instead as these are still around. Blood oranges are sweeter than the Sevilles so need a little less sugar and make a beautiful ruby-tinged preserve.

Chalked on the wall above the sink, I list what is available, ask for donations and leave out a jam jar of loose change.

Gilt & Flint Apple Juice
Haye Farm Eggs
Blood Orange Marmalade
Wild Garlic and Cheese Scones
Rhubarb and Ginger Muffins
Old Forge Bread

I am up at sunrise on Mothering Sunday to bake the first batch of scones and muffins and catch the early shoppers. Steve has promised to make bread, but he is still sleeping, adjusting to the rhythm of the pills that are keeping him up later in the evening. I prop a blackboard outside an hour later.

Honesty Store OPEN!!
(There will be bread too, but the baker didn't get up as early as the pastry chef)

Within a couple of hours, we have sold out of scones and apple juice, and the few eggs that are left will be beaten into an omelette for our breakfast. The bread sold straight from the oven, but Steve only made four loaves and two were on commission, hand-delivered piping hot to our neighbours, who were still in their pyjamas.

We eat the last of the muffins and think about what we can do for Easter. While we are waiting for our homegrown produce to burst forth, maybe a themed offering around a significant date is a more practical way to run this honesty box, judging from today's success. Steve and the kids cook a Mother's Day roast for me, with Jesse making the airiest Yorkshire puds the size of tennis balls, while I lounge on the sofa with a large glass of wine.

*

I don't have any work. What began as a predictably quiet start to the year has turned into tumbleweed bowling down my career path. As a writer, I have always had at least one project on the go. I know how fortunate I have been, and I am due a dip in employment, but this doesn't help quell the cold panic that rises as quickly as our mortgage interest rate. Steve says he can cover all the bills in the short term, but being self-employed too makes it a nail-biting time for us both. In fact, there are a few things he doesn't cover, but he doesn't tell me or admit it to himself, until I see the court summons for the council tax.

For a couple of months, our accountant, David, has been asking me to pop in so I finally go to see him. I am full of excuses about a book deadline that had kept me busy at the tail end of last year, and he wants to know what it was about.

'How to be good with your money,' I say without irony.

'Did you include the part where you should reply to your accountant's emails?' he asks, and we both laugh.

Then I feel like poking myself in the eye because I am a total idiot and David doesn't deserve to be stood up by an ostrich writer with her head in the sand. Steve calls him 'Finance Dad'. He is the only one with a clear overview of our money, and he spends longer sorting us both out than he will ever be properly rewarded for. In addition, Steve has told him about his ADHD diagnosis, and he has recommended an online accounting system that may be more suitable for the way Steve's brain works.

Today, Finance Dad is giving me lots of sage advice about treating myself as a business and setting money aside for tax before it is due. I say I am scared I will never work again. He stops just short of telling me I am being ridiculous and sends me off with a rallying speech of support. I am reminded of my old boss and friend, Dallas, the agent I worked for before I became an agent in my own right. When we had meetings with actors who were bemoaning their lack of auditions or questioning their hit rate, Dall would open a bottle of his favourite

Chardonnay and allay as many of their fears as possible. As they left, he would give them a hug and say the same thing – 'Keep the faith' – and now I say that to myself every single day.

I continue to hustle for writing jobs while scanning the local ads for short-term solutions, deciding to start with the things I like most: books and food. I get an interview at a local bookshop, but I don't get the job, even though I spend an inordinate amount of time in there, can find each section blindfolded and am eager to take on the hoovering. Perhaps I was too eager? This does nothing for my confidence.

I bump into a friend outside Waitrose in Bridport, who is popping in to buy an organic chicken, as I am building up the nerve to go and ask about shifts. I make the mistake of telling him this and he thinks I am joking.

'Oh, how the mighty have fallen,' he says, when he realises I am not.

'I should be so lucky to work there,' I say archly, and am proved right. There are no jobs.

My career started at the BBC, and it was a dream come true. It may have been a lowly schedules clerk position at the rocky bottom of the pay scale, but every morning I got to walk into the good ship Broadcasting House and up to the Radio Drama department. Fresh from A Levels, this was my university. The pals I made thirty-five years ago – Cath, Nicki and Elaine – have been my best friends ever since.

The department was a creative and half-cut law unto itself, where many directors, producers and writers began or ended their careers. The young and ambitious clipped the heels of the once-renowned, and got drunk together in the smoke-filled circular office of John

Tydeman, the head of drama, at the far end of the sixth-floor corridor.

John's office was the venue for celebrations, showdowns, job interviews, disciplinaries, staff appraisals, hosting dignitaries and visiting press, watched over by a shelf of teddy bears. I often helped unload the weekly booze delivery of gin, vodka, whisky and wine, listed under 'corporate entertainment' on expenses, and marvelled at the speed the drinks cabinet would empty.

When John wasn't there, we used it as a luxurious staff room, lolling on the sofas and watching daytime telly as we ate lunch. When he was there, we steered clear in case of any shouting, storming out, crying or congratulatory back slapping. John's voice boomed above all, and he prowled the corridors tiddly-pomming like Winnie-the-Pooh when he was happy, and roaring like an antagonised grizzly when he was not.

His was a gang you wished you were in but had no hope of joining unless you were fearsomely intelligent, side-splittingly funny or related to someone he knew, and I was none of those things. The *Who's Who* would be out on the desk after interviewing for producer positions. One marvellous woman, who shall remain nameless, (ironically) had no relation to a famous writer she shared an unusual surname with. It was just a fluke. The senior management team assumed she was his daughter or his niece and gave her the job, so it was only when he was mentioned at a later stage that she stated dismissively, 'Oh, I've never met the man. No relation to me.'

Towards the end of my second year there, I had a message that John, who never remembered my name, was going to do my annual appraisal. After an uncomfortable preamble of small talk, paper-shuffling and box-ticking, he perked up.

'I see you have taken advantage of the secondment system and popped off to our colleagues in other departments. I bet *EastEnders* was fascinating,' he said, skim-reading the document. 'Good for you! That's one of the marvellous things about the BBC, encouraging you to flourish. What did you discover?'

'Well,' my voice wavered nervously, 'I have decided not to pursue a production-based career. I enjoyed working with actors the most, so I want to be a casting director. Or an agent.'

John's dark caterpillar eyebrows shot up in surprise. 'Oh no, darling, that's not right for you,' he said, taking a long drag on his cigarette. 'You see, you aren't anyone. You have no family connections in the business or people to help you network. Not like Cecelia. Her parents, her stepfather, her siblings, her boyfriend, they are all immersed in this industry, so she is exactly the sort of person who can do it. Not you, I'm afraid. You will get married and have babies.'

He smiled at me encouragingly and signed his name with a flourish at the bottom of my appraisal report.

He died a few years ago. I was heartened to read in his obituary that, as a board member at the Garrick Club, as well as arguing for the rule on neck ties to be loosened, he also wanted women to be allowed to join. It appears you can teach an old bear new tricks.

*

Our neighbour's magnolia tree is blooming; our kitchen window is filled with a curtain of pink-edged blossom.

It is putting on the sort of display that stops me in my tracks, and I regularly pop out to take photographs of it against various colours of sky. The magnificence of it makes me feel spring-like, even if the weather doesn't. March is such a tease.

This is exactly the point of the year when I am not sure if I can continue living in the countryside. You would think I would have learnt by now. I have been waiting patiently, expecting things to change, and then they don't. It is still miserably cold, wet and muddy. My reward for surviving the long winter comes in tiny increments: the fulsome magnolia, the early daffodils, chirruping blackbirds at first light and the promise of the clocks going forward. It is all there if I remember to look for it.

The track out of the village is at peak swamp. The landscape is broad brushstrokes of bleak browns, greys and greens, and the hedgerows are speckled with the confetti blossom of the spiky blackthorn. There is definitely more this year, so does this mean we will be inundated with their sloe berries in the autumn? I hope so.

From the ridge on the old cart road, I can look out across the valley to the white cottage nestled in the dip, a whisper of smoke rising from the chimney. The fields slope and rise towards the sea, which is tucked just out of sight behind the cliffs where matchbox-sized caravans are set in a herringbone formation looking out to the ocean horizon. I recently saw an owl here, pale and snowy, swooping low from a distant tree, and for a few weeks there was a rare white pheasant flitting around the field, somehow evading predators. Both ghostly birds were vivid in the winter dirge.

MARCH

I record a voice note for Thea announcing that spring is almost here, way behind London of course, but nevertheless something to remark upon before I launch into an update on Steve. Thea knows about the psychiatrist appointment and that Steve has been taking medication. I tell her how we are both pretending not to monitor it too closely, but its significance for him and for us as a couple is hard to be breezy about. So far, Steve is feeling more focused and productive and there have been no significant mood swings. He says he has a newfound sense of balance. I don't think it has been the miracle he expected, but it is definitely helping. I mention that I can't feel anything but caution right now, which I am assuming is normal.

I press send on a message that has somehow come in at twenty-three minutes. That is a lot of me, particularly at 7 a.m. on a Monday morning. I leave another voice note apologising for the length of the last one.

Thea and I leave regular morning voice notes for each other as we walk our dogs, with 160 miles of fields, motorways, small towns and big cities between us. I am usually out first, breathlessly climbing grassy mounds, turning an ankle in muddy furrows and tucking my phone into my hood to mute the background wind as I speak. Thea listens to my ramblings an hour later when she is striding around Wandsworth Common with her pup, Cosmo, and sends a reply, complete with audible coffee sips and words lost to emergency service sirens. There are a lot of pauses while one of us stops to shout at their dog who has chased a squirrel (mine) or a jogger (hers), and we often lose our train of thought as we stoop to pick up dog poo, repeatedly apologising for terrible menopausal memory.

I only tend to use the voice note messaging system with Thea in what feels like an intimate, intense podcast between us both: one where you speak for as long as you like without interruption. I think this is a key element to its power and why it can feel like therapy. What begins as an offload or a rant about something can head in a direction I wasn't prepared for, and often, as I have spoken something out loud, I realise what is actually frustrating me.

I am amazed by thoughts and feelings I didn't know I had, as they tumble out of my head and land in that unjudgemental space. I can also waffle away from a subject so badly that I bore myself, so I always delete those messages and record again, snappier, briefer and with a clearer idea of what I am trying to say, already feeling lighter after a rant that no longer exists. Thea and I cover all the big stuff, but we always chuck in a bit of popular culture too, gossiping about celebrity news and discussing a favourite podcast, film, book or telly programme. I can about-turn on something I had been ignoring if she says she likes it.

This year, more than ever, we have been each other's safe place, both of us in relationships with recently diagnosed ADHD men. We can recount situations to each other and know, without further explanation, how Steve or Adam reacted, how we felt and what we might be able to do to resolve it. So many times, we start our responses with: 'I know exactly what you mean.'

*

I should be using my unwanted free time constructively in the garden, but this is a tricky month of guessing if the final frost is indeed the very final frost. How are you

MARCH

supposed to know? If there is another icy morning, the magnolia has had it.

I flick through my garden books and google seasonal checklists in case I am missing 'A Big Horticultural Job' and will kick myself come July. We don't have rose bushes to prune, alpines to tidy up or borders to mulch, and I feel curiously lonely in the veg patch without Steve tutting loudly. He is at work during the week, and I know he would rather me not do anything significant without him there. Such as misplant the legumes.

My mojo is in the doldrums. Morosely, I weed and listen to a podcast by two funny, smart women, Fi Glover and Jane Garvey, whose effortless banter makes them feel like they could be my friends as they talk about a recent night out together. It is too early for a glass of wine, or is it?

I decide not to put the rainbow chard seedlings into the raised bed until the last day of the month. Just in case. Or at least until Monty Don tells me to on BBC's *Gardener's World*. Although, like the thrill-seeking risk taker that I am, I do put the pea seeds in. They could turn out to be mouse food, but I want to start a first crop and see what happens. After measuring out some space for the beetroot, my nerve fails me as these are Steve's favourite, so I leave them for him to sow because I do not want to be responsible for ballsing it up.

The winter salad leaves are beginning to bolt, reminding me to sow more, which I do in a large soil tray and leave in the lean-to. Another thing to juggle out there. This is the point in our own gardener's world, where we are sick of the sight of all the leggy seedlings dotted around on windowsills but are too nervous to plant them out yet.

When Steve gets home, he acts happy at the progress I have made in the veg patch, but he disappears off to strim some nettles. I can see he is reinstating himself in the space, so I leave him to it and go inside to cook dinner. I had this image of us working side by side in the garden, rebuilding our broken relationship in companionable silence or deep conversation as we dug, planted and filled the honesty box. Instead, we both retreat to separate familiar spaces: me in the kitchen chopping onions; and him on the garden bank, eternally cutting back brambles.

*

I am on the phone about a potential new writing project. Just the possibility of it lifts my spirits. I go into the sitting room and shut the door, desperately hoping the internet connection will hold long enough for me to finish the call. Midway through, my middle child Hebe comes in, tights laddered (mine as it happens, so I won't be wanting them back) and school skirt spattered with paint from her beloved art class. She stands in front of me.

I try to ignore her. When I turn the other way, she sidles into my line of sight. I have to consider that someone may be dying so I look at her with an expression that says 'someone better be dying' and she mimes the dog being sick all over the kitchen floor. I pull a face that implores her to deal with it, and she mimes herself puking and leaves me alone. The rest of the conversation is tinged with the knowledge that once I have been a groovy professional talking about exciting career things, I will need to go back into the kitchen and scoop dog vomit off the terracotta tiles.

We all love Margot. She is the most spoilt member of our family. Initially we made great strides with her training: blowing a whistle before all commands, sending her to her bed when we ate, teaching her to walk to heel on the lead. Then Covid hit, we went into lockdown and the five of us were at home a lot, each with our own ideas on puppy discipline. In turn, she cornered us with such expressive, adoring looks, sideways head-tilting and an offered paw, that we were powerless in the face of her golden charms.

I said she wasn't allowed on the furniture, as she curled up in the corner of the sofa. I said no feeding her from the table, as she rested her noble head on my leg, waiting for my toast crust. I said no going upstairs, and this rule has, for the most part, remained because everyone gets tired of losing socks that have been carried around the house sandwiched between her soggy jaws.

I have never known a dog with as many nicknames as Margot has. The children named her after Margot in *The Durrells*, and Steve and I named her after Penelope Keith's character in *The Good Life*. I wanted Barbara, but I was over-ruled. Margot was shortened to Margs for ease when shouting across a field. Then it quickly turned to Moose when she grew bigger than anticipated and surprised me as much as the time I saw a real-life moose, expecting it to be the size of a deer rather than an elephant. It was a natural progression to Moosingtons and Margotines.

From this point, it goes wayward, with TikTok and social media taking some of the blame. Floof, Floon, Chonky, Chonky-Floon and Mrs Chonnington-Floof (a particular favourite). Somewhere, dog became Nog, Noggin the Nog and Kenny Noggins (as in Loggins, the American musician). We deviated to Moons, Mooningtons, Noon, Da Noon, Fatty, Fattypuss Platypus, Precious and, inexplicably, Sooty SooSoo. And after the revelation one night that she looked the minutest bit like the jacket potatoes we were eating, she became Jacky Tayto. It is unsurprising she has trouble responding to her actual name.

Someone once described their friend's dog as an overexcited child on a campsite, who has no personal space boundaries and goes to visit people in their tents assuming they will be warmly received. This is our dog, the meeter and greeter of the canine world. Forever friendly. Steve calls her his therapy dog. It is true that she seems particularly in tune with his frequency and can sense his mood. There is a distinctive tone to his voice when he is stressed, and she is alert to it, coming to find me before trying to clamber onto my lap. She doesn't do this at any other time, so I know this is an anxious reaction to his behaviour and makes me think she doesn't want to assume a support role. It doesn't feel very fair for her to shoulder that responsibility. She should just be a happy dog doing fun things, enjoying all her nicknames, praying for toast crusts, rolling in cowpats, chewing other dogs' bones and sleeping a lot.

It makes me think about the responsibility the children take on. If this is the dog's reaction, then how about them? Steve is an amazing father, with qualities that our kids love and have benefited from, but they have also been on the frontline of a few of his darker days.

The catalyst for them happened one recent Saturday, before diagnosis, when they all took the dog to the beach while I stayed at home to work or maybe just lie down for a bit. Within the hour, they stormed back into the house, the three siblings joined together in indignation and fury because Steve had lost his temper and shouted at them in public. I listened to both sides. Yes, the kids had been irritating and played a stupid game of who they could wind up the quickest. Yes, it turned out that backfired because the only one they succeeded in upsetting was their father. And no, it didn't warrant his volcanic response.

I made everyone sit around the table to talk it out. The teenagers did a much better job of this than Steve to begin with, who sat stony-faced, holding his humiliation tightly within his crossed arms. Each said how his reaction had made them feel, that they knew about his mental-health issues and mood disregulation, but his behaviour wasn't OK. My heart cracked with the confusing cocktail of pride, love, shame and sadness.

It was simultaneously one of my lowest parenting experiences, and the best, because what shone out of it, as well as the love and care they showed him, was how they were able to speak up. They were not diminished by his behaviour, and they could say, clearly and confidently, 'This is your issue; it is not mine.' They harnessed a power that I hope they never let go of.

Steve listened to everything they said. He broke down, apologised and everyone hugged. This experience reached into his core and changed him and the memory of it, and the strong relationship they have with him, sustains and reassures me that they are OK. More than OK, in fact. It is the dog I worry about.

April

The oilseed rape fields on the coast road glow luminescent in the early sea mist as I drive back after my morning swim. The garden is also punctuated by yellow: the furry heads of the dandelions, the last of the breezy daffodils, tiny fried-egg daisies and pockets of sweet primroses that pop up along the bank bordering the field and skip out across the grass. The forsythia tree is the first to bring colour into the garden, but the plucky blossom can't quite hang to meet the bluebells. In the veg plot, the mixed salad leaves are bolting, and their resulting flaxen flowers bob triumphantly, reminding me I am not in control.

I join Steve in the garden. He is yet another yellow thing, in his moth-eaten lemon sweater. He has owned this, or a version of it, since we got together over twenty years ago. It is a comfort blanket of a jumper, just like his orange bobble hat, and he has worn it a lot recently, as he waits to settle into the medication or until it settles into him. The pills catapult him out of bed in the morning and keep him going long after I have collapsed on the sofa. They have given him a pronounced tic, which makes his mouth purse tightly and his jaw clench, as if he is in a permanent state of disapproval. His appetite has dulled, which means he has to remind himself to eat by taking lunch into the office every day.

APRIL

These are some of the side effects that are supposed to calm down, but are a reminder of how full-on these amphetamines are. For someone who inhales linseed and chia seeds, rarely eats meat, wages a war against ultra-processed food, doesn't drink, practises yoga daily and recycles everything, this feels like a physical assault on his being. It is the very opposite of who he is, and yet he is fully invested in this salvation and is willing to put up with the short-term side effects, in order to maintain this new equilibrium. He says the benefits outweigh the negatives, even when he is in danger of losing a filling because of grinding his teeth at night.

Anyway, today it is me who struggles. I am questioning everything, spooling back in my head through life choices. It is tricky right now. Our personal money worries are magnified against the backdrop of a country slipping deeper into a cost-of-living crisis, interest rates jumping and the world wobbling on the axis of war. I feel like I am missing my skin – a raw, exposed human mess, flinching at every tiny thing. Steve meticulously sieves through the soil with his hands, picking out chunks of stone and roots and tossing them into the rusty wheelbarrow. I stop pulling dandelions out of the gravel.

'I thought by the time I was in my fifties, everything would be different, better somehow.' I sit back on my heels. 'I mean, not perfect obviously, but balanced. I wouldn't have to panic about finding next month's mortgage or drive a car that's a pothole away from being condemned or secure a slipped pane of glass in a child's bedroom window with duct tape. I know we have so many things to be grateful for but, right now, I spend my days prodded by burst underwire in my bra, and my nights sleeping on a mattress with a busted spring – I'm skewered! Surely that is a metaphor for something? I mean, did you think this is where you would be?'

'Me?' Steve says cheerfully. 'Me?! I thought I would be dead by now, so every day is a bonus.' He grins and returns to his monotonously pleasing chore. He isn't joking. I return to the weeds with renewed vigour.

*

Later that day, I am still in a funk. I can't shake the dread that has lodged in the pit of my stomach. I hide in the cabin on the pretext of doing some work and sit in front of my open laptop staring out of the window, at a view that hasn't changed much for centuries, down the village past the church spire and beyond the fields and valley to the medieval mound, known as the castle. Everything here seems to have a different name from the thing it actually is. The 'village' is really a hamlet. The road junction is called 'the square' and the village pond is known as 'the harbour'. And this cabin is really just a large shed.

The shed was built for Rosa, a professor of something and a friend of Sally, who owned the house before we did. They lived together in the house for several years until, rumour has it, there was a humdinger of a row and they fell out spectacularly. It appears Rosa had nowhere to go, so Sally built her a small cabin in the garden and hooked it up to the house amenities.

When we came to view the cottage and walked up to Rosa's place, we were confronted with a life on pause. The shelf-lined walls were toppling with books, and in the middle of the space was a big double-sided mahogany partner's desk, which made it impossible to swing any one of the multitude of cats who lived on the property. Rosa's living needs were rammed around the edges like an afterthought, with a sink under the window, a single bed in the corner and a strange half-bath next to the loo. Her rain mac was still hanging on a hook on the door, her hat sat on the desk on top of yellowing papers, and her mug was upturned on the tiny draining board. It was as if she had just popped out, but by then she had been dead for several years. Now Sally was too, so the house was up for sale and we bought it.

After we had revamped it, we rented the cabin out as a sort of glamping B&B for over nine years and were restricted to when we could access the veg patch, so when Covid hit we were more than ready for a break. In reclaiming the shed and the garden, it gave us the extra space we needed with three children rapidly growing up. The almost impossible dream for a writing spot for me, and a teen hangout at the weekend, became a happy reality, encouraged by Finance Dad, who said we weren't making enough money to justify turning it back into a holiday let. I guess the homemade granola, time-consuming sourdough and organic farm eggs didn't help balance the books.

Now, we can use every part of our tiered garden, including the raised beds and the sunny, sheltered courtyard spot in front of the shed, which has become a popular family hang-out. Here, there is a rusted garden table, mismatching chairs, a fire bowl that doubles as a BBQ and a sun awning fashioned from a large tablecloth clipped to rope. It isn't chic, but it is unbeatable for early-morning summer breakfasts and end-of-the-day dinner, when we bet on what time the sun will finally disappear behind Otter Hill.

This is exactly where I hoped I would be. With a family. A dog. In an area of outstanding natural beauty with the sea ten minutes away. Both of us doing jobs we love. So why doesn't it feel as idyllic as it looks when I write it down? Why do I sometimes hanker after my old London life and career? When I am asked by people considering making the same move or who have just done it and are taking some time to adjust, it is hard to know what to say. The honest response is that you may never know if you did the right thing, but continuing to let the 'what ifs' catch you out, like I have today, is the worst answer of all.

*

I have come into town to pick Steve up from work and manage to nab a parking space near his office. The skateboarder is out again, poised at the top of the steep high street, waiting for a lull in the traffic before he takes off down the hill, his posture nonchalant as he picks up speed. He is in jeans, a T-shirt and no helmet, his closely shaved head revealing a long, puckered train-track scar from the time he fell off and was rushed to hospital.

I watch him from the rearview mirror as he whizzes past and track his progress, my heart in my mouth, to his safe arrival at the bottom of the road by the clock tower, before he strides back up the long street ready to do the same all over again. At one point, he hitches a lift with an unsuspecting Range Rover, hanging on to the tow bar at the back. He is often here, and I can't tear my eyes away from him. This is what it feels like to be an adult, I think. Big hills to trudge up, getting the timing right, taking a risk, feeling the adrenaline rush and then, too soon, the bottom. No protection, never

APRIL

dressed in the appropriate clothing. Repeat ad infinitum in the hope you don't fall.

*

The Easter school holidays have begun. Raff is tormented by A Level revision and a mother who can't trust that he is really getting on with it. He is exasperated by the regularity with which I pop my head around his bedroom door with the excuse of delivering a treat each time I check up on him: a small pot of strong black coffee, a toasted hot cross bun soggy with melted butter, a handful of almonds, a packet of jelly sweets.

The rest of us are a little aimless in the face of important work going on. We don't want to go off on fun day trips and rub salt in his wound, but nor do we want to be kicking our heels for a fortnight. I am also waiting to hear about a job. As a watched inbox never delivers, I need to shift my focus on to something other than emails and a teenager in exam crisis. Time for another honesty box.

It is unseasonably warm, so I decide to move the honesty box from the lean-to to the front of the house where the tulips are putting on a fine display, despite Sheila's misgivings. She and I do not speak of my floral success when she passes, as tempted as I am to point at them smugly. I drag the uncomfortable iron garden bench from under the window and position it at the bottom of our path, facing the road. As we live on the village square (junction), there is no danger of the bench being missed. I lean a gifted sack of dusty potatoes up against it and add the remaining few bottles of apple juice. Most excitingly, I have beautiful ceramic beakers made by my potter friend, Alice Herbert. She says they are seconds, but I can't detect a single fault with them. She has also wrapped fist-size pieces of clay for craft projects, and I know several children (and adults) who will grab these. This reminds me of the honesty shelves I read about outside a ceramic studio in Japan which was selling off seconds, a widespread custom in the country. In Kochi Prefecture, on the island of Shikoku, Japanese farmers also use the stalls to sell excess and imperfect vegetables, fruit and flowers – the community embraces the honesty box values. Alice does too. She thinks it is a marvellous idea and promises more stock for my next one.

The slate sign is propped up against the bench leg. Steve adds a seed swap tray where people can pick up a packet they fancy and leave something they have too much of. Runner beans get swapped for zinnias, courgettes for cosmos and chillies for sunflowers. Nobody seems to want the calendula we have donated, which is a prolific grower but always makes me happy. Maybe I will sprinkle them liberally around the village in a late-night fit of guerrilla gardening.

While I bake a couple of batches of hot cross buns to add to the bench, I listen to a podcast chat between Angela Hartnett, Nick Grimshaw and Stanley Tucci as they eat spaghetti alle vongole and drink potent negronis. It feels like they are sitting at my kitchen table. I wish they were. I love that podcast. A brief village WhatsApp heralds the buns coming out of the oven, and they are gone within the hour.

A couple of days later, I receive a complaint. Not to my face obviously. Village etiquette means it should be delivered third hand. I bump into my parish council neighbour, Nigel, as I am coming back from my dog walk. He congratulates me on 'trying your hand at hedge laying' and tells me about the new weed puller machine he has ordered, which I am hoping isn't a subtle dig about our jungle garden. Then, as if the thought has just occurred to him, he says how sorry he is to hear of the complaint and hopes it doesn't stop me doing my honesty box thingy. He and his wife are in total agreement about its welcome place in the village.

Complaint?! I tell him this is the first I have heard of it, and I would like to know who has said what. Nigel is flustered. He begins to backtrack and mumbles something about somebody – he can't remember who – who has told his wife that *they* heard somebody – again he can't remember who *exactly* – had complained directly to me.

'No. They, whoever *they* are, have not said anything to me. I have not received a single complaint. What are they unhappy about?' Nigel pauses for a moment, knowing he is too far in to pretend he has made a mistake, and looks like he is weighing up how to deliver the news.

'They – someone, I don't know who – says the bench is causing a village congestion on the junction.' We both look at each other for a moment.

'You mean, like a disturbance?' I can't quite understand what he is saying. There has been no inkling of any issue.

'No, no, not like that, just a, well, an obstruction…' Nigel peters out.

'Oh,' I say. 'Thanks for letting me know.'

I realise as I walk the rest of the way home that I am thrilled my honesty box has created a bit of a stir. Maybe I shouldn't be, but it is fascinating to see how people respond. This now feels like a real thing, that has been received for better and worse, in the community. Nothing says you have made it in a small village until someone moans about whatever the 'it' is. I wonder what could have created a congestion. It was probably the queue for my hot cross buns because if those babies don't incite a bit of a riot, I don't know what will.

*

Still in baking mode, I make simnel cupcakes to take to Rob and Ali's for our Easter weekend celebration. These have a hidden fat layer of marzipan that surprises with almond sweetness when you bite into them. I decide not to make any for the honesty box because dried fruit is expensive, and I know marzipan divides people. Rob waits for them every year. Or he thinks I like to make them for him every year, so we are trapped in this cycle of seasonal bunnery. I thought about buying him an Italian Colomba di Pasqua instead. These cloud-light cakes baked in the shape of a dove, with candied peel and a sugar-and-almond crust, are the Easter cousin of the panettone. I am a big fan, so I buy one for myself, hide it at the back of the cupboard in the kitchen and tear chunks off it while I am waiting for the kettle to boil. I should have bought two.

Steve's medication has run out. While he waits for the prescription to arrive, he sinks into amphetamine-withdrawal oblivion. I know it is bad when he doesn't even speak to Margot, the dog. This is worse than before the diagnosis. It has come at exactly the wrong moment, with another family gathering ahead.

He spends the weekend either snoring on Rob and Ali's sofa or hunched in a chair, fixatedly darning his moth-eaten old jumper. When he gets to the final hole, his bottom lip wobbles, so Ali finds him a pair of her most threadbare socks and her bag of wool. He gratefully continues to weave, creating tiny patches of gold, bubble-gum pink, forest green and turquoise that transform the grey socks into a piece of artwork. The six kids bounce around him, involving him where they can and retreating when they see he is overwhelmed.

Living with ADHD can be hard. For the person who has it, and for those who love them. Like us. Like me. Like now.

*

Are dead birds significant in some way? An omen or a message from the spirit world, perhaps. Steve says it is bird flu, but I am not so sure. Raff sees a crow suspended from a branch in a tree, wings outstretched as if paused in the middle of take-off. One morning, I nip down to the house from my desk in the shed to make a coffee, and as I walk back up there is an expired fat pheasant stretched out on the path that was certainly not there five minutes earlier. Returning from a morning dog walk, a pigeon is lying on the road, and it takes all my might to stop Margot picking it up. A few strides on, there is a robin too – beak open, eyes blank. It is unnerving for birds to be dropping out of the sky all over the place, and strange to see something up close that is normally too fast to get a proper look at.

The birdsong is incredible at this time of year. My pal, Tara, suggests a dawn-chorus walk, which I readily agree to because she is the one with the most knowledge of their calls, and I like an early-morning mission. Our friends, Miranda, TV Lucy (because she works in telly) and I meet Tara in the pot-holey car park of an ancient hillfort in nearby Marshwood Vale at 4.45 a.m. We have timed it to arrive just before first light, so we can hear the very moment the birds begin.

The dog has come with me, which is not ideal because she tends to spook-bark in the dark, but I have also turned up with a flask and a tin of biscuits in my rucksack by way of recompense for irritating canine behaviour. TV Lucy is in her big parka, the one with the soft fur around the hood that I have always coveted, and she looks lovely and snug for the bone-aching chill at this time of the morning, unlike me. Yet again, I am in the wrong coat.

As we walk, Tara points out where the annual country fair used to be held, every June for over 300 years until the mid-fifties. The field full of rural stalls was centred around the horse-racing track, which is now the flat piece of grassland we are striding across. In the gloaming, we are silent, and I imagine the cheers from the crowd, pounding hooves and the land vibrating under our feet.

The first bird to speak up is the keen robin, followed by the pretty chatter of the blue tit and chaffinch, punctuated by the occasional screech of crow and rook. And the owl signing off after a heavy night. We stand in a clutch of trees, heads angled upwards, and listen intently before the dog begins to circle, whining her impatience. On a fallen tree trunk, looking out over the patchwork landscape of the vale and beyond to the sea, I pour hot chocolate into red enamel mugs and pass the biscuit tin around. This is not the ideal snack at 6 a.m, but it does the job, particularly for Miranda's hangover.

We decide to make this an annual event and force our other friend Susie out of bed next time. Tara suggests we go wild camping together; two of us pretend to seriously consider the idea while TV Lucy looks appalled. We choose our favourite bird call. I say mine is the peacock's – an eery medieval wail.

We used to have a peacock. Technically it wasn't ours; it belonged to our ex-neighbour, Brenda, from the farm up the lane. And it was a peahen, a very large, aggressive, noisy bird that would wander into our garden, calling mournfully. Brenda was furious because she thought the children encouraged it to stay. I am not sure how well she knew her peahen, because from the little contact we had with that bird, it was clear it did exactly what it wanted to do. Brenda and her husband, Roger, would drive down, manhandle the peahen into the car and take it back, only for the bird to spring up from behind our silver birch tree a couple of days later.

Then, like being in a bad horror film, it chose our garden to lay its eggs in, nesting in a patch of ferns very close to the cabin, which was then rented to paying guests. We had to keep making excuses for the peahen, as it strutted territorially and launched itself at unsuspecting holidaymakers.

'Hello, welcome to our village! How lovely that the sun is out for you. This is your cabin, the key is in the door, milk in the fridge, homemade sourdough and granola on the table, let us know if you need anything. Oh, and by the way, nothing to be alarmed by, but you may meet a grumpy roosting peahen. Whatever you do, do not engage with her. Do not look her in the eye. Do not move the sun lounger from its current spot, and you will be absolutely fine. She's not ours, but now she has laid eggs we can't shift her.'

I dread to think what the Tripadvisor reviews said at the time – I couldn't bring myself to read them.

The bird had full-on settled in. She had her eggs and sat on them. She had her quivering subjects (us) and she had the run of the garden. Brenda accused us of feeding her to keep her. I said she was stealing food with menaces, which was an entirely different thing altogether. She said she loved that peahen more than any other animal on her farm, and she wanted her home. A quick google of moving a peahen nest told us what we already knew – that she would abandon her eggs – and, although she was pushing her luck with us and breaking Brenda's heart, we had no choice but to wake up to her plaintive call each morning.

Secretly, I grew rather fond of her, as she strutted around, trailing her dingy brown feathers behind her, looking as aloof as a Hollywood diva. I began to feel that the bird liking us best was another reason for Brenda to have little digs at us about farm gates, children on the lane, where we parked our car and how city people would never fit into country life. She was unrelenting in her ability to make us feel like hopeless, disrespectful townies and gave us the impression she wasn't the only villager who felt like that. Once, she instructed a workman to loop barbed wire along the top of the five-bar gate next to our house, which led into her field. She had driven past and spotted the children hanging over it, picking blackberries. We knew she had a complicated relationship with other neighbours too, but it didn't stop me taking to heart what she said and feeling like an unwelcome incomer.

Then something awful happened. The peahen died. One moment, it was on yet another military manoeuvre to annex one half of the garden from humans; the next, it was lying at the side of the road. Initially, I thought it was sun bathing on the hot tarmac, but it was at a strange angle with its head stuck in the verge. My first thought was for Brenda and how devastated she would be. My second thought was how we would be blamed for the unexplained death. As I had a third thought, I raced up to the nest and gingerly checked on the eggs. There were four of them, now looking forlorn and orphaned. I wasn't sure how I was going to break this to Brenda. I called her immediately and explained that I didn't really know what had happened, other than assuming the peahen had been the victim of a hit and run.

'And that's really all I can tell you, Brenda. I am so sorry. I know how upset you'll be. The eggs are still here so I wonder if you can move them to an incubator? And if you want to come and pick up...' I stopped because I wasn't sure the bird had a name, '... and take her away to bury her.' There was silence on the other end of the phone.

'I see,' Brenda said. 'Well, thank you for letting me know. You can keep the eggs, they are impossible to move, and why don't you just sling the bird into the hedgerow?'

No way was I going to touch that carcass. It was huge, smelly and not my problem. It would be worse than the time Raff disposed of a dead pheasant by chucking it in our wheelie bin, in a heatwave, with two weeks until the refuse collectors swung by. I suggested that Brenda might want to dispose of her beloved bird in an appropriate way, befitting to her grief, and give it a proper burial.

'OK,' she said. 'I will send Roger down on the quad bike to collect her. We can sling her in our own hedgerow instead.'

*

I am overwhelmed by responsibility for people. Steve. Kids. Sometimes motherhood is about going around and turning things off that have been left on: lights in empty rooms, heating mysteriously switched to constant, hair straighteners dangerously near clothes on the floor, games consoles buzzing, toasted sandwich maker burning. It is also about relentless laundry and being asked for last-minute lifts, what is for dinner (please no couscous) and where things are (usually sports kits). So many things. All the things.

There are moments when I think my family are my day job and my actual work is just a nice hobby.

*

The warmth of a proper sun arrives, and I bask in the combined utter relief of better weather and a couple of work offers. Steve and I walk together, past the crab apple tree, which is resplendent in a flurry of acid-green leaves and bursts of magenta buds, the colour of an ice lolly I used to have after school. The flower's dainty white-pink petals are beginning to unfurl, but the branches still clasp hold of the last few wizened fruits. So last season.

There are fresh cow pats down the lane, and we follow the trail from the farm to the field where the cows have been moved to their summer hangout. They observe us with vague curiosity as they pull foliage out of the hedgerows, big raspy tongues twisting around the leaves. Margot tries to squeeze her head through a gap to say hello and gets a big lick on the top of her head, which was more than she bargained for.

We amble along the crusted soil of the track and across the fields, disturbing the nesting pheasants who rise, pulling their rotund grain-heavy bellies up into the air and lumbering over the hedges down into the valley. Steve's eyesight is sharper than mine, and he points out a patch of earth with a large hole and an imprint of the impatient muzzle of a badger and a clawed paw.

Margot bounces ahead of us, through the vapour that sits hazily over the meadow, and into the woods full of the most fragrant bluebells, which we brush past, staying on the narrow path. Apparently standing on a bluebell crushes its spirit and makes it harder for the plant to return the following year. I do not want that on my conscience.

A woodpecker is drumming in the trees. I don't have the bird call phone app yet, but I have downloaded the plant identifier and can tell those bluebells are the wild English type and that the daisy-like flowers peppered amongst them are meadow ragwort. I find three-cornered leeks for the first time, with their triangular stalks and flowers like a white bluebell. Near the tiny stream is a patch of garlic mustard, its leaves reminiscent of nettles. God, this app is addictive. I can't stop pointing it at any foliage or flower I see, even when I know what it is.

After a difficult start to the month with a blip in his prescription and a dosage adjustment, Steve wants to know if I have seen a difference since he has been on the medication. I say yes with the cautionary note that it is still early days. I want to be positively noncommittal because I have no idea how this is going to pan out, for him or for us as a couple. The withdrawal that descends without the pills is darker and scarier than life before them. The thought of that doesn't make Steve feel great either but it is making a difference, although there is something niggling at him that he can't quite put his finger on. There are still elements in his life that he can't get a handle on. Give it time, I say.

He is also doing a lot of research and reading around ADHD. He wants to know why and how. He discovers that current thinking is that this is how the brain is made, rather than something it develops, although in contradiction, he also reads that it can be exacerbated by a trauma.

We head for home, and I talk about how important this route is becoming to me. I am aware of every change in my surroundings and, if I wake up in the middle of the night, I try to stop my mind racing through my worries and push it down the track to the meadow instead. Imagining walking past sheep rather than counting them seems to do the trick. Steve says if he can't sleep or feels stressed, he 'walks' around the street in Pimlico where he spent the first nine years of his life and never wanted to leave. The buildings are his way-markers, which he follows in his memory, feeling like he is searching for something, but he isn't sure what.

Steve grew up in the flat above the wine shop, which his father ran, standing behind a dark wooden counter, ringing sales up on a clunky electric till with a cash drawer that kerchinged, and wrapping bottles in tissue paper while he chatted to customers. At the back of the shelf-lined shop, through an arch, was a desk and a clever mirror that meant you could look out but nobody could look in. That was where Steve sat, drawing buildings on Cinzano-branded paper with a blue Bic biro. Or he would brave it in the cellar, to give the returnable soda syphons a squirt and get as close as he dared to the coal bunkers under the pavement that opened into the very bowels of the earth.

When his dad made wine deliveries, Steve would sometimes tag along, especially if he was going to Ristorante Continental, the smart Italian restaurant owned by Marino, who laid the tables with crisp linen and fed Steve grissini while the grown-ups chatted. Once, a visit coincided with Steve's birthday and Marino brought out a papered slice of cassatta Siciliana, with a matchstick for a pole and a crisp pound note for a flag. Steve says the pure thrill of this has been unmatched since. On the opposite side of the street was Chalky White's barbers where he had his first haircut, and Herbert's corner shop where his parents found him when he had gone missing, being bought an ice cream by the bin man.

In Steve's mind, he regularly slides along to the launderette, the Conservative Club, the Constitution pub, the florist owned by his friend Barry's mum, and Grumbles restaurant (famously known for its sixties' clientele such as The Beatles), which is still going almost sixty years later. He walks into the Italian deli, plastic hams swinging in the window, and watches coffee beans being poured into the big, red grinder and thinly sliced prosciutto being laid out on waxed paper. When he was dying of bowel cancer, Steve's dad asked his sister, Steve's Aunt Helen, to pop to the deli and buy him some salami. She told him he wasn't allowed it, but he said what harm can it do now?

I had heard most of these stories before, particularly the one about the pound-note flag in the cake, to the point where I think this might have happened to me. What I didn't know was that Steve had found an archive of photographs online. Somebody had captured his street in 1968, when he was two years old, and again, in 1974, the year before he, his sister and his mother moved away. He tells me he scoured them in case they had captured his dad going about his business, popping into the barbers, or nipping out to see Marino, carrying a case of wine with a small boy trailing behind.

There is one picture he returned to again and again. It was a photograph of Herbert's shopfront and a blurry group of people standing outside chatting. Amongst them, he thought he could just make out a man holding a small child. I put my arms around him, and we stand in a long hug before Margot jumps up at us in irritation and I let go. Steve takes hold of my hand tightly as we walk home together. 'I think it's warm enough to ditch the bobble hat,' I say to him casually.

May

I keep trying to find a word that isn't 'frothy' to describe the cow parsley that lines the hedgerows in such abundance. A local friend, Grace, says when the cow parsley is in full bloom it transports her back to her late teens and being driven around country lanes in an old open-top sports car by an ex-boyfriend. It conjures up a carefree youth and the promise of summer days ahead, and I can't think of a better way to describe cow parsley than that. Now, after the rain, there is nothing frothy about the cow parsley as it hangs heavy with fat water droplets sparkling in the first sun for days, like a dowager's chandelier.

I stop the car and jump out to capture the glinting hedgerow on the camera on my phone but, later, when I look back at the photos, there are just heads of soggy blossom without the twinkle. There is too much water around after not enough for weeks.

'It's good for the garden!' says everyone over the age of forty.

I nod in agreement, water seeping through the cracked crease in my welly boot. Although maybe we have all had too much of a good thing, I think, as I assess the muddy path across our 'No Mow May' lawn, hammocks of water in the tarpaulin and puddles at the base of my sweet peas.

Grace is also a seed merchant (as well as a psychologist, writer and Jilly Cooper fan) from whom I score my sweet pea seeds with names such as 'Piggy Sue', 'Lisa Marie', 'Little Red Riding Hood', 'Black Knight' and 'Dusty Springfield'. I love them. One of my neighbours in the old estate cottages opposite hates sweet peas. She says she doesn't trust them. She visibly recoils at the thought of the tangled, creeping stems reaching out to her with their delicate petals and heady fragrance – as if she has been caught with a blast of something cloying from an over-eager sales assistant on a perfume counter. Their unruly joys are not welcome in her polite flower beds – and neither will there be any spilling out on to the razored lawn, thank you very much. I can see her from my window, weeding borders with the intensity of a dentist performing a root canal.

I am not sure I trust someone who doesn't like sweet peas. How can you dismiss a plant that is so eager to please? These easy-to-grow annuals, with their climbing curiosity and candy-coloured butterfly flowers, are as beautiful winding up a rickety hazel wigwam as they are in a jam jar on the kitchen table. They fall into the magic horticultural section of 'cut and come again', which means we must absolutely pick them to encourage further growth. The intoxicating floral formula of the more we take, the more we get.

Each year, I increase my sweet pea planting. What started as a galvanised pot of them by the front door has become tripod towers dotted about and a triumphant profusion clambering up the celestial hazel arch straddling two raised beds in the veg patch. I constructed it that way because I had visions of lying underneath a roof of sweet peas last summer, but I didn't prune them, so they grew outwards, stretching to either side of the garden. I had to tread carefully on the gravel path as they crossed it, winding through courgette plants and tucking themselves up with the kale. Self-seeded calendula emerged through the web of stems. At the other end of the raised bed, the glorious Italian white sunflowers stood lookout, their neat little heads angled towards the warmth. It wasn't how I planned it, but it was glorious all the same.

I am expecting similar scenes this year. Since starting the honesty box, I like to do an early-morning wander with a mug of tea, check on progress, chuck the occasional snail over the hedge into the field and settle into an old camping chair to watch the swallows flit from the telegraph line to the roof ridge of the old barn next door. Nobody told me how wonderful first light is in the spring either. There is a stilling moment when the birds greet the sunrise, and the sky begins to lift. At this point in the season, I always try and catch it, whether on a dog walk, in the sea or in the garden, because it gives a soft, secret blessing to the tone of my day. There is no app on your phone to alert you to a spectacular sunrise either. You take your chances and show up as often as you can. I can spot the pinkish glow from the bathroom window, and by the time I have dashed out it has faded into the greys and blues of a working day. The sweet peas I grow echo the morning and evening skies – from the corals, bubble-gum pinks and pale lilacs to the cloudy whites, dark bruised purples and almost blacks.

Monty Don recommends cutting them early while there is moisture in the air, and this has become part of my ritual. The long-stemmed are full of bloom and have a subtler aroma – I bunch these in jugs for the kitchen and sitting room. The short-stemmed are fragrant so I separate them into small bottles and put them in each bedroom as they are a useful antidote to teenage trainers and sports socks. I include them in my honesty box too. Who can resist a posy for a pound? Well, my neighbour can, of course. Now she has another thing to rail against because she says she isn't a fan of honesty boxes either, and she is living opposite one.

*

More rain. We have experienced a deluge on Bank Holiday Monday, which is often when these extreme weather conditions occur. Raff is revising, and Hebe and Jesse have gone to Anna and Dan's house to play table tennis with their kids. Steve fusses around the kitchen, frustrated at not being able to spend his bonus day off in the garden and worried about the lack of produce for our next honesty box. I suggest a list of chores we could be doing, such as beginning to clear the attic, repainting the downstairs loo or scrubbing the terracotta kitchen floor tiles with a special cleaner. The idea of attempting any of those things sends both of our moods plummeting. I want dappled sunlight, a riverbank edged with wild flowers, a large picnic hamper full of posh sandwiches and a good book. Steve wants to sow more beetroot seeds and build a log wall to screen the large compost heap. I can see how much he needs to be outside.

The division of labour for the honesty box is developing in an organic way, with Steve as head grower and me as retail manager and chef. OK, so this is not what I expected when we started this experiment and, although it isn't turning out to be as collaborative as

I had hoped, we are a team of sorts focused on a shared end goal.

A stream of water runs down the lane past our house, dragging stones, sticks and leaves from the verge, swerving the storm drain and carrying it around the corner towards the church. Just as I am hoping my seedlings are robust enough to cope with the battering, I catch an update from Stowford Flowers on Instagram. They have less of a stream and more of a torrent washing through their flower fields: the river running alongside their land has overflowed and is coursing a new journey. They post a video of the tractor making waves down the flooded track, and share shots of submerged flower fields while the vulnerable green shoots cling to the shifting soil beneath them. I show Steve, and it makes us gasp out loud.

Stowford Farm is the sort of place that would turn you to a life of agriculture if you didn't already know what a bloody grind it is. It is picture-perfect in a 'neat, red-brick, tidy farmyard and great views' sort of a way. I had only visited the honesty shed of the owner and florist, Liv Carter, a month earlier, on a promise of peach melba tulips. My youngest, Jesse, came too, although he objected for most of the way there until I took an emergency diversion to get petrol and bought him a packet of wine gums. He was happily silent for the rest of the journey, and when we arrived at the farm he was suitably impressed.

'Blimey, Muv, you need to up your honesty box game! Can I have one of these cakes?'

Annoyingly, he was right. In the old farrowing shed, Liv has set up a stall selling home-grown flowers and a 'help yourself' café with kettle, teabags and treats.

Ideal for the parched walker, less so for a middle-aged woman whose jeans are too tight. I resisted the apple-and-sultana cake and bought a bunch of deep amethyst ranunculus instead. I was too late for the tulips, but I still felt like a winner.

I join with many others in sending a message of solidarity and offer of help to Liv. Luckily, it appears that most of her field is salvageable, and the losses are relatively minor, but as she quite rightly says, flower growing is not for the faint-hearted. Steve and I are galvanised, get into waterproofs (well, he does because he has all the kit) and go out in the rain to check on our sweet peas. We don't achieve much, but it feels good to be outside for a bit, and we come back in soaked to the skin (me), light the fire and don't clean the kitchen floor.

*

The allotments in Lyme Regis have a sea view. They are raked from the edge of the cliff, back up a slope towards a large water butt and beyond to the road. From the car park, you can see the roofs of the little wooden sheds facing out to sea, higgledy piggledy amongst the veg plots interrupted by the occasional wicker spire of a wigwam structure. I have always wanted to go through the locked gate set into the thick hedge and wander around. I can't imagine a nicer thing than taking a breather in the middle of some back-breaking digging and looking up to see a circle of yachts from the sailing club or the Popeye-armed gig rowers cutting through the rough swell. Any thoughts of joining the waiting list for a plot are always dashed when I go into my own garden and see how much work I have to do there.

MAY

I had mentioned this to Miranda on our dawn-chorus walk, knowing she had an allotment and angling for an invitation. As luck would have it, I bump into her on the beach as she is on the way to pick the first of her broad beans.

'Come and have a look around,' she says.

We weave past holidaymakers and up the steep steps to the car park, Margot attempting to hoover up any stray chips before the seagulls. Going through the secret door is better than I imagined. Beyond it is an entire world of knowledgeable toiling gardeners who have created small plots of abundant happiness. Miranda leads me around, pointing out who is who and what they are growing.

Many of the patches are separated by rusty corrugated iron panels, blossomy apple trees and salt-licked wooden sheds. Forget-me-nots scramble between upturned wheelbarrows, and there are strategically placed benches for sunset viewing and weary gulls. Margot is thrilled to find several allotments have chickens, and she strains on the leash, nose pushed through wire fencing. Of course, the allotment owned by the architect has the best shed. And some sheds, such as Miranda's, have bottles of wine tucked in buckets. This is a little slice of horticultural heaven.

Miranda is crouching in the midst of the broad beans, plucking pods for me and telling me to plant the seeds on Remembrance Day as I bemoan my late crop. This is one of many tips she has learned from the allotment elders who have helped her traverse the highs and lows of veg growing. She gives me enough beans for several suppers and to provide for the honesty box too. I promise that next time I come I will bring a bottle of wine to add to her stash, and she promises that she will open it and share it with me as the sun goes down.

*

By the time we decided to move to Dorset, I had been a theatrical agent for over twelve years. I loved my job. I had a great list of clients. I worked hard and I cared a lot, maybe a bit too much. I took a maternal approach to the people I represented, which was fine when I wasn't somebody's mother, but once I was, I couldn't seem to switch between the two. I know agents who have been able to juggle the combination of parenthood and agenting, and I am envious of their skill. I also know agents who have not, and their children have grown up in the shadow of their most famous clients, confused by the position they hold on the scale of unconditional love.

One weekend, when I had a pile of scripts to read and a screening I should have gone to, I went to a children's birthday party with Steve and Raff instead and tried to squash the work guilt. Raff wasn't even two at this point, so he was toddling around on the eternal hunt for toy cars and biscuits. He tripped up in the host's garden, scraping his palms on the gravelled path, before getting up and wobbling towards us, deep brown eyes brimming with tears. I opened my arms to scoop him up, and he ran straight to Steve. This happened a lot.

Steve had changed career and retrained so he was at the beginning of his earning potential, whereas I had gained a level of success with the capacity to keep growing. It made sense for him to work part-time and be a stay-at-home dad, and for me to continue with my more-than-full-time career. This plan doesn't seem strange in today's world, thank goodness, but twenty years ago it was still unusual, and we received a fair bit of judgement and criticism.

Steve embraced his role with all the zest, irreverence and gratefulness that has made him a brilliant dad ever since. He attempted several baby and toddler groups but was largely ignored as the only man there, until he was scooped up by a friend who had a baby the same age and took Steve and Raff along with her to meet-ups. If any of the other mothers had a problem with it, they didn't say so.

For a while, the division of labour was a success, but it was too extreme to be a long-term option. Both of us wanted a little of what the other had. I wanted more time with Raff, and Steve wanted to establish himself in a profession he had spent several years training for. My initial warning bell was when I took my first big work trip since having Raff, to LA with one of my clients, Anna Maxwell Martin. I couldn't have been going with a better person to a more exciting place, but I sobbed all the way to Heathrow. I managed to sort myself out by the time I met Anna, but she already knew this was going to be an emotional wrench for me, and she greeted me with the warmest hug of understanding.

'You need an upgrade,' she said, and the nice airline staff took one look at me and agreed.

When we were settled on the plane in our business-class seats, Anna said, 'Now you need a drink and one of those little packets of nuts.'

By the time we arrived in LA, I was back in control. I propped a photo of Raff on my bedside table in the hotel room and embraced my working week with my usual professional energy. There, I thought, nothing has changed – what on earth was I worried about? I thought I could do it all.

The second warning bell clanged some months later when I was away with my best friends from BBC days: Elaine, Cath and Nicki. A group of us had rented a big house in Bridport for the weekend to celebrate Elaine's birthday, and several of them saw it as the perfect opportunity, in the nicest possible way, to escape their children. It was the opposite for me. The weekend was the only time I spent with Raff, and even that was often compromised by a work event or the *News of the World* or *Sunday Mirror* calling me about a client. I would get an inkling of this on a Friday night, it would then explode on Saturday morning, and we had until 7 p.m. that evening to deal with the situation before the story went to press. Occasionally we could get it pulled, but too many times the piece was in the Sunday papers, and I would spend the day talking to the client, legal support and PR gurus to decide how best to deal with the fallout. This was becoming more and more common, and I spent an inordinate amount of time on the phone at weekends. A phone that it now transpires (after the police contacted me several years later) was regularly being hacked.

On this occasion, I couldn't go away for the weekend without my eighteen-month-old and, as I was with my closest friends, I knew they would understand me bringing him along. I had never been to Bridport before, but it is uncanny that my second emotional wobble would happen in a place that was to become my future home. I spent the weekend trying to be all things – a mother, a friend and a person who just needs a long bath or a bit of a lie-in – made worse by the fact I had to leave early to drive back to London for the BAFTAs. I was wretched and self-pitying all the way home at the impossible juggle of job, parenting and being social, and also cross with myself for being so ungrateful for the life I had. At the BAFTAs, Anna won the Best Actress Award for BBC's *Bleak House*, and pride and joy for her burst forth from my core, but it didn't drown out the little voice inside my head that said my agenting days were numbered. Instead, it said, what a moment to go out on. Financially I couldn't stop work, and even if that had been an option, I didn't want to. I just needed to find a job that would utilise all the (weird) skills I had, feel vaguely like a career, but also give me evenings and weekends free. Ideally, in the countryside, where we could have some space without needing to earn the amount it took to survive in London, and somewhere Steve could work. It felt pretty impossible. Where on earth could I find a media job that wasn't in a city?

When I heard that the food writer and campaigner, Hugh Fearnley-Whittingstall, was looking for someone to work with him at River Cottage on media projects, I jumped at the chance of an introduction through a mutual friend. I thought it would be a nice chat over a cup of tea at their new HQ on the Dorset/Devon border. Instead, I was instructed to turn up at West Bay harbour and look for a boat.

There weren't many opportunities to get out on the water growing up in London, other than the occasional pedalo treat on the Serpentine, a River Thames cruise and a couple of ferry trips. I was lacking in sea legs and wouldn't have chosen to have my job interview on a fishing boat. Lurching around on board the fumy old vessel, I made small talk with the crew as I kept one wary eye on the horizon and the other on my fraying mackerel line. Hair crunchy with sea spray, and stomach tight with the unfamiliar tidal swell, I caught my first fish that day. It was a beauty. A silvery mackerel that gawped hopelessly for air and whose glassy stare I could still see when I shut my eyes that night. It was apparently customary for the accidental fishergirl to kiss her first slithering catch on the nose before being shown how to humanely despatch it with bare, London-livered hands. Which I did, proud and repulsed, before chucking it in the battered bucket to add to the day's haul.

When the engine shuddered to a halt, I was preoccupied with the desire and fear of catching another fish. There was an angry debate about why the boat had stopped, and I realised this wasn't planned and we were a long way from land. I was an even longer way from shore in all senses, completely adrift in my own life. Was I really going to leave my hard-earned showbiz career for this?

Hugh stripped to his pants, dived straight into the freezing spring sea and ducked under the boat. After several attempts, he successfully unravelled a length of old rope that had snarled around the propeller, and held it aloft to relieved cheers from deck. Pulled back up into the boat, Hugh stood shivering while we searched the tiny cabin and bench seats for anything that could be used as a towel. Nothing. I realised he was staring at the pale pink scarf around my neck, the little bit of cashmere luxury that had been an unaffordable treat. Slowly, I unwound it, handed it over and watched him briskly dry off, seesawing it across his back and between his legs.

As we headed to the harbour, against the backdrop of a spring sunset smudged a faint peach, there was a production line of gutting, filleting and cleaning before some of the catch was chopped and doused in lime juice and thinly sliced red chilli, ceviche style. I had never eaten fish like it – so fresh, subtle, the taste on my tongue matching the briny air, making it confusing to distinguish between senses. It was the first time I had been responsible for catching, killing, cooking and eating my own food, the complete circle. We shared it between us like an initiation, and I got the job. I just had to decide if I wanted it.

*

Steve and I are in a local town where we don't normally shop so we make a detour to the butcher, who we have heard makes great pies. The sign on his window says they are award-winning. We go in to buy a couple.

'Hey, so what makes your pies award-winning?' Steve asks in what I perceive to be a confrontational manner.

I can't tell why they are award-winning because I don't listen to the butcher's brusque reply. Instead, I try to make light of it, push the conversation along and pay quickly. On the pavement, we have an argument about why we can't just go into a shop, be polite, buy what we need and leave. Why the questions? Why the tone?

I have hit on a calcified element of his neurodivergence and think of the countless times we have had this disagreement in the past. Me thinking he has been rude or insensitive and being amazed that he can't see this. I am also painfully aware of my own paranoia about the best way to communicate with people, so maybe I am being neurotic. As for the pies, Steve has no idea what I am talking about.

'I just wanted to know why they won awards,' he says, mystified by my reaction.

*

Raff is bang-smack in the middle of exam revision, so he has developed a close relationship with the fridge and opens it every hour, staring meaningfully at the contents in case someone has miraculously provided something exciting since the last time he looked. When he asks when I am going shopping, I know I have taken it down to the scrapings. A heel of parmesan, a quarter of discolouring red cabbage and a lank spring onion isn't going to cut it. I can make a meal out of almost nothing, but then there's really nothing, and this is one of those times.

I head out to the veg patch. I know this isn't what Raff had in mind for revision grazing. He wants a family-size packet of Doritos, chunks of sweet melon and a box of Maltesers, but what he gets are a handful of plump pea pods, several premature radishes and two small, pale strawberries. I can't feed my family from our veg patch, so how in the god of green things' name am I going to fill an honesty box? The high hopes I had for a bumper summer crop are teetering.

Hebe gives me a hand with honesty box prep for this month. Rain is forecast so we tidy up the lean-to. She cuts armfuls of spiky, coconut-scented gorse from the field at the other end of the village, ties the branches in bunches and hangs them from the timber beams. The tight, yellow buds glow in the sunlight streaming through the corrugated plastic roof. Anything to give it a bit of a lift and attract people walking past. We cover the scruffy Formica work surface with a piece of fabric, and use an apple crate as a shelf. I want a spring theme, so there are jars of lemon-and-lime marmalade, tight-budded tulips, a tin of lemon shortbread biscuits, and Hebe has hand-painted blown eggs and displayed them in Alice the potter's brown-glazed egg cups. My parents have sent some packets of seeds as a donation, and Steve's mum has knitted several yellow dishcloths to add to the stall. It is a family affair.

When Steve gets back from the office, he pulls up the remaining leeks, which are on the cusp of leathery, and adds these to the table. Other than the ceramics, which are priced, everything else is pay-what-you-can, although it seems the leeks don't raise as much enthusiasm as the biscuits. We should have picked them a month ago. Another lesson learned.

*

There is uproar in the neurodivergent community over the recent BBC *Panorama* documentary 'Private ADHD Clinics Exposed', which has resulted in clickbait headlines and media debate. Those with ADHD call the investigation distressing and triggering, making them feel misunderstood and furious that the real issues are being ignored.

I watch it so Steve doesn't have to. I follow the journalist's quest to expose a health scandal where those who believe they have ADHD avoid the long NHS waiting lists by paying money they don't have to three companies that allegedly do not have the qualifications to give a diagnosis. The repeated claim is that these private clinics diagnose almost every patient they see and give a prescription for serious medication that may not be appropriate.

While I can see the point the programme is making, they seem to be missing the point too. One NHS consultant says the number of people coming forward to seek diagnosis is twenty times what it was five years ago, describing it as a trickle turning into a stream. Now waiting lists are too long and full of desperate people who are forced to consider private solutions to an issue that threatens their existence. Surely, this is more worthy of investigation? How to receive, process, diagnose and protect before some are scooped up by unscrupulous practitioners. Desperation can lead us to make ill-advised judgements. The silver lining of wading through the noise that comes following the transmission is the discovery of the ADHD Foundation online, which publishes a clear and deft response to the programme.

I tell Steve he doesn't need to watch *Panorama*. It will just make him angry and, worse, it will make him look suspiciously at the scaffolding he has been building at a point when his trust and openness has been rewarded. Now is not the time for him to second-guess himself or question the decision he took. We have faith in the private psychiatrist he saw and the process he went through, but then again we don't really have a choice.

*

The rain has stopped, for now. It is the big conversation of the village. Have we ever known a spring as wet as this one, we disappointedly ask each other. Maybe this means we are in for a good summer, we say optimistically. The lane outside our house is covered in debris again, tugged from the hedgerows by the insistent water that streams down the road in a deluge. I record a voice note for Thea. When she listens back, she tells me later, as she walks up Clapham High Street, she can hear the squelching as I cross the field, mud sucking at my wellies.

Margot stops abruptly and sits at the entrance to the meadow. She can instantly see what it takes me a while to spot. A deer is grazing at the edge of the woodland, its head dipping into the long grass. It stares at us, and we stare back. I quietly command the dog to stay put, but she is unsure if this is friend or foe, so she isn't budging. From the trees, a single rasping loud bark echoes around the valley, an alert from another deer. It is a strange sound, a bit like a dog, in the same way people say crocodile tastes a bit like chicken. It is an almost fantastical call, and the other deer answers to it by darting into the woods.

The Irish setter, Darren, bounds up, breaking the spell, followed by Keith on his quad bike, skidding to a halt in a spray of muddy water. He looks like he has been in a fight, with deep scratches across his face, and tells me he had almost come a cropper earlier in the week. He had been on the quad bike coming down the track and thought he could safely brush past the overhanging brambles. He underestimated them and they ensnared him, almost pulling him off his seat and taking a chunk of his ear in the bargain.

He rushes the story because he has something more interesting to report: he has found an old map of the village, from 1845. There aren't many houses on it, but ours is marked, he says as a single-storey blacksmith. More importantly, there is a cart track that has surprised him. It used to run above the meadow we are standing in, through the woods and out over the fields towards the town. He has a plan to follow the ghost of it with a metal detector. I ask if I can join him when he does. In the late 1960s, a farmer he knows a few miles away found a section of Roman mosaic pavement. This triggered a dig by the Devon Archaeological Society and the amazing discovery of not only a Roman villa, but underneath, an Iron Age settlement.

'The place was crawling with English Heritage people and the like. And do you know what they did once they had finished the dig? You won't believe it. They just covered it all back up. Why would they do a thing like that? I can't understand it.' He looks wistfully towards the horizon. 'Can you imagine what could be buried under our feet right now?' His eyes sparkle with the thought of treasure.

As I head back up the lane, eyeing stubborn brambles warily, Gerry chugs past in one of his vintage tractors. He raises a hand in greeting, but he doesn't stop to chat. He is on a regular route, back and forth, collecting logs, cutting hedges and surveying the place where he was born almost seventy years ago and has kept a shed full of tractors. No matter how interested I am in the history of this village, our house and the ghosts of long-departed people, it isn't enough. I wasn't born here, and there is nothing I can do to change that.

Margot has dug up Darren's bone again. She carries it awkwardly, dropping it every few yards before trying a new way of grasping it in her jaw. This is becoming a bit of a habit. She obsessively seeks the damn thing out, wherever I may try and dispose of it, so we have a stand-off next to it, before she reluctantly follows me, empty-mouthed. Just before the village pond is a bank of wild garlic in full flower and pungent with maturity. The smell is enveloping, reminding me of walking past a French or Italian restaurant on a balmy summer evening in the city. I go home thinking about Roman treasures and what to cook for dinner.

*

Questions I get asked a lot about my honesty box crusade include how people pay when they no longer carry cash. Some honesty boxes display QR codes but the majority, like mine, rely on old-fashioned coins and notes. I would prefer to remind people to keep a fiver in cash in their car or rucksack or tell them to leave an IOU rather than suggest complicated payment methods. As someone who still likes using real money and thinks it is important that we do so, that is my only real answer.

'OK,' they say, 'but think of all the light-fingered, untrustworthy folk and the stories of them taking screwdrivers/chainsaws/diggers to the secured cash boxes? Doesn't that worry you?' Well, no.

Stories of deceit still seem so rare that they make the local news, with one dairy farmer branding thieves of his cashbox 'brazen toerags' but vowing not to be put off from honesty-selling his small batches of handmade ice cream. That's the spirit! It seems this happens to each of us occasionally, but not enough to make most of us want to stop – other than those who are systematically targeted, and if their trust is repeatedly broken, I can see why they give up.

Another question is whether there is a place for honesty boxes in built-up areas. Do those that thrive do so because of the cemented or chained cash boxes and the unblinking eye of CCTV? I had hoped to get more positive urban feedback when I put a shout-out via social media, but instead I get lots of photos of honesty boxes, stands and cupboards in rural places.

I didn't want this to be the answer to my question, and maybe I am missing something. Then an email from a friend pings up with a photo attached, showing how his West London allotment adopts the honesty box system. As well as a table full of gluts, one of the growers sells plants from her bike basket. I can see from the picture that she has pots of sharp, lemony lovage for a pound a pop. Stuck on the side of her basket is a sign that reads: *Lovage pairs perfectly with potatoes, is a superb addition to soups and did you know the stalks are hollow and make great straws for a Bloody Mary?!*

Underneath she has typed out a quote from my old boss, Hugh Fearnley-Whittingstall, confessing his lovage love, just in case the cocktail tip is not encouraging enough. The honesty cash tin is padlocked to her basket, and her bike is padlocked to the railings. If anyone does steal the lovage, I hope they make a bloody good Mary, and if they steal her bike, I hope they get an almighty puncture.

June

I am sitting on a plastic chair outside the local hospital, with my face turned to the sun. It is what they used to call a cottage hospital, which makes me think of woodsmoke, crochet blankets and purple foxgloves towering over white picket fences. I came here a few times when the children were little, dragging one or other of them in with raging earache, unexplained sickness bug or suspected broken finger. Usually on a Sunday and always in through the main entrance. Where I sit now is tucked around the side of the building, by a door with a sign above saying *Mental Health Unit*. I have never noticed this before.

Steve is here for an appointment. After his private ADHD diagnosis, he is being handed over to the NHS. This forty-five-minute assessment with the psychiatrist should be a simple matter of a confirmation and a repeat prescription for medication. His GP was furious that Steve circumnavigated the system and hopped out to go privately before attempting to slip back in again for a shared care agreement. Steve agreed. This wasn't how he wanted it to be either, but he said his marriage was on the rocks and so was his energy for any future. In the face of a two-year waiting list, he didn't think he had a choice.

I accept any criticism or judgement thrown our way. I can see how hard this is for the NHS and those waiting patiently on the list, but the system is broken and breaking people. We have performed a selfish act in the name of survival, and we are not the only ones.

I am waiting for Steve, and then we will go to Soulshine café and drink coffee in the courtyard, maybe with one of those warm, flaky Portuguese custard tarts. The door swings open and he comes out, ashen and silent. Too soon. The psychiatrist appears behind him, and for a moment I wonder if Steve has walked out and he is chasing after him. The psychiatrist asks me to join them both in his office. Something is wrong, but I follow calmly through a waiting room of silent people staring at their phones. This is beginning to feel like an apocalyptic film, where there will soon be a big explosion and a sudden invasion of zombies. I think I am supposed to be the heroine, but nobody has given me the script or a weapon.

In the consulting room, we sit opposite a photograph on the wall of what may be the Alps. The psychiatrist sits at his desk, but swivels to face us so there is no barrier between us. I could reach out and pat his knee reassuringly. I am not sure how I can feel scared and safe at the same time. Perhaps it is the combination of his kind face and furrowed brow.

'I've had a chat with your husband, and we thought it may be helpful for you to join us at this point.' The psychiatrist looks thoughtfully at his notes. 'There are a few questions that he's not able to answer.'

I look at Steve. He is poker straight, hands wrapped around his body in a self-hug. He looks at me blankly. I have never seen someone quite so absent from themselves. I can't be sure he knows who I am, let alone who he is. Neither of us were expecting this. He has only been in here twenty minutes. What the hell could go wrong in that short space of time? I am suddenly furious with them both, these middle-aged men, one in a suit, the other in an anorak, for letting it get to this and now expecting me to have the answers. And I am tired of being the answer.

'I have been through a list of standard questions with your husband, and I think we may be dealing with a more complex diagnosis than he was initially given. He's found it increasingly hard to talk about. I would appreciate your perspective.' The psychiatrist looks at me encouragingly.

'Fire away,' I say, as the word 'complex' ricochets around my brain.

Steve stares straight ahead at the picture. Maybe he is halfway up one of those picturesque mountains rather than in this stuffy room being told things have got complicated.

I hope so.

There are many questions, and I answer them truthfully, at times feeling uncomfortable and disloyal when Steve is sitting next to me. Occasionally I turn to him, to check it is OK to continue, and he nods. I can see he is relaxing a little as I do what he is unable to, and I am surprised at how much better I begin to feel. It is an utter relief to talk to a professional who represents trust and rescue. It is as if he has come along beside me and taken one handle of a heavy bag that I have been carrying, for how long I forget, or is helping me push an overflowing wheelbarrow over bumps in the garden. I realise that in all the years Steve and I have been together, I have never been part of a therapy session or psychological evaluation. This now seems a massive oversight.

The psychiatrist asks about Steve's ability to communicate, which makes me want to crack some sort of silly gag as I sit there talking on his behalf. I tell him how hard he finds social situations and that he struggles with the complexities and nuance of relationships. He can get confused and irritable. Sometimes he finds it problematic to regulate his mood. He often hates himself. I run through this list, but I also say he is funny, kind, loving, a wonderful dad. I want to give the psychiatrist the full picture.

'So yes, communication can be challenging. Except around death, he's very good at speaking to people who are grieving, and he isn't scared by it. Whatever holds him back in the everyday doesn't exist in the face of loss.'

This is because he knows how it feels: he has lost several key beloved figures in his life, including his father and then his stepfather. When Steve was twenty-one and his sister was eighteen, she was rushed to hospital with what turned out to be meningitis. He was away working on a Cumbrian farm as part of his agricultural college education and was called home. When he arrived, his grandmother asked if he had brought his suit back with him, and that is how he knew his sister wasn't going to make it.

The psychiatrist is scribbling notes, focused both on what I am saying and Steve's gradual return to his body. When Steve begins to cry a little, I think the psychiatrist is as relieved as I am. He checks his watch.

'OK, we're way over time now, which is not a problem, but I wasn't envisaging the consultation going in this direction.' The psychiatrist is using a 'let's wrap this up now' voice. 'So we'll need to book in another session once you've filled in the forms I'm going to send you away with. I think we have a little more work to do on understanding your situation.'

'Are you telling me I don't have ADHD?' Steve sounds panicky. 'Only I need that medication. It has really helped. I am able to function better at work, it has regulated my mood, I think I am calmer, happier, easier to be around... I only came here so you could sign the forms.'

We are not leaving without these drugs, which have given him (and me) some respite, and if he isn't able to fight for them, then I will. The psychiatrist is quiet for a moment, clearly considering how much he should share.

'Look, I can't tell you anything for sure until we have been through the process, but based on this session, I think we need to look beyond ADHD. I'll give you a prescription for the medication. I just...' He pauses. 'I hate to say this without all the facts in front of me, but I think you have ADHD and ASD."

'ASD? Autism? You think I am autistic?' Steve asks, eyes wide.

'Yes.' The psychiatrist nods.

Steve looks at me as if he is expecting me to disagree with the psychiatrist, but I am a step ahead of him.

'Autism,' he rolls the word around his mouth, 'and is there medication for that too?'

'No,' the psychiatrist says. 'It's just something you have to live with. It's not uncommon for someone with ASD to have ADHD too. And trauma and autism can go hand in hand; they sometimes share similar characteristics, which makes it tricky to unravel one from the other.'

'So there's nothing I can do to alleviate the autism?' Steve isn't prepared for this change of events.

'You'll need to learn coping mechanisms. We can cover this next time I see you. I'm sorry if this comes as a shock to you.'

I feel the finality and surety of this complete diagnosis. It is no surprise that ADHD is only part of the picture and an explanation as to why the medication has partly helped but not fully. This is why neither of us were totally convinced by its powers. As the final pieces are gently put in place there is an overwhelming rightness about what we are being told. Now we have all the facts and know what we are dealing with, this could be revolutionary for us both. Steve shakes his head sadly.

'This has come as a big blow,' he says, and the psychiatrist sees my eyebrows shoot up in disbelief.

We walk back to the car and sit in silence for a few moments.

'Isn't this a good thing?' I resist the urge to pick up my phone and google 'ASD diagnosis'. 'We have all the facts now. The final piece of the jigsaw. No more surprises.'

'Well, that was a fucking big one. No way out of this with fancy meds.' Steve is gloomy, frustration overriding acceptance. 'Maybe he is wrong. I will fill in the forms, but maybe he is wrong.'

Without discussing it, we ditch the idea of coffee and head home.

*

A soft light halos the sunrise, promising a fierce heat later. In a couple of weeks, we will celebrate the summer solstice, swiftly followed by midsummer. We have so much still to plant in the raised beds that my list now seems unfeasible verging on ridiculous. I listen to a garden podcast where someone who knows what they are talking about says exactly what I need to hear. I summarise the gist for Steve later. Be ambitious but know when to settle because time, weather and budget are always against us, and we will never achieve what we think we can at the beginning of the season. He looks like he agrees, but I know he is on a mission to fill every spare scrap of soil, particularly as I am hoping a third of what we produce will be honesty box stock.

Margot and I are coming back from our walk, and she has stopped by the pond, head slightly to one side, fixated on something in the water. A moorhen chick is pushing its way through the thick algae, squeaking its alarm. I can see a long trail of endurance in the treacle-thick slime where the fluffy black bird has persevered. It is clearly distressed. Its tiny beak is wide open as if in one long scream, and it brings both wings up together as it valiantly tries to push forward. The mother flits from the bank to a half-submerged tree trunk and then to the wall, calling to it.

When we first arrived in the village, the pond was open. We floated homemade paper boats, charted the progress of the frog spawn and watched avidly for fish in the clear water.

There was a big polystyrene hippopotamus wallowing amongst the weeds next to a sign saying 'PLEASE DON'T FEED THE HIPPO', but then the notice disappeared overnight. Maybe the hippo ate it. For Raff's tenth birthday, I asked the farmer if we could use his pond. He said, 'Yep, just as long as you promise not to sue me if someone dies.' It reminded me of the beginning of *Swallows and Amazons* when the father responds to the children's letter begging him to allow them to sail, and he tells them if they are not duffers then they will not drown.

I borrowed kayaks and surfboards and discovered two decaying pedaloes in the undergrowth on the far bank. Admittedly, it was a brave and ambitious undertaking, but the party was a big success, with kids gliding across the water before jumping off the edge of their watercrafts into the murky depths. We managed to get them all safely back on dry land and hosed them off in the road in case of leeches or undetermined germs, which they said was almost as much fun as messing around in the pond. The afternoon was exactly what I had imagined Raff's childhood would become when we decided to leave the city. It was a halcyon day in our country life.

Now, the pond is out of bounds. The official line is health-and-safety reasons because one can never be too sure who is a duffer, which is a fair point. Unofficially, there has been a village falling-out, and the heavy padlock slung around the iron gate is the clearest message to keep away. Even the hippo has slunk off somewhere.

Sheila, my neighbour who is still hoping I will stock tinned tomatoes in my honesty box, walks past cajoling her slow Labrador. He is behaving like he has been brought out against his will and uses us as a reason to stop, flopping down on my feet with a heavy sigh. I explain the moorhen chick's predicament to Sheila, but I stop short of asking her to give me a bunk up over the old stone wall. We both watch the exhausted bird slow down before frantically paddling again.

'I think we're scaring the mother away.' Sheila gestures to the moorhen, keeping its distance on the other side of the pond.

JUNE

Margot's snout is pushed through the bars of the wrought iron gate, as intent on the hopeless chick as we are, but for different reasons.

'I could hop over and clear a path in the water to the bank? Or lift it out on a long piece of wood?' I try to sound hopeful, without any clue of how I would execute either plan. The chick has travelled so far and is so close to solid ground, it is unbearable to watch.

'Then how does it get back round to its nest on the other side? Unless you try and carry it, but nobody has cleared these banks for years. When my children were little, they would swim in here...' Sheila trails off wistfully, nudges her dog and carries on down the lane, the Labrador lagging behind her like the train of a long dress.

I walk home, praying Mummy Moorhen knows what she is doing.

'Can we go back and help?' I know Steve will know what to do. He echoes Sheila.

'Don't interfere with nature. You may disturb the nest or the other chicks. The mother may disappear in a fright. I don't think you can do anything other than see how it plays out.'

I hadn't expected that. He loves his wild snake colony in our overgrown patch and is refusing to mow the grass or tidy around the compost heap, so they aren't disturbed during their nesting season. We are all banned from the back of the garden, to allow them to bask in peace, which I am beginning to object to, although I don't want to use it if it means a sudden slithering reptile stand-off. I mean to go back to the pond later, but I am distracted by work and testing Raff on some A-level revision for his last exam. I forget about the moorhen chick.

When I approach the pond the next morning, I can see the moorhen and her babies pottering around the far edge of the water in a shaft of beatific sunlight. Oh, thank you Mother Nature, you didn't forsake the little one. I lean over the gate, watching them scoot about. The green sludge is still scored after yesterday's heart-rending pilgrimage, and then I spot something black in the water, within touching distance of the bank. It is the keeling body of the lifeless chick.

*

Raff expected that the end of exams would be heralded by applause, fireworks, a mariachi band and maybe being driven around the village in an open-top car, having flowers thrown at him. But he can't shake the uneasy feeling that he should be revising, followed by a groggy inability to make any plans. As adults, we know an anti-climax when we see one, but he is still learning. Instead, the feeling of freedom creeps up on him slowly as more friends finish their A levels, we pop out for lunch midweek and his siblings fall off the school bus at the end of the day, racing each other to the loo for a poo. The penny finally drops for him after an all-night party with the rest of the ragged students.

The following morning, Raff is driven home by his friend, Merlin, and I pour them big mugs of tea that steam their bloodshot eyeballs. This is the stage of motherhood that I have been looking forward to, the late teens, the bit I thought I would be really good at, carrying more patience and energy than I had in the clamouring toddler years. Their early childhoods dragged so exhaustingly at times, clanging against work and establishing a social life in a new area, but now

JUNE

everything is on double speed and it is going too fast for me.

I fry the boys eggs while firing questions about who snogged who and were there any arguments. They are weak from cheap beer and lack of sleep, and sing like canaries. There was a pool, but they didn't swim in it. There was booze but very few of them got drunk, other than someone vomiting on someone else's tent. There were no drugs, but that's what teenagers tell parents so I can't vouch for that. Instead, they fed wood into the fire pit and talked about summer plans. Raff spent hours tucked up in a wheelbarrow wrapped in someone else's sleeping bag, watching the fire, and at first light they all piped down so they could listen to the dawn chorus. These beautiful creatures were suddenly spooked by the realities of what is ahead.

After we wave Merlin off, I don't want Raff to slink to bed until he has done something from our to-do list. This is how we are pacing this strange early summer, and it means that I can schedule work and still get to spend time with him before he flies the nest. We have a long agenda of things we want to do, or more accurately two lists of things we each want to do that intersect at points. On my list is fruit picking.

I can't pretend our fruit patch is a success. It isn't even a patch. There are a few strawberry plants, blackcurrant and redcurrant bushes and a gooseberry twig. So far, the harvest has given me a handful of strawberries to eat while contemplating whether we need to lift the plants and put them somewhere high and slug-proof. The blackcurrants have been a scattering over breakfast yoghurt. The gooseberries have been non-existent, so much so that I had to check if it was indeed a gooseberry plant.

The saving grace is about twenty minutes down the road in the form of a Pick Your Own (or Pick Your Nose as the kids called it years ago and this has stuck). The season starts with strawberries, crosses over with gooseberries, neatly segues into redcurrants, blackcurrants and ends with raspberries. To be guaranteed a good haul of each, it requires several trips between June and July, something I have never managed previously. This year, I am determined to catch them all, with a plan to make summer jam for the honesty box in lieu of a lack of my own fruitful harvest.

As I drive down country lanes, edges and corners blurred by the overgrown hedgerows, Raff talks about his friends' plans for the summer. There are holidays booked, part-time jobs secured, university offers accepted, deferments considered, and panics over whether the right course has been chosen or if they should go travelling around Indonesia instead. They are all steadfastly and sensibly ignoring the looming date for exam results.

The day is overcast and heavy with the threat of an unbroken storm, noisy crows scattering as a tractor turns into a neighbouring field. At the PYO, we pick strawberries from the chest-high gullies in companionable silence, only broken when we compete over finding the biggest and juiciest berries hiding under green-leaf umbrellas. We test several just to make sure, popping the whole fruit in, juice bursting in our mouths and staining the tips of our fingers.

I feel chilly so Raff gives me his jumper. The candy-floss scent from the strawberries mixes with last night's

JUNE

party woodsmoke that has seeped into the wool. I want to bury my nose in it, bottle the smell and preserve it as a tribute to midsummer and teenage rites of passage. And I want to stop time. No, more than that, I want to rewind the years, to the first time we came fruit-picking together and I was trying to find things to break up the very long summer. Why did I rush it all then? Why was I trying to make time pass quicker? Why was I hurrying them all to get bigger? I want to sob with longing for what is past, but if I do, I will break this spell between Raff and me, so I concentrate on plucking berry after berry, biting my lip, blinking back tears and rhythmically filling the basket.

We pick strawberries for jam and to eat throughout the week, and then move on to the gooseberries, which are fit to popping. Their shiny skins are threaded with veins, stretched but not quite ripe to split, like miniature pale watermelons. We grit our teeth through the spiky forage and find some the size of eyeballs. I am greedy with picking, thinking of all the recipes I want to try, but we stop once we get to what I estimate is a kilo. I have decided on using half for a sweet crumble and the rest for a salsa to go with chicken enchiladas or BBQ mackerel, if we get lucky with the fishing rod. With the cash left over after weighing the berries, we buy ice creams – double chocolate for Raff and hazelnut for me – and we eat them, sitting on the grass, watching other pickers traipse the tramlines of fruits.

'I was thinking how much I want to capture this moment.' My words are out before I can stop myself.

'Oh, Muv,' Raff says, jumping up and dusting off the grass from his jeans. 'Don't go all strange and soppy on me.'

Later, I am sitting outside, topping and tailing the gooseberries and listening to a literary podcast about the legendary countryman and author Ronald Blythe, who died recently at the telegram-receiving age of one hundred. He was a magnificent oak in the nature-writing world. Steve is in the kitchen, and I can hear his music from here, shaking the house. I will have to tell him to turn it down. He can't cope with loud noises, unless he instigates them – this includes, but is not limited to, him talking at volume, clanging pans and playing music at ear-deafening levels. Housebeats with repetitive mind-bending bolts of sound that calm and focus him yet send my brain into spasms. This is another thing I am now seeing from a different viewpoint, aware of it as a sensory need rather than an annoyance. All of these things are like breadcrumbs leading to the dual-diagnosis.

The music goes off abruptly as if Steve can tell what I am thinking, and he comes out flourishing a wodge of paper.

'My forms from the psychiatrist,' he says, stress etched across his face. 'I started to do this on my own, but I don't trust myself. They are asking me to grade characteristics and, if I am autistic, how am I supposed to be that self-aware? I want to give truthful answers. Can you help me?'

Thus begins a long process of him reading out each question and answering it with a grade of never, sometimes, often, always, followed by looking at me for validation. I am relieved that I have something meditative to do at the same time.

Raff wanders into the garden as we are halfway through. Steve is frustrated with the time it is taking and the way I am answering the spouse questions.

'No. On this form, it isn't "very occasionally", it's "rarely".' His patience is running out.

'OK, but you know what I mean.' I have moved on to hulling strawberries and trying not to overthink my responses in the hope they are as honest as possible.

'Please use the correct language,' he says, and I think we don't need these forms to tell us what I already know.

Raff looks at me in silent acknowledgement. His presence lightens the mood, and when Steve questions one of the answers in a 'I am not sure I do that' way, Raff and I look at each other and then at him, and say in unison that he absolutely does do that.

It is liberating to have someone else's support, but I am aware this is not Raff's responsibility, and some stuff may be uncomfortable for him to hear about his father. He seems unperturbed, and his caring yet irreverent approach tinges the experience with heart-lifting humour, proving my theory about finding the funny. It works in so many situations, and it makes this process we are flailing around in much easier. Steve has always found it hard to laugh at himself, it is a confusing thing to him, but he is getting better at it. I look at Raff and am overwhelmed by a feeling of missing him when he is right there in front of me. Sometimes it seems like there are only two adults in this house – and one of them isn't Steve.

*

Thea has left me a long voice note. I save it as a reward until I can escape my laptop in the afternoon heat. Margot and I head in the opposite direction from our usual morning walk onto the shady footpath that leads out of the village towards the coast road. There are bursts of late-blooming elderflower here, and I want to pick a few flower sprays to cook with the gooseberries. Thea responds to my morning message where I tell her about Steve's possible autism diagnosis. She is as unsurprised as me, and then updates me on what is going on at her end. I imagine us together, on a tiny rowing boat pitching in the dangerous swell of a cruel sea, each clinging to an oar with no idea what to do next.

'Anyway, in other news ... Oh, hang on, sip of coffee,' she slurps. 'I've just got a tattoo. I love it. It's perfect. It says *be here now* to remind me to stay in the moment. I wanted it somewhere I could easily read it so it is on my arm, except the only problem is the text is quite small so I can't see it without my glasses on. So much for middle-aged rebellion!'

This makes me chuckle all the way home.

*

Our knackered kitchen has become a symbol of our relationship. While we can potter around doing small jobs in other parts of the house, whenever we talk about renovating the kitchen it ends in an argument. Now I see it is where Steve's needs and my resistance to it meet. He demands perfection, stripping everything back to the joists and foundations to see the bare bones, expose any hidden problems and then rebuild, except this is too mammoth a task for us, financially and practically. It isn't possible, but this is where his expectation sits and he can't conceive of another way, certainly not the one I suggest, which is admittedly a frustrating piecemeal, out-of-synch approach but designed to get things done.

Over the years, various family and friends have mentioned our lack of DIY ability, the procrastination over home improvements, and when on earth do we plan to do the kitchen exactly? Through their eyes, I can see the patched holes in the ceiling, the random jutting pipework, the wobbly kitchen cabinets, the cutlery drawer that is sticky on its old runners, the blown plaster on the back wall, and the old porcelain butler's sink set in slowly rotting wood. When the subject comes up, it is as if I am sitting opposite the enquirer naked, or that Steve and I have been catapulted into Relate. How can I explain to them the psychological complexities behind it all when we are only just understanding them ourselves?

Before Steve, I got stuff done. It wasn't always pretty or practical or thought through, but I made decisions, I made mistakes and I got on with my life. Now I feel that any move I make will be a trigger and so it is easier not to do anything. Like last year, when I took the matter into my own hands and hired a builder to knock a hole in the wall and build a larder. This was something we had been talking about doing for ten years so I was hardly rushing into it, plus we had known the builder for the same length of time so I trusted him.

I told Steve we would start with this because I had the money to cover the whole job, it would give us more storage and mean that we could take the old kitchen cupboards out. Steve's reticence was palpable, and he dug his heels in – he wanted to draw detailed plans with measurements, but he couldn't pin himself down to do it. The builder was there in front of me with another job to rush on to, so I used my body as an approximate measure of where I wanted shelves. It got done. Had I waited for Steve we would still be without it.

Steve emanated fury for days. He couldn't walk past the larder without tutting, picking at a bit of plaster or going up close to examine a detail he found himself disappointed by. 'Why the architrave?' he asked me, as if I had decided to dye the dog neon pink.

My haphazard approach had sent him haywire. OK, yes, it could have been planned better, but I had utilised a dead space and ticked a chore off the list. Now we know what we know, I can see this was hard for him and he needed time to adjust to it and yet in that moment, I felt resentful, frustrated and then worse, I was convinced I had done the wrong thing. After a week of him circling the cupboard, refusing to use it, he started to rearrange the contents and then bought a label maker for the jars, spending a happy evening slapping stickers on everything.

'This larder space is very useful,' he said. 'We should have done this years ago.'

*

There is an ex-Londoner's bray that I can be just as guilty of slipping into: an expat language that city folk share when they are bemoaning the ninety-minute round trip to the nearest cinema, the fact that nobody knows how to make a decent cortado, or how impossible it is to find a good hairdresser. If ever I catch myself daring to compare the two places, I imagine boiling my own head as a punishment. I also try not to mention what I used to do for a living because I am aware, against the backdrop of slurry pits, that I might sound like a bit of a wanker.

When we first moved down, I was terribly tight-lipped about it because I was desperate to fit in. Steve, with his three years of agricultural college tucked in the pocket of his ancient Barbour, took to it all immediately. He has always been just as at home in a field of cattle as he is in late-night Soho. This is one of the things that first attracted me to him. His transition to rural living was effortless and stylish, while mine was a kick-bollocks-scramble, floundering around in a life that wasn't my own until I found a comfortable spot.

When I do slip back into a showbiz story or entertainment anecdote, I am careful to check my audience. I try not to let the tale turn into a long-winded monologue, because I love any excuse to wallow in the old days. And while it cheers me, it also boosts my ego to remind myself, and others, about what I used to do and I really don't like that about myself. Recently a friend mentioned an actor she loved, and before I could stop myself, I told her I used to represent him.

'Ooh, get you!' she said, and I shrunk to the size of a beetle, praying for a heavy boot to crush me into the flagstones.

I was annoyed with myself for showing off, and I was irritated with her for squashing my opportunity to share the other part of me, not just the country dweller selling jam outside her garden gate. I wasn't lying, it was the truth, I was that person, and I had those experiences. It was a timely reminder to keep it zipped as much as possible and save it for those who were there too. Such as my agent colleagues and friends.

Olivia and Suzanne left the industry just before I did, with babies tucked under their arms and their horizons set on a more balanced home life. They were trailblazers for me, showing how I could walk away, even if it meant leaving bits of myself behind. We have remained in touch with occasional city meet-ups and regular

WhatsApp communication for gossip. The messages are often prompted by someone we know being in the news, a glitzy awards ceremony or a death. Sometimes a sudden flashback will catch one of us unawares as we are ferrying teenagers around or boiling a vat of pasta. We reach for our phones, messaging each other, 'Do you remember when…?' Like pinning a set of paper-thin butterflies inside a display case.

Do you remember when (famous actor) was staying in a Gatwick hotel before his flight out to the film set, and he called me at 4 a.m. to tell me to ring air traffic control to stop the planes flying overhead because he couldn't sleep?!

Do you remember when we had that idea to set up the Dead Actors Agency and only look after the estates of deceased celebrities? Well, someone else has only gone and done it! Can you imagine all the good bits without clients calling asking why they haven't had any auditions recently? We should have taken that idea seriously.

Do you remember when I said I was so sick of going to the theatre that I never ever wanted to go again? Now I would do anything for four hours of Shakespeare. I would even watch A Midsummer Night's Dream *for the forty-fifth time.*

Do you remember the time (famous actor) rang and complained that his trailer was 5 cm shorter than (famous actress's) who was a much bigger star than him at the time. He must have got down on his hands and knees and measured it with a ruler!

JUNE

Sad to hear (famous actress) has died, even though she was an utter bitch when I was an assistant and made me kneel in front of her to apologise for forgetting to collect her dry cleaning.

Do you remember the time I had Kate Winslet's custom-made Oscar dress in the boot of my old Renault 5 and I went to the cinema and halfway through the film I remembered the car didn't lock and I ran all the way back to it with a bit of sick in my mouth? (This was me. Nobody had nicked the dress out of the car, but I drove home and slept with the dress laid out next to me in case of burglars. This memory still makes my toes curl.)

Do you remember my old boss saying we are not curing cancer, we are just getting actors work, which made me feel better about mistakes I made? Except she would then tell casting directors that I was on a day-release scheme and I didn't understand, so asked her day release from where?

Do you remember the client who wanted to change his name from Luke to Luc because he thought it looked sexier and would get him more work, and I thought in my head, 'No, talent will get you more work.'

Do you remember the time (famous American producer) tricked me into giving him (famous actor's) telephone number, and (famous actor) went mad and I thought I was going to be fired?

Do you remember the actress who had a big hit in that Sunday evening drama and thought she was ready for Hollywood? And the casting director said if she was going to LA, she would have to go via Lourdes because she would need a miracle to become a movie star?? Whatever happened to her?

Each to their own, and none of my beeswax, but WHY DID GORGEOUS (FAMOUS ACTOR) DO THIS TO HIS FACE?! #botoxblooper

Do you remember when (famous actor) popped around to my house to pick up a script, and my sister was there, and she was gobsmacked that anyone could talk about themselves in a monologue without drawing breath? She said he left without even asking her name.

Currently watching the BAFTAs, and eldest asked if Emma Thompson was drunk, and I said, 'No, just theatrical.'

Raff latest joke. When the news alert pings on his phone and he says, 'Oh no,' and I say 'What?!' and he says, 'Dame Judi Dench dead at 88,' and I get emotional. He is gearing up for Bill Nighy next, I just know it.

The knives are out for (famous actor). I have met him a couple of times and it was like shaking hands with Voldemort's brother.

Do you remember the time my old boss took (famous actor) out for lunch and halfway through he went to the loo and didn't return? She called me, worried sick, and then found him in the restaurant kitchen drinking with the chef.

JUNE

Do you remember the time (famous actor) came into the office and kept cadging cigarettes off me, and then he went out to replace them and returned with a packet of ten, opened them and took one out before he gave them to me because he had smoked nine of mine? He couldn't just give me the whole packet even though he was a multi-millionaire.

Do you remember the time I ended up in that hotel room with the American agent who said if I left, he could make things difficult for me career-wise? On second thoughts, maybe I didn't tell you about that. (This was also me.)

*

Summer Solstice. The longest day of the year begins with car issues, which is annoying on any day of the year but particularly on the lengthiest. The clutch has gone, and I have been manually reattaching it for the last week. This is as bad as – or worse than – it sounds, depending on what you know about cars. I know nothing.

My car is pretty old and has very little that is complicated or electric about it, other than the windows that have also been playing up by staying up. A while ago, I asked the mechanic at the end of the village if he could fix them, but he refused on the grounds of it costing more than the car was worth, and anyway I didn't need to open them.

'What about hot weather?' I asked, and he shrugged, 'or what about if I'm driving past a neighbour in the lane and want to say hello? I have to partially open my door.'

'So, don't chat,' he said.

'OK,' I said, 'what if my car topples into a fast-moving river and I need to escape through the window?'

'Well, if that happens,' he replied, 'then the electrics will fail anyway.'

I think there is something odd in trying to get a mechanic to do work that I am prepared to pay for, and him refusing.

The mechanic can't help with my clutch right now, he says, because he is too busy and has a back molar that is giving him gyp. So Steve shows me how to re-hook the pedal back on to the arm as though it is the most normal thing in the world. This involves contorting my body with half of it out of the car, lying on my side on the driver's seat and reaching my arms under the steering wheel. The sharp edges of the dashboard slice into my wrists and leave bloody streaks.

Once the clutch is secure, it will begin to slip before pinging off approximately fifteen minutes into a journey, so every ten minutes I pull over to push the lever back in place. This is not safe, I think. This is an understatement, I also think. Of course, I could take it elsewhere to another mechanic, but this causes its own issues around garage loyalty, so I persevere.

The clutch goes on a roundabout while I am on my way to a meeting. When I arrive, after causing a major traffic jam while fixing the sodding car, I babble about clutch trouble and laugh, showing my slashed wrists in what I think is a mildly amusing anecdote. Everyone looks aghast. I break down twice on the way home – car and emotions – and freewheel through the village and straight to the mechanic. I am fifty-fucking-two, and I should not be driving around in this sort of half-arsed situation. I am irrationally cross with Steve because I need to blame someone. Maybe if we hadn't spent a load of money on therapy, I think, we could have afforded a better car ... but that's unfair and it doesn't solve anything.

Only the mechanic can help, and if blood and tears don't get me bumped up the waiting list, I don't know what will. I dump the car and stomp into his workshop, holding my wrists out like a Shakespearean queen.

The mechanic flinches. 'Steve didn't tell me it was that bad,' he says disapprovingly, 'which is unlike him, because your husband would get hot and bothered in the Antarctic.'

'That's because he has ADHD and autism,' I say before I can stop myself.

I immediately wish I hadn't, but it shuts the mechanic up. He mends the clutch in five minutes at the mere cost of a crisp tenner and a week of my life.

In the vehicle commotion, I have not had time to celebrate the Solstice. In previous years, I have marked it in various ways, including a group swim as the sun rises followed by a beach fire, BBQ sausages and floral crowns. One year, emboldened by a warm sky, sun salutations and deserted beach, we all stripped off, held hands and ran shrieking into the sea. Later that morning, as Steve was walking to work along the seafront, he passed a café owner chatting to a friend. 'You will never guess what I saw at dawn?! Eight naked ladies running into the sea...' The following year we did the same but did not bank on a group of sixth formers turning up as we were about to get out of the water. Those poor kids.

Ros and I catch the Solstice a day late, but carry the appropriate gratitude in our morning swim. We are on a different beach. It is a great spot, but less predictable in bad weather so we make it our summer destination, avoiding the fishermen lined up along the far end of the shore. There is rarely anyone else on the beach when we turn up, parking by the shuttered ice cream kiosk and the bins, overflowing with yesterday's greasy chip wrappers. If the waves are too punchy, we can be knocked off our feet and pounded against the shingle ledge, scrabbling inelegantly out of the water on all fours.

The sea is flat-calm today, as clear as Sundays, and we get in as an arrow of beautiful white light pierces the bay, gliding through the glassy quiet water and then back-pedalling into the sparkling path of the sun. A cormorant dives for its breakfast and resurfaces triumphantly with its beak clamped around a fish. A sailing boat is moored out past the buoys, and we express the hope that someone will beckon us on board, maybe for a breakfast of coffee, eggs and buttery croissants.

'I could swim much further for the dangling of a pastry,' I say sincerely.

'I wouldn't care if there were maverick dolphins in our way.' Ros looks hungrily at the boat.

We drape our swimmers over the shingle and sit, watching the light edge around the bay. I tell Ros about Steve's appointment with the psychiatrist as I pour out ginger-and-lemon tea. I give the bare bones of it because I don't want to monopolise these magical post-swim moments or smear them with real-life stuff, even though this is what we both use this time for. Taking it in turns to chew over the gristly bits that are troubling us.

'The thing about Steve,' Ros says, 'is that he's a tryer. In all these years, he hasn't given up trying to get to the bottom of things and now he has achieved it. It's such an admirable, impressive approach.'

JUNE

'I think that's why we are still together, because he is intent on answers and change, except knowing what we know now doesn't make things different, but it does make it something we can recognise and deal with.'
'It's a good thing for you both.' Ros smiles encouragingly at me and rolls up her swimsuit in her towel.
'It feels like it could be.' I shake the dregs from our cups. 'Sorry about the lack of hot chocolate today. I ran out. Won't be making that mistake again, I feel like I have just been sucking on a lukewarm lemon.'
'Metaphor for life,' Ros says as we trudge up the beach flicking pebbles from our sandals.

*

Steve has been doing a lot of googling and in-depth reading while he waits to be told what we already know. This is his answer to almost anything, and when faced with a possible dual diagnosis, he dives into the internet ocean of advice, philosophy and memes. He has been fascinated by all the symptoms of ADHD, but is finding autism less appealing to read about. Some of the most disabling effects of the former can be alleviated with medication, but the latter cannot, and I can understand why this flummoxes him. It also surprises us both that a dual diagnosis has only been available for ten years, as guidelines before this point meant that a medical professional would need to choose between one or the other. There are many autistic traits he doesn't connect with, which is also confusing and unsatisfying.

He finds a statement that stops him in his tracks. 'So, the quote is, "If you have met one person with autism, then you have met one person with autism." Do you get it? Do you see what it means? It's a play on the old "If you've met one person with whatever, then you have met them all," but not with neurodivergence. Everyone is unique. It's so fucking annoying. How am I supposed to solve this?'

'You're not – you're supposed to learn how to live with it. We're all going to have to learn how to live with it.' I don't want to be harsh, but this is the reality.

'You don't have to learn how to live with it. This is not your problem,' he says simply.

We have not talked about our marriage for quite some time. It has been filed in pending while Steve takes big strides in his diagnosis and understanding.

I don't think he is angling for an answer from me so I ignore the statement. 'Like the psychiatrist says, there are tools and coping mechanisms that you need to lean into. I read something recently about setting yourself small daily routines to calm your ASD responses, but leaving space in your day to feed your impulsive ADHD side. And there is a thing called body doubling, where you complete an action alongside someone, to help with distraction and inertia. Perhaps I can come in and we can put some admin processes in place in the office? And if you start your working week with a list of priorities that you schedule in before you start…'

Steve interrupts me – he has heard enough. I have already overloaded his brain and I can see he is thinking of reasons why my suggestions won't work. 'Well, I also read something recently about time blindness. It's an ADHD thing. I know you think I have an issue with punctuality and, well, this explains it.' He sounds triumphant.

JUNE

Oh good, I think to myself sarcastically. He has found the perfect excuse to live by his own clock, and there isn't a damn thing I can do about it because he is now telling me it is a condition.

I feel guilty thinking this and then frustrated, and wonder if time blindness is intermittent because Steve isn't always late. He can be bang on schedule for meetings and site visits, he switches the radio on ready for the Ashes commentary, and perfectly poaches an egg. And yet, when it comes to certain commitments, such as school pick-ups or being back at a time I have requested, he can't do it – and now that is because he has ADHD.

It is a family joke that on the rare occasion he was on primary school pick-up, our children were the last ones left standing in the playground. While I thought this happened a handful of times, it seems it happened most of the times he was in charge, but the children didn't want to dob him in. Steve can't hold the fact that they have to be at school by 8.40 a.m. and leave at 3.30 p.m., even though this has been the case for the last fourteen years. It is a fluid thing for him. I am trying to accept he has a different grip on the concept of time, but the fallout often lands in my lap. It just feels really disrespectful to whoever is kept waiting, which is usually me.

Without telling him, I do my own research to discover that time blindness is indeed a thing and associated with temporal processing. The internet is full of it, and I feel chastened for not taking it seriously but I don't admit this to Steve yet. I know I have to make allowances, and yet where does my frustration go? I am also envious. Steve is more able to live in the moment than I am.

Like the crocodile in *Peter Pan*, I have a clock ticking inside me, counting through the days and pushing me past moments I should savour, while Steve pauses by cracks in the pavement. And this isn't a euphemism, because he will often stop and look at cracks in a wall and wonder how they happened. Or stand and have a conversation with someone and be surprised when he misses the train. Or think anything that will clearly take all morning will only be an hour. Alternatively, things that should only take an hour can go on all day. This is time blindness.

*

I have been looking for people who Steve can relate to. I come across an Instagram post from the writer Matt Haig, telling his followers that he was diagnosed with ADHD and ASD a year or so ago and it has taken him this long to talk about it. He writes in a raw, truthful and reassuring way, which I hope will be helpful for Steve, so I forward it to him. He needs to know there are others out there who can express how he feels, and maybe it will encourage him to accept the diagnosis.

It also helps me. Matt describes exactly what Steve has also gone through, from the long-term mental-health crisis that saw him on the very edge of his life, to the expected ADHD diagnosis and the 'shock' at finding out he was also autistic. Matt talks about his battle with trying to be neurotypical with a mind that isn't, and how he is trying to understand his autism and the social difficulties this brings. One part resonates more loudly than the rest. Matt says he is ridiculously literal and can find it hard to read people or situations, which means he comes across as 'either too shy or too rude'.

JUNE

He says, 'My ADHD likes fun, but my autism means that it exhausts me because I really need a routine. I am a continual tug of war.' He signs off on the post with, 'I really hope this helps someone.'

After I have sent all of this to Steve and get no response, I follow up with an impatient 'Well??! Isn't this amazing! And he has a golden retriever too!' text. He sends a non-committal thumbs up. Not the reaction I wanted. I thought he would display a sense of relief, recognise a kindred spirit bravely making a very public statement and showing it is going to be OK.

Look! I want to say, you are not alone in your tug of war! But Steve doesn't want to hear this because he still doesn't think it applies to him. Yes, he is ADHD, but his mind can't seem to contemplate autism. It is as if it cuts off just before he gets there. Instead, he feels humiliation, inadequacy, as if he is letting us down by being both things rather than just one.

I return to Matt's words several times to read the messages posted by his followers in support. So many people pouring out their own stories of depression, shame and diagnosis. These ping up in real time in front of my eyes and I scan them all: a mosaic of tiny mirrors, each reflecting the same light in slightly different directions. The shared experience reaches far into me, breaking through my protective steel structure and touching the soft emotional core I keep hidden, even from myself. Especially from myself.

Sitting at the kitchen table, milk slowly forming a skin over my coffee, I feel such empathy for Steve, an emotion that has been suppressed by the stress and loneliness of being the strong one. Compassion is tough to muster when you are in survival mode, and parts of me have been stifled over the years. Other emotions bubble up, and I realise I have been scared of Steve's mental health and angry about it too. The one thing I am not supposed to feel in this situation: the least helpful reaction. I think I have squeezed these feelings inside me for so long that they have become impacted and misshapen, transforming into a sort of humming disappointment. If someone asked me how I feel right now, I couldn't answer truthfully because I have too many defences in place, both to protect Steve and to stop me facing it all. I don't know how to access my honest self.

July

The village loves a good knees-up. In the past, we have come together for big events such as Bonfire Night, the last minutes of New Year's Eve, royal celebrations and tractor rallies. Most of us have taken it in turns to host them, with mixed results.

About a year after we arrived and had resurfaced from the fuss of getting the house habitable and turning the shed into an Airbnb, we invited everyone over for tea and cake. It was an opportunity to meet the neighbours who had been slowing down as they drove past and, that afternoon, after polite chitter chatter, they swarmed over the half-finished house and garden.

I thought it went awfully well, helped by the large jugs of Pimms swiftly followed by the PG Tips, until a couple of days later when we received a call from the local council saying someone had reported us, suggesting we might be running a B&B without planning consent. We couldn't quite believe it. Firstly, it wasn't true, and secondly, we wanted to know who the hell had enjoyed our homemade scones and coffee-and-walnut cake and then waddled straight home to protest behind our backs.

We had a list of suspects, and at the top was Margaret. When we first moved in, she had popped round on the pretext of welcoming us but with the obvious intention of checking the cut of our jib and spelling out the village rules. She had clearly found us wanting. While we couldn't openly accuse her, we could ask her if, as the self-appointed spokesperson of the village, she might know who was unhappy.

'Me,' she said, chin tipped defiantly in the air. 'I called the council.'

'But why, Margaret?' Steve asked.

'Because I can,' she replied.

A few years later, when Margaret had left for a retirement home (God save them), our friends Anna and Dan moved into the village and offered to host that year's bonfire party. The festivities were interrupted by irate peacock-owner Brenda, parked on the field next to their house, full-beam headlights shining uncomfortably on the party for the duration, convinced we were about to traumatise the farm animals. We had already assured her we would behave responsibly and stick to sparklers. That is until one neighbour arrived a little the worse for wear holding banned fireworks and chucked a box of them straight on the fire as Anna and I ran around scooping up children in the path of the rockets and shoving them in the house.

When Sheila threw a summer garden party, another neighbour was disgruntled to find that what she assumed was a quiche Lorraine was in fact a salmon-and-broccoli tart, which was her favourite. 'If only someone had labelled each buffet plate, then I would not have missed out,' she huffed.

All the big issues down our way. The biggest was that finding a place we could all gather in was becoming increasingly fraught, and we needed a new village location on safe, neutral territory in time for the next celebration, which was the Queen's Platinum Jubilee. There was a lot of speculation about how and where

JULY

the village would commemorate the right royal date. Everyone had an opinion on what to do, but nobody wanted to get lumbered with being the one to organise it. Conversations were full of half-finished comments, like an alternative game of pass the parcel, where whoever completes a sentence gets stuck with a job to do.

There were whisperings from the incomers that the locals wouldn't want us to join their celebrations, and mutterings from the locals that the incomers wouldn't turn up. I flagged down Quad Bike Keith – of the 'born and bred' contingent – as he rounded the corner in his car, one hand on the steering wheel, the other clutching a scotch egg he was munching on.

'Keith, some of us at this end of the village have been chatting about the Jubilee and wanted to know whether there were any plans afoot? We would love to be involved.'

'So, we thought four days of celebrations,' Keith said.

'Gosh, four? OK, we were thinking more like … one?' I couldn't face spending four days of relentless partying with people I loved, let alone with my idiosyncratic neighbours.

'Yeah, well, we don't do small. Gerry is getting his tractor out to take everyone up to the café for breakfast. Special village deal of a fiver for a bacon sandwich and coffee. Beacon lighting in my field one evening. Maybe a jumble sale the following day. The finale will be a big rounders match and BBQ on Gerry's field.'

Keith didn't need my input. The best news was that we had a place for villagers to head to. Well done, Gerry, and thank you.

'Lovely, great, I'll talk to everyone this end and let you know what they think,' I said, doing a double thumbs up, which is what I had started doing when I was really not sure of anything.

That afternoon, I drove through the village to see a timetable of events tucked under car windscreen wipers and posted outside the church. Decision already made. That's how things get done here. In fairness, the rest of us had not taken the initiative, and it took the pressure off to know that there was a plan.

Gerry and Keith turned out to be the Ant and Dec of the village celebrations. They met as teenagers at the Young Farmers' Association and have been friends ever since, talking in anecdotes about people with nicknames such as 'Spiker', 'Growler' and 'Old Man'. Any opportunity I get, I plug them for more stories, one of my favourites being the time the combine harvester was up on Otter Hill in front of our house. The driver took too sharp a turn, lost control, and the beast of a vehicle rolled down the hill. He called for everyone to bail, which they did, catapulting into the grass and watching helplessly as the mechanical monster picked up speed, passed clean through the hedgerow, out on to the road, through the front wall of the cottage garden and came to rest inches from the house. Incredibly, nobody was hurt, and someone even has a photograph of the disaster.

There is something so familiar about these two men. They remind me of my grandfather, Sidney Hinks, who was passionate about his London heritage and loved a good yarn. He had nicknames for people too, particularly cocky sorts who he called 'Charley Big Spuds'. I think he would have liked Keith and Gerry, even though they speak a different sort of English and are settled in such opposite landscapes. They are all fixed to their place,

JULY

with the blood of their ancestors steeped in the Devon soil or the Acton pavements.

The day before the festivities began, Gerry spent hours assembling the sides and roof of his trailer, filling it with straw-bale seating and stringing red, white and blue bunting along the sides. There was a piece of floorboard tied to the back, with the words 'hand signals only' painted on to it. Gerry had several old pride-and-joy tractors to choose from and had polished up his blue Fordson Major for the job, tying a large Union Jack flag to the fender. He beamed with delight at his transport as we piled on and off to head to the café the next morning and then, just before sunset, to beacon lighting.

I took a dusty bottle of sloe gin that I had found in the back of the cupboard and was just the thing to toast Her Majesty. As we left later that evening, I prised the booze out of teenage hands and left the rest of it with Keith. We walked back up the village, the moon suspended from a blanket of cloud in a dying orange sky, and looked out for bats in the creeping darkness. When I turned my bedside lamp off, I could hear Gerry trundling back up the lane in his trusty tractor. It made me feel secure.

The finale of all celebrations, the rounders game, was on the Glebe Field. Throughout the afternoon, people arrived, beer bottles clinking, heavy picnic hampers bashing shins and dogs straining on leads. Gerry and Keith had put up a gazebo, plugged in a sound system and set up several BBQs, which were lit ready for people to cook their sausages on. There were bottles of wine lined up, crates of beer and a table full of homemade cakes and bakes that we had all donated.

Caroline, from the old manor, sat in a capacious throne-like deckchair looking like our very own queen of the village. Everyone agreed that Sheila's sausage rolls were the best. Nigel rallied the troops for the rounders match, which was raucous, hilarious and tinged with danger, not helped by sugar-fuelled children and feral dogs. Steve got bitten by a competitive collie as they both tried to catch the rounders ball, and Harry's wife broke her toe sliding to second base. Of all the village celebrations we had been part of over the years, this felt like the most successful: a definitive example of how a group of people brought together by the accident of sharing a postcode could become a community. I reckoned this country weekend would burn brighter than any other in our children's memories.

Before we left, I looked for Gerry so I could thank him. Past the vegetable beds in the corner, the stacked log pile, the tractors tucked away for the night and the decking where camping chairs were set out around a keg of beer, there was a door at the far end of the barn. An alluring golden light seeped out around the edges. I peeped in, and there was Gerry in what I expected to be some sort of workshop for broken machinery, but instead looked more like an upmarket ski chalet. The walls were panelled with offcuts of wood and hung with paintings and photographs. There was a beautiful eight-foot pine table with benches ('from our house in France') at one end, and at the other was a blazing log burner with an armchair either side of it.

'Gerry, this is amazing,' I said in awe and jealousy, sitting in one of the chairs. This was not what I expected. 'All it needs is a drinks cabi—'

Gerry lifted a bottle from the hidden wine rack.

His family originally owned the farm in the middle of the village until it was gradually sold off, much

JULY

to his dismay. All he had left was a black-and-white photograph of how it used to look, which he had pinned to the wall of his shed. He released it from the rusted drawing pins so I could get a closer look, and showed me where he kept pigs as a young boy, tracing the route he would take in the tractor, from the farm to the gate in front of our cottage that leads into Blacksmith's Field. Someone reported Gerry to Cyril Hodges, the local constable, for being thirteen years old in charge of a vehicle. Cyril hid his regulation police motorbike in the hedgerow and lay in wait, but a village network of whispers warned Gerry, so he went by foot to feed the pigs for a week and evaded capture.

Gerry's wife, Jane, had grown up in the Old Rectory, which was perched high on the hill, raised above the rest of us and facing the direction of the sea. Jane's father had been the vicar. Gerry's father was the farmer. They first met when she was five and he was ten. They had been grubby-kneed, tree-climbing village kids who grew up to leave the place, marry other people and have children. Throughout, Gerry kept hold of the Glebe field and then by a great strike of luck, he got hold of Jane too. Theirs was a burning middle-aged love of homecoming. They had a flat in the local town, a farmhouse in France, and Jane's horses were stabled alongside Gerry's tractors on the Glebe field. They had completed a glorious circle. Jane was only sixty-two when she died of cancer, and Gerry's heart broke clean in two.

'My Jane,' he calls her when he talks about her, never just 'Jane'.

He tells me this story as we look at photographs of her, straight-backed in hunting regalia, sipping from a silver cup, in her jeans leaning forward on her horse and laughing, her hair and the horse's mane intertwined. I understand it now. The way he drives his tractors around the village as though he owns it. He does.

It doesn't mean that I am not worthy of a place in this rich village history, but my story is tentative and recent in comparison to Gerry's, whose roots spiral down through the flinty soil. His ancestors rest in the small graveyard, his soul is embedded in the land, and his memories roam free, like his beautiful Jane, who I imagine galloping across the fields of her childhood, leaping high over hedges and gates on her chestnut horse, no longer contained by physical things.

*

We are going camping in Cornwall. When I say we, I don't include Raff because he saved up and has gone off on a solo backpacking trip around Italy for several weeks. The original plan was to meet up with him out there, but our finances won't stretch to it, which means we won't get a family holiday this year. This makes me feel particularly sorry for myself because there can't be many opportunities left for the five of us to go away. I wanted this summer to be special for Raff, although he is doing a good job of that on his own, and with a fellow traveller, a lovely French-Canadian girl who he met in Florence. The truth is, I wanted the summer to be special for me before Raff heads to uni.

Also, when I say 'we', I don't include Steve either because he is topping and tailing the trip by driving, putting the tent up, staying the night and then heading home to work before coming back out at the end of the week to do everything in reverse. He has a lot on, and we are camping with three other families, which may present social challenges that he hasn't yet worked out how to navigate. We decide it is better for him to be there for some of the time with the ability to retreat, which feels like a good compromise. As for camping, he loves it and approaches it in the sort of Ray Mears-meets-SAS manner that leaves me cold. It is a serious business, which I ruin when I swap my sleeping bag for a duvet and bring digestive biscuits as a main food group, so I am looking forward to holidaying under canvas in my own haphazard 'wellies left outside the tent in the rain' way. It is going to be like a school field trip when the teachers go off to the pub.

I hate camping almost as much as I hate going up into the attic. I have to do the latter to get the stuff for the former, which makes me cross. I prefer standing on the narrow, wobbly ladder with my head stuck through the hatch and giving directions, rather than climbing up into the rafters and facing our nostalgic dumping ground. The battered suitcases bulging with baby clothes, Steve's family trunk housing his Scout blanket covered in good-deed badges, plastic tubs of old school reports and letters, a large toy kitchen that all the kids adored playing with, and boxes of Christmas decorations. I sincerely hope that the insects up there are cluster flies not bluebottles, which rise lazily and get caught in my hair. It could be the forgotten backroom of a badly organised museum.

Steve is up there huffing and puffing. He can't just pull out the camping equipment and get the hell out of there, as I would do. He makes a meal of taking the hoover up and tackling the flies with Indiana Jones ferocity, and then he rearranges boxes to find what was right in front of him all along. This fuels his irritation so he then rails against my (our) hoarding issues and throws a few things down on the landing that we can't possibly need to keep. It is also ironic because many of the items in the loft have come from hobbies that he has excitedly started before losing interest or finding a reason why he can't continue. The set of expensive golf clubs, the fly-fishing kit, the sea-fishing equipment and the riding boots, jodhpurs and whip. There is a large cardboard box of half-finished Airfix models, an ice-cream maker and steel toe-capped boots. None of these things are mine.

He has been pretty monosyllabic for the last week, and now we are not speaking after a tired argument about how him not invoicing clients means no money, so the trip up to the attic just compounds it. I can't imagine how we are going to get everything organised in this fug of discontent, so I suggest we both go and pick up a gas bottle for the camping stove and then we can have a row in the car without the kids overhearing us. We drive to the farm shop in silence.

The rain is torrential, and this exacerbates my gloom about a week under canvas and a marriage on the precipice. I plan to treat myself to a couple of cheery geraniums or a synthetic iced cake when we get there, but I don't even have the spirit for that, so we pick up the gas bottle and a packet of biscuits, maintaining a polite but frosty manner in public. Back in the car, we stare straight ahead through the rainy windscreen, watching customers make a dash for the shop through deep puddles. It would be quite entertaining if we weren't ignoring each other. I don't start the engine so we continue to sit until Steve is ready to talk.

'I just don't understand what I am doing wrong. These drugs I am on aren't a miracle cure for ADHD. They don't erase it. They help with my concentration, my maddening impulsivity and clearing my dopamine pathway, but sometimes I still make the same mistakes. How?'

We come back to the conversation about finding tools to support him, particularly in his working day, such as writing a plan, scheduling projects, and changing how he deals with distractions. He has an unfounded fear of invoicing clients and asking for money so Finance Dad has given him a pep talk. I am frustrated on Steve's behalf because he is so good at what he does, his attention to detail is unparalleled, his care for his clients goes above and beyond and yet he can scupper himself in an instant. This is all for nothing if he doesn't feel he deserves to be paid. I also suggest that anyone with the amount of work he has might feel like this. What if it wasn't a neurodivergent thing, but just a 'far too busy for the number of hours in a day' scenario?

Again, I offer to come into the office a day a week to help with the admin, which neither of us really wants, although it is a constructive possibility. We agree that we feel like terrible adults, ricocheting from one issue to the next, just about scraping through, but with no future safety net. Hand to mouth. I feel Steve's fury desert him and know we are finally getting to the root of his recent mood. It often takes a roundabout route.

'By the way, I heard back from the psychiatrist, and I am definitely autistic,' he says flatly, 'with a side order of ADHD. The thing is, I can get my head around the ADHD because of the pill. Autism is different. It's for life and there's no escape.' He turns to look at me. 'I don't want to be autistic.'

*

I wake up feeling tired. My stomach is still anchored by last night's fish and chips, and the pink wine I drank a glass too much of has a tight grip around my head. I can't hear the birds, and the tent is shrouded in darkness, so I know it is not quite dawn. My airbed is flat as a pancake to the stony ground, making it impossible to get back to sleep, so I quietly feel around for my glasses, jacket and phone and pull on my damp wellies at the tent flap.

The campsite is completely still. There are footballs discarded in the dew-soaked grass, swimsuits and towels optimistically hanging over guy ropes and chairs upturned in case of rain overnight. Out to sea, the sky is the softest and palest strips of blues, pinks and corals with ribbons of hazy cloud. It will be a while before the sun comes up, but it is light enough for me to leave the campsite and head along the worn path diagonally across the fields to the cliff edge and the wide ocean beyond.

Leading down into the town is a steep overgrown cave-type path of perpetual shadow, which is dangerously slippery underfoot, so I hang on to the chunks of slate, laid herringbone-style, which make a wall to my right and pop out on to the harbour road. The white Victorian villas and Cornish stone cottages looking out to sea, with their pale blue or arsenic green faded window frames, are mainly for holidaymakers at this time of year, their front gardens full of abandoned paddle boards and flip-flops. I want to get to the beach before the sun rises, so I turn right before the Boathouse restaurant and the pub, and hurry past the succession of small art galleries and the vintage shop on the corner.

Empty beer bottles are lined up neatly outside the sailing club at the top end of the private lane. Here, there is a mix of architecture: on one side, the houses are built high above the road facing the horizon, and on the other they are almost touching the sea wall, giving glimpses of waves and boats through the gaps. In the gardens and on the verges are white and purply blue agapanthus flowers the size of my head, blowsy hydrangeas with nasturtium fringing, and an old fishing boat that has been used as a flower bed.

The road becomes a narrow footpath with a sentinel of spiky Bear's Breeches, which look like vicious lupins, that block the ocean view from the benches set at intervals and dedicated to long-dead members of the community. Beyond, the track is overgrown, smattered with a few early sour little blackberries, luscious ferns and brittle sepia cow parsley before the way opens out into a field of rabbits, bursts of sunny ragwort and sloe bushes nurturing hard berries. I squeeze a sloe between my thumb and finger and reckon these will need a couple more weeks of plumping before they are ready to pick.

From the top of the concrete staircase, I can see that not only is the beach empty this morning, but I am the first one down, the sand smooth and untouched until my footprints. Yesterday, later than now but still early, I had come here with Steve, and there were three women in swim caps doing a serene breaststroke across the bay. Two yachts were moored up, and a tender nipped from one to the other for what I imagined was a shared breakfast on deck. We went to the furthest end of the beach, stripped naked and raced into the sea, Margot paddling furiously behind us. Then the refuse collectors turned up, and a man appeared and began doing yoga moves while his dog chased seagulls.

'We will never see these people again,' I said, reassuring myself more than Steve. 'Make a run for it!' We dashed out to our pile of sand-blown clothes, giddy with joy and liberation, grabbing at pants, Margot dancing around us while we tried to pull our socks on. Holding hands, we walked back along the cliff into the little town just as the coffee hut opened. Steve ordered and I pulled up two stools at the counter hewn from a slab of tree trunk, looking out to sea while Margot took lapping gulps from the dog water bowl before settling down in the shade. It was blissful.

The sun, hot on our faces, cast a shimmering ribbon across the water, broken by swimmers launching themselves from the tiny harbour beach. A boat puttered out, keeping its distance from the group of paddleboarders and kayakers who were wobbling in its wake. Steve and I talked idly about retiring here, which house we would live in and how we would enjoy a simple life, eating fish we caught from the jetty and joining the film club in the local church hall. Margot would like it, we said, ignoring the fact that it would make her at least 175 in dog years. If anyone overheard us, they would think we were happily married. I think we were in that moment. A tenuous bubble of togetherness that dissipated when we got back to the campsite.

Steve's mood shifted while he tried to maintain his usual breakfast routine of yoghurt, muesli and

JULY

carefully peeled-and-segmented orange, in a tent kitchen shared with sixteen other people. In this situation, it is impossible to expect what we always do to be the same, but he didn't think this as he searched for a bowl, spoon, cereal and knife, and he wasn't the only one in our camping gang who found this change of routine challenging. Yet when it is Steve, I feel like his carer, every fibre of my being tuned to his emotional responses, thinking ahead to what may trip him up. He doesn't want to be singled out, nor does he know how to fit in. Now, with more understanding of who he is, we need to learn how to traverse these situations, but it is early days. When he drove back home, I waved him off with relief, the morning strands that bound us unravelling after a stressful breakfast.

Now I am ecstatically alone. No Steve, no boats, no swimmers, no beach visitors, no worried dog. My hangover and indigestion have evaporated. I stride into the water, feeling the mild shock as it breaks against my thighs and swallows me whole, closing over my nakedness. My breath is in motion with the wave, and I swim through fronds of pink seaweed into an open sky and pure happiness, the town and life behind me. I imagine my bare bottom shining brightly through the clear water, but I don't care.

I am belligerent in my nudity, and without glasses I am braver still because I can't see very much. I have tipped into that age where I am too old to care what people think, and I welcome it, wishing I had had this power when I was younger. My bosoms are two bobbing inflatables as I lie back, looking through my toes at the horizon, the heavy menopausal weight of me suspended, the cool air refreshing after the musty tent and sleepless night. I will be ready to head back to my campmates once I have had a coffee at the kiosk in town.

Don't think, just be, I think.

I thank the sea before leaving it, misjudging the tide, so my wellies come to greet me in the shallows. I tip the water out of them and wring out my socks, which had been tucked inside. The rest of my clothes are higher on the rock, and I am in underwear by the time two dogs bound over to see me. Their owner is meandering along the sand, head down, looking for shells, and we both simultaneously call 'hello!' cheerily.

'I just saw you from the cliff. How brave of you to get into the water!' she says, which I take to mean, 'How brave of you to skinny dip.'

'Ah yes, I'm sorry about my bare bottom.'

She brushes the comment off with a wave of her hand. 'Oh, I couldn't tell if you were in a swimming costume or not, I have terrible eyesight,' she says diplomatically.

I wander slowly back along the coastal path, not wanting to leave my magical solitary morning. I am too early for coffee, so when I get to the hut I pull up a stool as the staff are unloading trays of buttery pastries from the back of a van, and lay my wet socks out in the sun. I am in no rush for them to crank up the coffee machine. I could sit here all day. I simultaneously wish Steve was with me, and am also glad he isn't. It is very confusing.

I take a photo of the view on my phone and send it to him.

He instantly replies: *I miss you*

I respond with a pulsating red love heart.

*

Alice pops by with squash plants for me, and another cardboard box of ceramics that I carefully unpack in front of her, oohing and aahing over each piece. This time she has brought me porcelain pots, as delicate as eggshells with the same whites and pale green-blue tones. I am nervous about putting them out on the honesty bench. What if they get stolen or broken? She waves away my anxiety. She wants to have a look around the veg patch, so we wander with mugs of tea, and she talks gently about her slow but steady recovery from cancer.

'There's so much I want to do, now I feel better and more able, but I also want to relish the lazy summer living. Hang out with my boys, potter around the garden, fire up my new kiln, swim in the sea and read. So many books! So much life to enjoy.'

We choose a spot for the squash. Before she leaves, I hug her tightly, her usually robust frame feeling as fragile as the porcelain pieces she has created but both bursting with spirit.

*

We are in the middle of the traditional honesty box season. From June to September, it is likely that there will be a bounty of fresh produce available with a particular focus on August for gluts. This is exactly the time to keep your wits about you, eyes peeled, and actual cash in your pocket. I have picked courgettes, sweet peas and the first of the runner beans and pop them out on the bench, but right now, I am more interested in other people's honesty boxes than my own. I have so much still to learn about veg growing. From good soil management and succession planting to predators and blights, progress is slow and flawed and I am already thinking about doing better next year. I reckon that makes me a proper gardener.

I potter around the raised beds, plucking out weeds, pulling up more radishes and cutting a bunch of sweet peas for a vase in the shed. Before I sit at my desk, I clear up the wine bottle and glasses left from last night and chip the candle wax off the table. Miranda, TV Lucy and Susie came over for dinner. We sat outside, determined to catch every drop of summer warmth and my pretty-in-pink climbing roses, which were at optimum lush levels, demanding to be worshipped. We stayed out until late, edging chairs closer to the fire, talking about past lives and future trips, heads tilted back watching for shooting stars. Now, in the morning light, I should get the secateurs out and have a tidy up, but I have a writing deadline and can't be distracted. I look around me at all we still need to do in the garden.

Everything turns wild so fast with a shot of sun and drenching of rain. The self-seeded apple tree already has gobstopper-sized fruits that I am supposed to begin thinning, discarding the weak, malformed and blemished to allow the strong, beautiful apples to thrive. I decide to leave that job to nature. Or Steve, if he remembers. The honeysuckle and deep purple clematis flowers are beginning to wither, while the first cobnuts, in their downy jackets, poke through the hedge. Everything is still the greenest green, but the sturdy brambles are scattered with the last of their petals as the tight buds of the first blackberries push through. The light has changed too. It feels lower, wider, somehow.

At my desk, deep in work, I have to remind myself not to hunch, as my shoulders gradually rise to my

JULY

ears, which exacerbates an awful stiffness in my neck. It could be the way I sit at my computer or the many-symptomed menopause. Maybe if I go to the chiropractor, they will tell me it is because I am carrying a heavy emotional weight, which they will then offer to carefully prise off me and pop in a corner or obliterate with a laser beam.

This reminds me of the chiropodist I went to many years ago, after a verruca multiplied in front of my eyes. By the time I turned up for the appointment, the sole of my foot was covered in them. The chiropodist took a medical approach first, and then she took a holistic view, examining me with a fervour and fascination that made me think I might have a rare condition, before asking me what I did for a living. I told her I was an agent, giving a brief description of what this entailed, leaving out details such as a client ringing me from a police cell, having to go to another client's house to physically get them to a film set and spending countless evenings standing outside restaurants on my phone watching my friends through the glass eating dinner. Throughout the appointment, I could hear my Blackberry (yep, that long ago) buzzing relentlessly in my bag. The chiropodist asked me how many clients I had, and I told her as she counted the verrucas. One for every client. Proof that the body does indeed keep the score.

I have been writing for less than an hour before I am interrupted. Steve has asked a company to come and quote on replacing our windows. He has worked with them before and recommended them to family and friends with resounding success so it is our turn to get excited. Except, like everything about this house, which isn't supposed to be a house, it isn't easy or straightforward.

I make coffee, and everyone is jolly, especially Steve, who is buzzing with hope. Things go downhill quickly. I watch their cheery demeanour slip as they study every window, shaking their heads, sucking in breath, speaking quietly to each other about what might be possible. I know this troubled look and the shift in energy, so I go back to my desk until I hear loud bangs and the sound of something smashing on the lane.

I almost don't go back down, but I am a fifty-something woman who used to manage a client list fraught with regular catastrophe (as just mentioned). If I can deal with an actor being arrested, a celebrity AWOL from a big press conference, or a paparazzi car chase in a London cab with a drunk actress, I can face a few men with a hammer and good intentions.

Chunks of render have been chipped away from the corner of each ground-floor window. This is worse than I thought. I am almost wishing for a group of gobby paparazzi instead. Much easier to deal with. The men turn to look at me: the light has gone out in their eyes, and the boss sees my return as an opportunity to make an escape.

'Bad news.' This discovery appears to have hit him harder than it will hit us. 'These window frames are not properly fixed into the walls. We can't do anything until you have chipped the render off and a builder has taken a look.'

I laugh in a knowing 'oh this silly house always keeping us on our toes' sort of way, although it really has come up trumps this time. Windows not fitting in walls has to be up there in the list of serious defaults.

JULY

The boss is a good man and an excellent professional, but he can't hide his dismay. 'I have to be honest,' he says, and I want to say *no, no, no, please don't*, 'this is the first time in my window-fitting career that I have been utterly stumped by a set of French doors.' Once they have left us for dust, wheel-spinning out of the village, likely patting this cautionary tale in their top pockets ready to share with head-shaking disbelief when they get back to HQ, Steve is clinging on to the belief that he can solve the problem.

He decides he will tackle the render himself and should get it done in a couple of weekends. The following Saturday, he spends several hours in the heat of the day, chipping away at the wall outside, exposing a wide margin of brick around the edge of one window. That night, he can't sleep because of the pain in his shoulder from a historic injury. I suggest we take a financial hit and pay someone to do it for us, but he won't be beaten. The following day, he continues for a couple more hours before retiring in agony and despair, and promises he will ring a builder.

We add this job to the list of all the other things that haven't been done, like the leaky gutter, the broken cistern and, of course, the entire kitchen. I remind myself of my mantra to 'find the funny', but it feels about as hilarious as an Edinburgh fringe show performing to a snoozing audience of one pissed person at midnight.

*

As I learn more about neurodivergence, people from my past pop into my head like characters wandering aimlessly onto a stage. A nice man I was trapped in a corner with at a party who told me everything he knew about cloud formations. A builder who emotionally overshared and didn't finish any of the jobs he started. A famous actor who was deemed 'trouble' because of his erratic mental state. An anarchic friend who pushed all the boundaries – when I went out partying with her, I half-expected to wake up in a skip in the morning or on a ferry to Bruges. Countless moments swim up from the unfathomable depths of my terrible memory and sharpen my senses in the everyday. So much has changed around neurodivergence in the last thirty years, but still not enough. I look at Steve as he rails against his disordered mind and I think about how valiantly he keeps going, pedalling twice as fast.

*

Steve tells the kids about his double diagnosis. It isn't an announcement, more like a 'by the way' confirmation of what they already know. Their generation is largely better at accepting difference without judgement. Or at least, all the teenagers I know are. This gives me hope for the future, even when there are so many red flags from the media and the global political climate saying the opposite. Our three are supportive. They are well versed in neurodivergence, whether with Steve at home or amongst their friends, and they are also not that bothered. Let everyone be who they are. But I have to interject when Steve begins to run through his mental-health history and the journey he took to get to this point. There are some things they really don't need to know, and I don't want to be reminded of.

He says he is coming to terms with being autistic, but that it will take him some time.

'I think it's the word I struggle with too. The connotations that come with the label "autistic". It's a disability. Just one you can't see or work out the limits of. When I was younger, I remember the misunderstanding and judgement around it. I suppose I could stick to ASD, or try AutiHD, which sounds jaunty?' He looks around the table at all of us.

'Why don't we call it something else?' Hebe suggests. 'You think you have Mediterranean genes so let's see what the Italians call it.' She googles on her phone. 'Autismo!'

Maybe searching for a euphemism for 'autism' means Steve is ashamed. So too the way he jokes about it, but while he carries complex feelings of shame, confusion and fear around the diagnosis, he also has a sense of humour that has not been dulled in the darkest times, and he relies on it. In the past, he has found it hard to laugh at himself and yet this experience is opening him up. We tiptoe across the minefield of appropriate language, but to Steve it is just a field.

'I am *in* the neurodivergent community, and if I can't make a joke about myself then how am I supposed to accept who I am?' he says.

August

The dog is whining. A low, insistent sound that launches me out of bed, grabbing clothes as I go. Her tone can mean one of several things: she wants to go outside to sniff the air, return to a rotten apple she was chewing, or she is busting for a wee. As I come downstairs, she abandons her usual routine of searching for a shoe to gift me and legs it to the back door. She gallops up the stone steps and squats in the long grass, blinking at me in what seems like an apology.

No point going back to bed, so I pull on my wellies and we head down the village, past the house where, almost a century ago, the owners allegedly buried their dead horse in the back garden. This was followed some years later by another neighbour burying their piano, presumably also dead, in their front garden. I often wonder about this as I walk past, because I have a hell of a job hacking at the stony earth to plant a mere crocus bulb. Horses and pianos are not small.

Overnight, the powering rain has flattened the hollyhocks next to the church, leaving them indecently splayed on the road. Everything about the morning is soft: the blue of the sky, the wispy clouds, the birdsong, the early warmth. The deep green foliage sags and drips loudly after the deluge. It is also the end of things: the cow parsley, the wild honeysuckle, my much-admired climbing roses. The crab apple tree now has hard olive-size golden fruits. I can feel autumn waiting in the wings, impatiently hopping from one burnished boot to the other while chewing on a handful of roasted chestnuts.

The moorhen chicks have grown. From the other side of the pond, I can't quite tell them apart from their mother. Suddenly, there is a flash of brown fur ahead of us and Margot crouches, adopting her coiled-spring approach. A young deer, small hooves clattering on the tarmac, skitters off down the road. Despite my whispered shout at the dog, she takes off after it, a lumbering barrel in comparison. I am not worried that she will ever catch up with a deer or want to do anything other than play with it, but I don't want the wild animal to feel any more fear than it already does in its everyday battle for survival.

On the track lie several fallen apples, knocked down in yesterday's storm. These are already a healthy size, tinged red and calling to me. I can immediately taste apple crumble. A handful are unscathed, no bruising or maggoty holes, as if the soft thuds happened just before I turned the corner. I pile a few up to collect on my way back.

The tall grass in the meadow is suffused with light, and tiny white butterflies rise up as I brush past. In the woodland, the ferns have stretched out, laddered leaves catching the filtered rays and shading the dank undergrowth. My morning walk crosses the land of five different owners, and I feel lucky that I haven't been stopped by any of them so far. They could build gates and put up 'Keep Out' signs, but they haven't yet – and I hope they don't, at least not before I see the hazel and oak turn in autumn.

Treading the same steps every day makes me more attentive to the almost imperceptible changes in nature, and I try to take as much notice as possible. Give or take recording the odd voice-note message to Thea.

This time, I walk down to the bottom of the field to the old railway line. Up until the mid-sixties, the Puffing Billy steam train used to chug past on the branch line from the local town, through our village and along to the coast. I drive past a small section of railway bridge every day, have walked some of the old track reclaimed by inhospitable brambles and unpredictable landslides, and stood under the soaring viaduct that straddles the local farmland. The ghost of Puffing Billy is everywhere, remnants of the railway border the village, and the station house at the top of the lane has an old carriage in the garden. Someone gave me a black-and-white postcard of the steam train moving at full, leisurely pelt through the outskirts of the village. I vow to try and trace the route on one of my walks soon.

The local builder tells me about his father who, at five years old, would wait on the side of the track for Puffing Billy. The conductor on the train would reach out and grab his tiny, outstretched hand and pull him up into the cabin. He would jump off at the next junction and walk the rest of the way to school. Every afternoon, he did the same on his way home, except this time the train driver would give him the heavy shovel and he would feed coal into the mouth of the ravenous beast, returning home every evening covered in a layer of soot.

I turn around and collect the apples on the way back. It is still early, everyone is in bed, so I make tea as quietly as possible and take it up to the veg patch. It is a mess here. Too much rain and too little time to roll up my sleeves and get in it have left it neglected. It looks rough and not in a good rural magazine-shoot way. The sweet peas are over before the ones by the house have yet to flower, and the forlorn broad beans have rusted while the climbing beans spread territorially over everything with no sign of producing.

The kids pulled their old bikes out of the shed to mend punctures and have abandoned them stacked on top of each other, pedals caught in chains, blocking the path. Steve fastened nets over two of the raised beds in the vain hope of protecting our crops from the long list of birds, snails, slugs, squirrels, rabbits, mice and deer, but now we can't see the exciting growth underneath.

All in all, this garden is not what I imagined when we set out on our mission. I think that is the nature of veg growing. We are making a regular note of the failures as well as the successes to refer back to. It feels trite to use this analogy for our marriage too, but I will. As we scribble in a notebook about our disaster with the borlotti beans (planted too late? Not enough water? Wrong position?), I also want to write about the pointless row we just had and how we didn't listen to what the other one was trying to say. Who would get the notebook if we split up?

One plant thrives in the damp: the gunnera. It has always been a favourite of mine; even in my tiny London courtyard, I planted one in a big pot. Its mighty, majestic, dinosaur leaves scoop up to the sky, ready to catch the rain like upturned umbrellas, and it magnifies the sound of the fat water droplets. I think this plant represents protection from the elements. Each year, it grows back bigger and stronger.

'Isn't the gunnera amazing again this year,' I say to Steve when I go back in the house. 'Incredible really – because it is so low maintenance, we don't have to do anything to it.'

'Well, no, other than cutting back the leaves in the autumn and covering the stem of the plant with them to protect it over winter.'

'Oh, I don't even do that,' I say dismissively. 'It just returns again in spring.'

'No ... *you* don't.' Steve slathers his usual rye bread with the usual honey. '*I* do.'

'Oh...'

'Yep. Anyway, did you pick anything for the honesty box?'

The honesty box is limping through a month it should be thriving in. I can't fake it. By now, I had envisaged an offering similar to the church altar at a harvest festival, but instead the veg patch is barely keeping five of us in runner beans. To make myself feel better, later that morning I mention it on Instagram and ask people to keep an eye out for honesty boxes and share their favourites.

I am overwhelmed by the responses and the photos that ping up on my phone. Zooming in, I pore over the produce, the signs, the money-taking methods and the different boxes. Some are tables, or stalls, old cupboards or sheds. It is utterly inspiring. There is also a lot of chat about difficult growing conditions this year and the struggle for certain plants to get going. The collective mantra – 'Everything is late because of the weather' – gives me hope for my future crops.

In my search for other devotees, I discover Jill Mead, a photographer who shares my obsession with honesty boxes and captures fab shots of them wherever she goes. Her love for them was ignited over thirty-five years ago in the village of Great Broughton in North Yorkshire, where she grew up. Back then, she would pop down to her neighbour, William, with a handful of coins, and wait in his shed while he picked tomatoes for her from his greenhouse. He told customers that if he wasn't around, they could just weigh what they wanted and leave the money. Happily, it sounds like he and his honesty shed are still there.

Over the years, Jill has photographed several of these sheds in her home county of Yorkshire, complete with members of her family – her beloved brother and son – grinning and holding aloft eggs and jars of chutney. She has captured a well-stocked shed in Sussex with a sign reading *The rural crime team patrols here*, and another that boasts CCTV. This elicits sadness in her, as it does me. She admits that she always has to buy something, even if it is a vegetable or pickle she isn't keen on. Same same.

Jill has snapped a friend buying jam from a pretty roadside cupboard on the Isle of Wight, large jars of pickled onions in an honesty box near Padstow in Cornwall, and marrows in Cambridgeshire. There is even a fossil stall in Staithes, North Yorkshire. On the Lizard in Cornwall is a clever payment system that involves dropping your cash down a drainpipe. Poignantly, the duck food being sold on the Isle of Wight is in aid of the Alex Hulme Foundation: this was established in memory of Alex, who died in 2011 at the age of twelve. All proceeds go to research into non-Hodgkin lymphoma.

At the egg shop in Newport in Essex, Jill didn't have enough change and was generously waved away with a cheery, 'Just bring it back another time.' Her one wish is that more boxes were stocked with home-baked cakes and biscuits. She says that if her mum had set one up, it 'would have needed a bouncer'. I am inspired by these insights and Jill's photographs on the *Guardian* website. None of these honesty boxes are picture perfect, but they shine with the trust and soul that reminds me why I love them and why I have my own.

*

The summer limps on at home. Other than the camping trip to Cornwall. This was the opposite of a relaxing break because there was rain at some point every day, sometimes all of the day. It was only saved by the group of mates we went with, and the campfire spirit. By which I mean vodka. I don't want to go anywhere unless it is hot, or culturally interesting or somewhere I don't have to cook, and we don't have the budget for any of those places.

Last year's attempt at a cheap holiday is still ingrained in my mind. We had driven to Scotland for a week and hired a lovely cottage for a few days while the rest of the time we planned to camp. Steve had always wanted to stay in a bothy, and after a bit of research, I found a place that appealed to me too: Queen Victoria's bothy on the Balmoral Estate. It was tucked behind her lodge house, Glas-allt-Shiel, on the bank of Loch Muick, which the Queen had built as a widow's escape where she could mope around in peace. She wasn't completely alone. There were ghillies catching trout for her supper and, as the light began to fade, a billion tiny midges came out to play. Or at least that was my experience when I went there, minus the strapping kilted men hoisting fish out of the loch.

AUGUST

It was Steve's dream to walk all day and bed down in a bothy at night. It was my dream to walk a shorter distance, find a bothy with an open fire and hope to meet a royal ghost when I popped out for an al fresco wee. It didn't live up to either of our expectations. As amateurs to this game, one of whom ill-advisedly but resolutely carried her duvet and pillow on her back in an Ikea bag for several miles, we were woefully under-prepared.

We certainly didn't expect to be sharing the bothy with strangers, even though this is sort of the whole point of it because you can't book – you just pitch up as a weary hiker. Lee and Scott, ex-army and experienced bothy dwellers, were also not prepared for a rookie family of five and a soggy, over-friendly retriever who bounded into the place, only to ricochet straight back out when their dog snarled its disapproval.

The loch, woods and land around the lodge were outstandingly, breathtakingly beautiful and exactly the backdrop I had imagined for our picnic supper, but the midges attacked us in the same way I go through a box of After Eights. Inside the bothy, the only lights came from the glow of the fire that Lee and Scott had lit, and the orange tip of the spliff they were sharing.

We all squeezed around the table, and I took out a Camembert that I had picked up for pennies because it was out of date. The pungent smell filled the room, making everyone gag, and Lee and Scott decided the midges were better company. They sat out on a log, dejectedly smoking and probably slagging us off for crashing their party. We felt bad about it, so when they came back in, we offered them a dram from the whisky we had fortuitously packed, even though Lee said after a couple of sips that he was a recovering alcoholic, which made me feel even worse. Lee did all the talking. Scott just made the odd comment from the depths of his hoodie, which may or may not have been jokes, so I gave the odd half-laugh to cover either option.

There was nothing to do so we went to bed. Steve slept on the floor with Margot, laid out next to the bunk bed where the men were sleeping, because we couldn't get the dog up the treacherous ladder to the mezzanine level in the rafters where the children and I were setting up. We organised makeshift beds in a haphazard fashion, every so often catching each other's eye, raising brows and silently agreeing about the weirdness of the situation. I wasn't sure whether to feel safer that Lee and Scott were there, or unnerved, but when Hebe whispered the same fears, I reassured her they were good people, and promised to sleep with one eye open.

That day was also my birthday.

At first light, we were all awake because none of us had slept, so we packed up as quietly as we could while Lee, Scott and even their dog pretended to be asleep. We slipped out straight into torrential rain and a several-mile return to the car park. On the way back, much to everyone's annoyance, I picked handfuls of rowan berries because I can't pass up a foraging opportunity, even in a storm, and I took a sprig of heather for luck, which still sits in a small pot in our kitchen.

I asked Steve if the bothy had cured him of his fascination or encouraged him to do more of these sorts of holidays, which, for the avoidance of doubt, would be without me. His eyes lit up at the idea of further wild Scottish adventures, minus a woman lugging her bedding in a plastic carrier bag fashioned into a makeshift rucksack.

AUGUST

'I loved it,' he said. 'The only bit that wasn't great was in the middle of the night when Lee or Scott, I am not sure which, pissed in a bottle quite near my head.'

*

Painfully aware of last year's disaster, because of the number of times I have retold the bothy story with the inflection on it being my *birthday*, Steve asks me how I want to spend it this year. We are both August-born, him before me, so he always feels the pressure of doing something nice because I will have already made a fuss of him.

I am irresistibly disposed to make a thing of events, coming from a working-class family who always scraped some money together for 'a bit of a do', whatever the celebration. Steve can't handle this stress, so every year there is a last-minute panic and an accusation that I am 'impossible to buy for' (not true because, you know, books, candles, cashmere socks) and I don't like 'surprises' (that depends on the surprise). Admittedly, I give mixed messages every year, because half of me wants the day to disappear without fanfare, and the other half wants to ride into a party on a horse in the way Madonna did for her birthday. These two parts of myself are tricky to reconcile.

This year, I really want to have a nice day without the panic this brings Steve and, in turn, me, so I take matters into my own hands and book a table at a restaurant I have wanted to go to for ages. It is on the edge of Dartmoor, which means we can spend the day walking and exploring before pitching up for a lovely dinner at the end of it. Steve is relieved not to be the organiser.

'And I want to find as many honesty boxes as possible,' I say, knowing he would drive me to the ends of the earth on this endeavour.

The day itself is grimy, with drizzle in the sharp moorland wind, so we take a shorter hike from a car park that I know has a coffee van. When we arrive, there is just a pale gravel space where the van should be, and everyone's shoulders slump in despair. We begin our walk, and Hebe realises she has forgotten her camera, so we all groan as she runs back to get it, and loiter by a stream while Margot races around, excited by the unfamiliar landscape and strange smells.

'Guess what?!' Hebe bounds back with the camera and a big grin. 'The best news ever! The coffee van has arrived!' We all cheer with relief and gratitude like the scene in my favourite film, *Meet Me in St Louis*, when the father tells his family he is not making them move to New York after all, and everyone begins talking at once. Spirits soar as we reach the van and order coffees and wrap squares of brownies in paper napkins for our walker's snack.

As the morning wears on, the sun builds strength and we shed layers. After the walk, we drive around for a bit, village-hopping in the hunt for honesty boxes, and buy eggs, jam, a lemon drizzle cake and, at one roadside stall, an enormous bunch of soil-encrusted carrots with leafy green fronds. We eat pasties the size of our heads in Ashburton, and wander around Totnes in the late-afternoon warmth, where Raff buys a suit in a charity shop and changes into it in the car park before dinner.

As the evening sun dips, I sit in a bunting-festooned square with my funny, infuriating, brilliant family, a glass of ice-cold vermouth and a very tired dog who has stretched out in everyone's way so moving her is like turning a ship. As birthdays go, it is pretty unbeatable and definitely better than lying in a dark, dank hut that stinks of runny Camembert, mouldy dogs and marijuana. Steve is on good form too, happy that the pressure of arranging the celebration is off his shoulders.

I can see how immobilised he has become over the years in all sorts of situations. His trust in himself, his ability and his instinct have been eroded to the point of having so little that sometimes he pretends to have a lot. The nine-year-old boy inside him crouches behind a wall of bluster, praying not to be found out.

The dual diagnosis has made so much sense and, even though Steve isn't really aware of it yet, he is beginning to move and stretch into a new space. He looks in the mirror and finally sees himself. And I see him too, in many ways no different from before, but now lit from within by a secret revealed. I wonder what I could have done differently over the years to ease the mental maelstrom, rather than unwittingly exacerbate it.

Kindness – I could have been kinder. I am trying, but my fighting instinct obscures the softer, subtler feelings in case they behave like bindweed, wrapping around all the practical things I need to do and weakening my ability to achieve them.

I am tasked with too much responsibility and always pick up the slack of Steve's unfinished business, whether this is around the house, our finances, decisions to be made, cooking supper, hanging out laundry... no job too small for him to be distracted from. I can't be sure that Steve would be able to catch us if we fell, so I muddle us all through, month after month, often with barely disguised frustration or annoyance. Now, with a clearer understanding of who Steve is, we both need to accept what this means, and I need to make peace with it. I can feel the fossilised anger within me begin to crumble a little at the edges.

But right now, it is my birthday so I am going to save challenging thoughts for another time and ask to see the wine list.

*

Steve rings while I am in the middle of making dinner.

'I have done something which is probably incredibly stupid,' he says, and my heart sinks. It often does with these sorts of declarations, and I go and stand in the garden so the children can't earwig. 'James called me today and we had a chat and I think maybe I was a little too honest.'

James and his wife Rachel are good friends of ours. When they employed Steve to work on a build project for them, I had my reservations. Working for friends is often ill-advised, particularly when you really like them. It is a gamble and I didn't want to lose them in some sort of personal roulette game of professional disgruntlement. We all discussed it one night over wine and posh crisps and assured each other it wouldn't be a disaster.

'You've gone quiet,' Steve says.

I know not to hit him with the panic I am feeling. I am learning how to manage my emotional reaction so it doesn't overwhelm him, and he needs to be able to tell me the facts without being thrown into a panic.

'I'm listening.' I watch a robin hop onto the fence. I had always thought these birds represented the loved ones who are no longer with us, but recently I had also learned they are vicious aggressors in the bird world.

'So, James was asking about where I was with the project, and I was feeling pretty stressed about the workload and timings and whether I could deliver on the schedule we discussed... Anyway, one thing led to another, so I told him I had been diagnosed with ADHD...'

OK, I had told Rachel about this diagnosis, so it was likely James already knew. I breathed out slowly...

'... and autism. I told him I had just found out I was autistic.'

I had not told her that. I wanted to be able to talk myself through it before I began to explain it to others and I wanted Steve to be ready to speak openly.

'Lucy? It's bad, isn't it? I shouldn't have said anything, should I? I mean, I know he is a friend, but right now he is a client, and he is waiting for me to deliver work. Now he will think I am incapable, unprofessional, mentally unsound...'

I think quickly. 'What did he say?'

James is a man who makes things happen. A husband, father, classic-car lover, sailor and red-wine drinker. He is re-reading Proust.

'He said he understood. He said he could help. He has offered to give me a few sessions on managing my business and I said yes, because I could really do with the help, and now I am freaking out because I am completely exposed. But I am also excited at the prospect of him working with me on how I communicate with my clients. I really admire and respect him. I trust him.'

'Well then, you've done the right thing.'

I wait for the familiar queasiness of a Steve Situation, but it doesn't come. He has been honest, vulnerable, accepted the help that has been offered. I mentally nominate James for a Nobel Peace Prize.

'Are you sure I have done the right thing?' Steve sounds anxious.

'Yep.' I am sincere. 'You've been brave and true. I couldn't have done what you just did. I am really proud of you.'

I also think this shows how Steve has started to face his autistic self, but I don't say this. I want his realisation of this to go at his pace, not mine.

*

The light is dreamy, pigeons cooing, a gentle August ending. It is a significant point in the year, with a new school term and first year at university on the horizon, and the cusp of seasons. Autumn in the morning, reverting to summer by lunchtime, before tipping back into autumn as the sun sets.

I head off down the lane, breaking overnight cobwebs like crossing invisible finishing lines. The landscape is heavy with thorny branches of blackberries, a scatter of elderberries and the sloes the spring blossom had promised. Everything is slower to mature along the canopied track, growth shaded by growth. I find an arch of blackberries – speckled green and pink, with some berries already turning a deep aubergine – entwined in elder, which are the ingredients for bramble jelly in one spot. The scent of fermenting apples is sharp, sweet and waspish, and there is an abundance of holly above the ferns, which jut out of the old stone wall of the ancient cart track. I could keep walking straight into the eighteenth century.

Back at home, I pick runner and climbing beans, the last of the sweet peas, perky sunflowers and bunches of tied herbs for the honesty box. There have been courgettes too, and I left a couple to transform into marrows just for us. Apparently, overgrown courgettes aren't actually marrows. You need to plant marrow seeds to grow the real thing, but I am happy with a fake marrow. It is a full-circle moment to harvest my own, after bringing home the Dartmoor marrow along with the conviction to set up my honesty box a year ago. I transform this one with the same recipe I used then: an old Delia Smith Provençale classic with onions, a couple of tins of tomatoes and coriander seeds, ladled onto a mound of rice for dinner and coated with the usual over-grating of cheese by the kids – their answer to things they aren't keen on.

I make a runner bean pickle and courgette chutney to store in the back of the larder, ready to fill the honesty box in November when there is little else available. In our scrappy garden notebook, I jot down a reminder to prioritise tomatoes next year. There are not nearly enough to share beyond the kitchen, and even then, they are so precious that we eat them off the vine as a treat. I am now on a mission to find honesty boxes stocking tomatoes.

I don't have to wait long.

*

Every summer, I have a routine with my friends Cat and Jessamy, who I met when we worked at River Cottage together. They were a big reason for me not to run for the hills (A40 flyover) in the early days when my body was in Dorset and my heart was in Shepherd's Bush. Having left a lovely group of friends behind, it was a leap into the unknown, but it turned out that Cat and Jessamy were there to catch me. Their friendship reassured me that I could start again, in a new place, with new people who would become important to me.

Several times over the school holiday, we meet at Cat's parents' idyllic farm to splash around in the old swimming pool in their orchard and picnic in the shade of the apple trees.

A bottle of Cava and a Victoria sponge for Cat's birthday at the beginning of the school holiday sets the tone, and we do the same for mine at the end. When it is hot, we all get in the pool. The adults wallow at the side, catching up on news, and when it rains, we huddle under the awning with mugs of tea while the children dive-bomb each other and bob around on inflatables. I imagine the kids, years from now, reminiscing about these times, and each summer I take the same photo of them all lined up and jumping into the water. Incrementally bigger each time the swallows prepare to leave.

Now it is our final swim of the season and we all linger, not quite wanting it to be over, as we pack up and have to shout at the kids to get them out of the pool. Cat's mum comes to tell us not to leave without helping ourselves from the basket of tomatoes she has left in the porch. Tomatoes! I fast-walk there and politely pick a salad's amount, until she urges me to take more because she has a greenhouse full of ripening beauties. She says they just need eating.

AUGUST

Why can't I be drowning in tomatoes, I wonder out loud. It turns out she changes the soil every year, feeds the plants, plays Bach to them (OK, maybe not this) so like most things, hard graft pays off. Damn. I fill the bag I am given, the car full of the evocative smell of tomato leaf as we drive home. A few punnets of tomatoes go in the honesty box, but I roast the rest with a bulb of smoked garlic and a good handful of marjoram, before blitzing this into litres of passata oblivion and decanting into old yoghurt pots for the freezer. This winter, I will thank my summer self.

Several days later, I drive past an honesty box selling tomatoes, as well as cucumbers, sunflowers, pots of parsley and eggs. I screech to a halt, and as sedately and safely as I can, I reverse. Someone coming the other way does the same and we stop, almost bumper to bumper, and get out of our cars, sheepishly. Now comes the etiquette of approaching the table of produce and splitting the spoils. Luckily, my opponent doesn't want tomatoes (weird), but she does want sunflowers, cucumbers and eggs so we split those between us.

I want to chat about honesty boxes, but she can see the obsession in my eyes and beats a hasty retreat. I scoop up all the 50p bags of tomatoes and make a big salad with mozzarella and herbs from the garden for dinner.

*

I am woken by suffocating humidity, which is either a menopausal flush or heavy weather, after a storm in the early hours. In a clammy half-sleep, my head somersaults around all the issues; when I run out of things to worry about, I find some more. When is the car tax due, or have I missed it? Where can I find a dentist now that ours has retired? Does the sewage tank need emptying? This is really no good. I heave myself out of bed and into yesterday's pants.

There is no change in the air temperature as I dodge the big monsoon-style puddles and water drips from every leaf, the downpour freshening the scent of the hedgerows. The owls are calling in the half-light. After a conversation with Steve about the possibility of selling up, the village is doing a very good job of encouraging me to stay. I walk under open bedroom windows and sense the true stillness of deep sleepers. This is freedom, to move unseen and uninterrupted, and my thoughts are now jumping instead of spiralling as they were when I was in bed. It begins to rain again, and the dog looks at me, expecting to turn back.

I shake my head. 'We're in it now, Margot – may as well push on.'

Someone once said that the early risers who venture out bring the day back with them. This is how I feel, as if I am tramping back to the house with the morning tucked under my arm ready to show and tell. By the time I return, whether from walking or swimming, everyone is up and in the kitchen, and wants to know what the day is like.

'I felt rain in the air,' I may say, or 'Thick cloud, but I reckon it will burn off,' or 'So cold, the pond has iced over,' or 'You will/won't need to take your coat to school,' or 'You missed the best sunrise.' At which point, they change the subject.

This morning, as I stomp back into the house to search for dog towels, Steve and Raff are talking about someone local with a serious drug problem. It is a sad story. Some London friends say we made the right decision, leaving the city and giving our kids a bucolic country upbringing. No gangs on the streets, they say. No knife crime. No drugs. They may be generally right about the first and second statements, but not the third because there are drugs everywhere if you know who to talk to and where to look. Sometimes, I think it may be worse for the country teenagers than their city contemporaries, because there is a lot less to do in a field. I also know this is a ridiculous generalisation, and I have no stats to back it up.

The drug culture here seems to be just as prevalent with the middle-aged middle classers. Covert invitations to boot rooms, loos in chic wine bars, summerhouses on rolling lawns or smart studies, including the same people who only buy organic chicken, eat fairtrade chocolate and practise an awful lot of yoga. While children as young as nine anxiously cross county lines clutching rucksacks hiding illegal substances.

In recent years there has also been a rise in magic mushroom-taking locally. This has been mentioned to Steve as an option to help with depression and now neurodivergence. Apparently micro-dosing is the way to go, but it is not something which appeals to him. He is putting all his faith into prescribed drugs.

*

Steve has decided to come off WhatsApp. Or at least he has exited a few groups that cause him stress. OK, the absolute truth is that I suggested he leave them. He is not comfortable in charge of an instant messaging system. He either gets stuck on a thread of lengthy responding, throwing in gifs and making jokes, or he turns it into a lecture. Which is fine if you are related to him (family threads), live next door to him (village neighbours' thread) or are good friends (London threads). However, some groups press his buttons in all the wrong ways, and he recounts long conversations to me, in which I am left thinking that the person who has complicated the chat is Steve himself. I don't think it is a healthy form of communication for him.

One of these days, he may get himself into trouble on this platform with his frankness or irony. I have said this before, when he did not have a diagnosis, and he refused to listen. Now, he sees it. He comes off a professional forum that has been bothering him, a place where he has shared helpful information, but with little return and a lot of frustration. He volunteers for the RNLI and has also stepped off their non-urgent thread, which is full of people discussing schedules and inconsequential news. At their next meeting, he explains to a room full of people that he has been diagnosed with ADHD and autism and finds WhatsApp communication can be distracting or triggering for him. His mum is there as he recounts this story later.

'You aren't telling people, are you?' his mum asks in surprise.

'Yes, I am, and the more I speak about it and get a positive reaction, the less ashamed I feel. In fact, a couple of the guys came up to me in the pub after and said they thought they may be neurodivergent too. And when I told my friend James, he offered to help me with a time-management plan for my business. The stigma around mental illness seems to have shifted in recent years. Yes, it's still complicated, but it's changed a lot since your day, Mum.'

AUGUST

This feels like another big step forward. He doesn't run up and down the high street telling people he is neurodivergent. He doesn't talk about it on Instagram. He just tells people when he gauges it is right to, and so far his instinct hasn't let him down.

At a friend's house for dinner, he sits next to a psychotherapist. They end up having an enlightening conversation about EMDR treatment, a therapy that targets PTSD with eye movement and focuses on trauma through a structured process. Both of them agree how valuable it is, and this is the first time I have heard Steve talk about it in relation to his diagnosis.

'In all the years of therapy, it was the only thing that really worked for me,' he says. 'It was like the end of an archaeological dig, after the excavation of all the other stuff I had to confront, and then the EMDR scraped away the rest of the soil and exposed what was hidden at the core. I think it prepared me for a neurodivergence diagnosis. I reckon without it, I might still be stuck. It was like an out-of-body experience so I am evangelical about the practice.'

*

Thea and Adam have separated, the ADHD diagnosis only one element of their mutual decision to take some time apart. It is incredibly emotional, difficult and painful for them both, but I am so proud of how they navigate the fracturing, as friends rather than thwarted lovers. Give or take the odd implosion, because who wouldn't succumb to that, they are steadfast in their love and care for each other.

I am not shocked by their decision, but I feel the foundations of my own marriage struggling to withstand the shock. Steve is sure they will get back together, partly for their own sakes – and also because if they don't, then what does that say about us? He doesn't articulate this, but I know what he is thinking, and his advice to Adam in the immediate aftermath is peppered with encouragement not to move too fast.

'Look at us,' he says to me encouragingly. 'We are finding a way through, aren't we?'

Are we? I don't know yet. Do I still love him, or are we delaying an inevitable ending? I wonder how much of our relationship is now held together in a co-dependent stranglehold.

I am worried for Thea and Adam, but there is also a shadier emotion at play: envy. Which is a ridiculous thing to say as they juggle sore hearts and family priorities with the practicalities of a split – it ain't no walk in the park for God's sake – but the truth is that I am curious about what it is like to be free from the weight of someone else.

Thea and Adam started dating several years before Steve and I got together. I was going out with a series of unsuitable men during this time, and I use the phrase 'going out' loosely while 'unsuitable' is an understatement. I kissed a lot of frogs, exactly because they were frogs and I knew they wouldn't turn into princes. There was a minorly famous flame-haired actor, an Irish builder who repeatedly reminded me that I was not his girlfriend, a theatre director with intense chat and unwashed bedsheets, a security guard who talked about his ex-wife, a work colleague of my brother who realised he was happy being single, an old pal of mine who was a mistake...

I am going to stop there before this becomes a different sort of story. But my point is that Adam and Thea saw me through them all. Then when they met Steve, their eyes lit up with the recognition of a good man. My brother Rob and his wife Ali felt the same way.

Our early relationship wasn't straightforward, but it was clear from the way we both felt about each other that it was special. Whatever the obstacles, we knew we shouldn't let it go, so we didn't. Steve had been through a difficult divorce, and I was an uncinematic version of Bridget Jones, where nobody threw anybody through a restaurant window to win my attention, so we were realistically romantic or romantically realistic.

So many of the things that attracted me to Steve, such as his impulsivity, unpredictability, brutal honesty, humour, clever brain, anarchic leanings and unabashed hyperfocus on whatever his new passion was (me), now seem to point in one direction. His neurodivergence was always hiding in plain sight and has hitchhiked with us throughout our relationship, for better and for worse. As it has done for Adam and Thea. It both amazes me, and is at the same time completely unsurprising, that we have journeyed this in tandem with them. Whatever happens between us as couples, we four friends hold each other up in this strange new world we find ourselves in, and we will not let each other fall.

September

I want this month's honesty box to have a harvest festival vibe. Steve is picking what is ready to eat, but the priority has to be on feeding us. For a week or so, there is nothing to share. Then he brings a glut of French beans into the kitchen. I bundle these into handfuls and pop them out on the bench.

One of the many things we have not got right this year is succession sowing. This is something we haven't worried about too much in the past but now, with an eye on providing for the honesty box 'business', we need a more regular supply of produce. I also want the honesty box to be the recipient of other people's gluts. While I have had some good guest donations this year – eggs, apple juice, ceramics, broad beans, tomatoes – I could do with more to fill the gaps.

I hatch a plan for apples.

Our apple tree is a dismal producer. Likely started by someone (probably one of the kids when they were small) chucking a core over the bank outside the shed, it has grown by accident, and the tasteless, fluffy, inedible fruits arrived a few years ago. Instead, I ask Caroline and Peter, our neighbours in the old manor with an orchard, if I can pick some apples. This is a risky move.

Ten years ago, when the children were still small and could be entertained by a scoot down the village, we bumped into Caroline's husband, Peter, who was throwing a chainsaw through some branches overhanging their drive. He mentioned being swamped with orchard fruits and invited us to pick what we wanted. I took him at his word.

We trundled down with a wheelbarrow the following day while Peter and Caroline were out, loaded it up with four different varieties of apples, and filled baskets with plums, damsons and medlars. There was still plenty left of everything. We may have even taken a flask with us and stretched out in the long grass underneath the trees – which feels presumptuous now I think about it. On our way back up the lane, wheelbarrow full, baskets groaning and damsons in our pockets, we waved thankfully to Caroline and Peter as they drove towards us. Peter grinned, but Caroline looked at me as if she had caught me walking up the road in her cashmere coat.

She wound down the car window. 'What on earth do you think you are doing?' She gesticulated at the wheelbarrow, which I instantly regretted taking.

'Peter said we could help ourselves...' I panicked and pushed Peter under the bus. 'There are still loads left.'

'We didn't mean you could take *that many*!'

Peter's beaming smile was cemented rigidly on his face.

'Oh, I am so sorry,' I said, as a few apples tumbled out of the barrow. The children looked on, mouths sticky from plum juice. 'I was going to make you some medlar jelly though...' I trailed off, realising this wasn't much of a swap.

'Oh lovely!' Peter said encouragingly. 'I've never had medlar jelly.'

'Don't be silly, Peter, of course you have.' And with that, Caroline rolled up the window and indicated for Peter to drive on.

'Oops,' said Hebe, biting into another plum as they disappeared down the lane.

While I have been invited back to their house in the decade that has followed, I have never been ushered through the garden arch until today. Caroline has offered me some apples and made me coffee, so I am hoping this means I have been forgiven. We wander past neat rows of beetroot and a curtain of runner beans with a calendula hem, then beyond to the orchard. I can suddenly picture my children, ten years younger at eight, five and three, darting behind tree trunks, throwing squished fruit at each other and perching on Steve's shoulders to pluck the perfect apple just out of reach.

'Thanks so much, Caroline. I won't be long. I'll pick a few and disappear out the back gate so I don't disturb you.' I set my modestly small basket down, next to rotting windfall apples that have been raked into a pile.

Caroline sits on a bench. She isn't going anywhere. She hasn't forgotten, and she is damned if it is happening again on her watch.

*

There is at least one local orchard I can go to any old time I want, although I am not allowed to pick apples there either. The community orchard in Bridport is tucked away behind the church on the high street. It is relatively small, but upholds a vital custom for the locals, where they host traditional events including the January wassail of tree blessing, celebrating the blossom on May Day, storytelling on warm summer evenings, and picking and pressing the bounty in autumn.

One Saturday, just before the harvest, the five of us and Margot head into town and pick up takeaway coffees

SEPTEMBER

and pastries from Soulshine Café. Then we wander around the corner to the orchard and a bench in the sun. The dog snuffles at the base of the apple trees as we read the beautifully simple wooden tags tied to branches that tell us which variety they are. Within a couple of weeks, these trees will be stripped of their fruit, the patch will be a hive of volunteer activity, and we will be dropping Raff off to start university. Right now, for one precious moment, we and the apples are all suspended in a shaft of light, togetherness and croissant crumbs before life forges ahead again.

*

There has been an influx of information about neurodivergence: a whole shelf of books is now dedicated to it in our local bookshop, and there has been a steady stream of media commentary in recent months. High-profile people are coming out as neurodivergent. It is brilliant and about time. I read articles that I then forward to Steve, suggest books he may want to get and trawl Instagram for positive portrayals of neurodivergence. I don't have to look far for a wealth of dynamic, supportive feeds that reflect facets of Steve's experience. In the process of wanting to learn more for him, I am also looking for myself in this research and how I can exist within our relationship. I read about partnerships of love, acceptance and understanding, but I can't seem to find those who are still trying to get their head around it and are being honest about that. Where are the people like me who are learning to live with recently diagnosed neurodivergent partners? How do I fit in? Am I able to say it is hard for me? Will I be allowed to voice that? I want to speak openly about my place in all of this, but I don't know how to.

*

As well as those I wrestle off Caroline, I pick apples off the lane where they have fallen from a neighbour's tree. Wherever I go, I am on high alert. Rob and Ali inherited several ancient apple trees and an annual wasp frenzy so, at their house, I play a dangerous game by going out in flip-flops and bare arms to fill a bag with the sweet cidery fruit. A few days later, my birding expert friend Tara turns up unannounced with an unravelling straw basket spilling apples and ripe damsons, the jewels of autumn.

I get a message from an old pal, Johnny, who I had asked to scout around his local area for honesty box stories. He comes back with a bit of Sussex glory. In Burwash village, the home of the author Rudyard Kipling, there is an honesty box fashioned from a rabbit hutch. The owners also have a seventeeth-century tile-hung Grade II-listed house, with a large orchard, and have bagged up their ancient apple varieties to sell for a suggested donation of £1.50 per kilo. All proceeds go to the village hall and the Burwash Horticultural Society. Johnny sends me photographs, including close-ups of every laminated sign. One proudly states the apples have not been treated with any chemical sprays. Another, in unmissable red font, reads:

> *Unfortunately, we have had money taken from this box, so if you have the right change please can you post your money for apples through the letterbox in the front door. Thank you.*

Then there are the signs for each of the apples, and my heart beats faster as I read them…

Northern Greening: very old 18th century cooking apple and forebear of many Victorian era culinary apples with a good acidic flavour.

Alfriston: introduced in the late 1700s in Uckfield, a sharp cooking apple that stores well, is very good baked and cooks down to a puree.

Newtons Wonder: first introduced in Derbyshire in 1870, a cooking apple with a sharp acidic flavour.

Winston: introduced in 1944, late keeping apple. Rain has smudged the rest of this sign, but I can make out the words: *firm flesh, sharp, mellowing to sweet.*

Burwash Allrounder: an unknown variety that eats and cooks well. Why not try this interesting apple?!

Annie Elizabeth: traditional cooking apple with a sweet flavour which keeps its shape when cooked. Believed to be a seedling of a Blenheim Orange.

I have an embarrassment of apples. Kilos are piled up in bowls around the kitchen and lined up in plastic trays in the lean-to. Yet I see the photographs and seriously consider driving four hours for a bag of Alfristons. I don't. I am not that silly, but that is how the desire grips me. Instead, I think about what I can do with the mountain I already have. This has earned me the new nickname, Greedy Gluts, as bestowed on me by my family, who are moving apples off the kitchen table so they can find space to do homework and balance their beans on toast. I put some in the honesty box (*free to a good home!*) and cook my way through the carousel of apple recipes, from crumbles (which is the law), pies and cakes to a breakfast compote or sliced and eaten off the tip of a knife with a chunk of crumbly cheddar.

They all come and go, but I need something to last longer than a short weekend and to add to the honesty box as the fresh produce begins to slow down in the weeks ahead. Apple-and-herb jelly is the answer. Harvest in aspic. The ideal accompaniment to Sunday roasts and cheese, spread thickly in sandwiches and added to sauces, with me always saying 'Go steady!' as the jar is passed around the table, spoon suckered into the jelly.

As well as apple jelly, I make a hedgerow version. This encompasses blackberries, elderberries, sloes and crab apples, depending on what I can forage. Like marmalade-making, there is a considered process to it. Boiling the fruits in a jam pan, scooping the resulting mush into a square of muslin, tying the four corners into a bag, suspending it over a bowl and watching its juices drip, drip, drip, before putting it back in the pan with sugar to rolling boil and transform into magic in a jar. This is my daily meditation for a week. I listen to Minnie Driver reading her exquisite memoir as I check apples for maggots and slice off blemishes, which feels like some sort of obvious metaphor for Hollywood, particularly when she gets to the bit about Harvey Weinstein.

*

It is not quite the equinox, but autumn is definitely here. I am back in my dog-walking coat, the one that doubles as extra insulation when we run out of oil. The air smells of the taste of cold cider as I walk through the village. Cheery sunflowers bob over fences, and some of the roses have a second bloom. On the pond, the moorhen chicks perch cockily on a half-submerged log, almost as big as their mother now, and I think of their poor sibling, swallowed by the lagoon. I bump into villager Harry, already on his way back from his very early dog walk. He tells me it was dark enough this morning for him to need his head torch, and we both say how much we love autumn. Harry says he is happy in every season, and I can see that. He used to work in IT before he realised his lifelong dreams of being a landsman, a job that requires you to embrace every weather.

As I walk past the smart parking lot for a newly renovated farmhouse, a long line of outdoor lights flash on. This hasn't happened before and it takes me by surprise, making me stop dead, like a raccoon caught in a spotlight. I know this because I once shone a torch on a raccoon as it went through my rucksack while I was camping with friends in Paradise Creek in California. I was tucked up in a sleeping bag under the stars, sleeping the sleep of someone who knows it is only a matter of time before they are woken by serial killers, bears or blood-sucking spiders.

When I heard a rustling, I thought I was done for, but it also sounded like someone setting out a picnic. I shone the torch, and a raccoon stared back, standing on two legs, its mouth full of my impending breakfast. Neither of us moved. It was motionless for several long seconds before nonchalantly wandering off into the vegetation with my bagel. In the morning, it looked like we had been burgled by a crack team of monkeys.

After almost nine months of walking the track out of the village, I am about to be rewarded with the best of the seasons. The mist lies low at the far end of the valley, and I can hear an industrious tractor in the distance. It is as if I am up in the clouds looking down, the tippety top of the trees just visible through the white gauze. This season plays tricks on me like no other. I am both willing it on and wanting to reverse it at the same time, back to an autumn past when the children were still at primary school and all we had to think about was finding the best conkers. I want to set time to half speed.

Nineteen years ago, I spent much of September heavily pregnant, in denial and chain-chewing Haribos. I had thought about the concept of having a baby, but not the reality. I told my agency colleagues when I'd got to five months, but I didn't tell my clients until I absolutely had to. I used to say the reason I kept quiet was because I was scared they would fire me, but this was unfair on them (other than the two who did leave me and who were also pregnant – which was unexpected). I think the real reason for my secrecy was more complicated. It was less about not wanting them to leave me, and more about me not wanting to leave them. I wanted to give birth in a parallel universe, without impacting my existing one.

This memory of trepidation sparks up every September. The moments are carved into my mind like initials scratched with a compass on a school desk. I can run my hands over the marks still. It stays with me in a way the build-up to Hebe and Jesse's births does not. That has got nothing to do with love and excitement; I just wasn't as scared by the time it was their turn. Fear, naivety and the unknown stapled the events of Raff's arrival into my memory. It was the moment I became a mother.

I hadn't read the childbirth books or gone to any classes. I hadn't joined the NCT for fear of being part of a group I would have to swiftly leave when I returned to work. Instead, I squished together all the stories and advice from my sister-in-law, Ali, and best friends, Nicki, Cath and Elaine, who had become mothers before me, and thought that would be enough. Only Elaine had experienced an emergency caesarean, which had been traumatic, so she really didn't want to talk about it.

Raff was cut out of me after a day of labour took a worrying turn and I found myself speeding by hospital bed into a theatre very unlike the ones I was used to. It was frightening for us and routine for the expert medical team, who greeted two of us and cheerfully sent three of us back to the ward. Before then, I just had a boyfriend, and now I had a family. We watched the sun coming up behind Wormwood Scrubs prison and I drank the best cup of sugary tea and ate the most delicious, heavily buttered, sliced white toast, only matched twice more in my life.

I asked to be discharged after a sleepless night of everyone else's babies crying except my own, and the interrogative glare of a bright spotlight that was angled directly at my pillow. As I lived down the road, the overworked midwives didn't put up a fight and let me leave early, if I promised to stay in bed over the weekend, which I mostly did. On Monday morning, a huge bunch of flowers was delivered, and ten minutes later I had a call from the client who sent them. She congratulated me without asking if I had a boy or a girl, and said she had given me the weekend to recover, but now she had a list of work things to discuss. I was on my email for every day of the three months I had taken as maternity leave, and it was a relief to return to the office without trying to type with a baby flopped over my shoulder.

I was absent for much of the first two years of Raff's life, until we left London, so I was determined to make up for it at the other end of his childhood. Working from home a lot makes me available to drink coffee with a sixth former on a part-time school schedule. I have made the most of that time with him, knowing the clock is ticking faster and faster to his adult beginnings. Now he is off to university, the confusing emotions swell inside me and threaten to drag me under. I understand what a lump in your throat means now – it is a physical thing – and when I stand in a supermarket aisle choosing Raff a spatula, I am overcome with the sensation that I want to lie down and wail as if someone has just ripped my baby from my arms. I take gulps of air and force myself to chuck things into the basket. It is the strangest combination of happiness for him and sadness for me; our family of five is morphing into something new. We had nineteen years, and there were so many things we didn't do. I didn't expect it to be over so fast. I want to celebrate his independence and I want to crush it.

Raff senses this but he does not want me to spell it out, nor do I want to spread it out in front of him. He moves fast and light through his final days at home, full of excitement. He is kind to me but holds my sorrow at arm's length, which is exactly as it should be. Someone clever once said having children is like watching your heart walk around outside your body. I imagine the pulsating crimson organ skipping off ahead of me and losing sight of it in a crowd. It is time

SEPTEMBER

for me to unshackle, step back and wave Raff off with love and pride – and I do. And in those moments, it breaks me.

I leave a voice note for Thea, my voice thick and wobbly. I need some perspective on it, but I also need to handle this carefully because she will be in my position in a year's time when she waves her eldest off, as well as going through a separation. A bit like not telling a pregnant woman every gory detail of your labour, I pick through what I share, and then I realise something else as I am speaking.

'It's just occurred to me as I say it out loud, but there's a clarity to this sadness. It's positive, right for him to go, it only means good things and so it's a powerful pain, not unlike childbirth. I've spent so long tussling with my emotions around Steve that it's refreshing to be feeling something else. Here's a different sort of personal pain, and I can do this version. This is my job as a mother. It makes me feel alive and in touch with my emotions in a way I don't need to hide from or redraw.'

I also tell Thea that I am keeping an eye on Steve. He is doing all the joy and thrill of Raff's new life, and none of the sadness. I wonder if he is bottling it up and it will come flooding out and drown the rest of us who are left. While I am processing it now, and pre-empting those sorrowful moments without my boy, is Steve in denial? Will this be his next downfall? I tiptoe around him, but I don't see anything hidden: sure, he is nervous for Raff, and he will miss him, but he is not sad.

Why would he be when this is not a bad thing, he says. I believe him. What is more, I hang on to his strength. I allow myself to collapse into the emotion because he isn't, and knowing he will hold me is an unusual and nice place for us both to be. I press send on the message to Thea and instantly feel lighter.

TV Lucy is doing the same with her daughter. She drops her at university a couple of days before Raff goes. On her way home, she calls me. We are both overcome by the emotion of her experience and the knowledge that it will be me next.

'Leaving the house with them is awful,' she says. 'Nobody tells you this. Shutting the front door knowing that when you step back through it again, it will be without them. Driving down the road trying to be cheery, with all their stuff piled so high that it is all you can see in the rear-view mirror. Be warned: take tissues.'

The day before Raff leaves, he and I go down to the The Kiosk on the beach for a breakfast of bacon bagels and milky coffees. We sit in deckchairs and look out to sea, watching the air ambulance hover, a geography field trip stride back and forth, and tourists get mugged by seagulls. We stay there until the car park ticket runs out.

I tell myself: *Don't panic about this coming to an end. Instead think about what is ahead, and how our relationship will strengthen in different ways. Right now, here he is, exist in the moment.*

In the evening, I cook a meal with many different types of vegetables in case they are the last green things Raff sees until reading week, and we open a bottle of champagne we have been saving for a special occasion. I want this moment to be a celebration. There is a knock at the door. Outside, Anna and Dan stand with all our neighbour friends and kids, and they sing 'We wish you a merry uni…' like surreal carollers, cheering Raff, patting him on the back and telling him not to do what they did at university, which I am hoping they don't elaborate on.

He is given gifts to remind him of home: a mug with a picture of the Cobb in Lyme Regis, and a coaster with the face of a golden retriever who looks very much like Margot. I can see how much this means to Raff, and I am too emotional to speak other than sink into the big empathetic hugs that come from the mums in the group.

Later, when Raff is upstairs packing the last few clothes, I go into the sitting room where Steve has stacked all the uni kitchen equipment, bedding and random items that Raff will probably never use. Steve is an intense packer. He packs like he will be subjected to a random check by a commanding officer. In the past, I would chuck stuff in with slovenly speed and an argument would ensue; now I have learnt not to disrupt his flow so I don't get involved.

Standing amongst the boxes, I take a photo to send to Elaine, Cath and Nicki with a 'he's off' caption and a crying emoji. They have been there before me and know the score. So too do Rob and Ali, who message and call to check up on us, knowing how oddly devastating this experience is. On Instagram, the writer Lorraine Candy shares free-flowing advice about uni drop-offs, full of warmth and understanding, as are the comments that follow, which help me feel less like I am making a silly fuss.

In the middle of all my emotion, Steve is still upbeat. He pulls me in for a big hug, and I cry silently into his shoulder.

'He will be fine,' he says. 'More than fine. He is so ready for this.'

I am grateful for his reassuring arms around me. 'Isn't it funny how good you can be with all the big life stuff and yet...'

'Yes, and hopeless in the everyday!'

*

It's Michaelmas. We are officially in autumn. There has been a storm overnight, and the wind continues to take cruel swipes at the apples while the rain turns the remaining blackberries mouldy. A tree is down, blocking the beginning of the track, and Margot and I look at each other in surprise. We are now so used to this walk that any change registers.

The following day, someone has taken the body of the trunk and left its frondy top branches strewn across the ground, causing a village uproar because the person who took it does not own the tree. Furthermore, this same person is suddenly offering logs for sale on Facebook. One of the main gripes is that this person couldn't even be bothered to clear up the rest of the tree, leaving it the way a fox leaves a chicken.

I walk over the fields. In the first, the cut grass has been swept up and baled in big, black plastic rolls. Margot uses her warning bark and dashes frantically between me and the one closest to us, until I walk up to it and pat it reassuringly to show her there is no danger. In the next field, the mounds of grass form neat lines, and the small, flattened path I used to follow has disappeared. In its place are wide stretches of short grass edged with piles of cuttings. I see no machinery, no baler, no farmer. It is stealth work around a bad-weather forecast. The dog sends up a clutter of pheasants, who fly low and noisy overhead.

SEPTEMBER

On the way past the crab apple tree, I check the size of the fruits. This variety doesn't get much bigger than a golf ball, so it will take quite a few to be useful. The question is whether I can take any apples from the low-hanging branch that stretches over the fence towards the road, or if this is technically classed as scrumping, an illegal act of theft if on someone's land.

A formidable local friend once caught someone at the top of her drive, picking damsons from her tree. To make matters worse, in a premeditated manner he was standing on the roof of his Land Rover, with a tarpaulin spread out to catch the plummy spoils. He wasn't just picking a few to stew for his breakfast – it looked like he was planning to feed an entire restaurant with them. She made him hand over every single one, which he did shamefacedly, after a half-hearted attempt to argue that he thought he was on a public highway before offering to pay for them. It fell on deaf ears as she estimated a kilo and gave that to him as payment for his labours.

'He was extremely lucky to leave there with anything at all,' she told me later. 'I was incensed. How dare he! Anyway, I suppose he has done me a favour, although I am now knee-deep in ripe damsons. Do you want a couple of kilos?'

We are almost home when Margot suddenly darts across the lane to the wall of the pond and shows great interest in something. It can't be a squirrel because they are too quick for her. Whatever it is, she has it cornered. She bows low and then jumps in the air before one paw playfully pats it. It must be a frog. This is the time of year when I always find one in my welly, returning like a hibernating homing instinct. The dog is not listening to my command to leave. She has her eyes on the prize, which turns out to be, horror of absolute horrors, a moorhen chick.

I have not forgiven myself for the last tragedy so I am damned if I will be responsible for a second. I yank Margot back by her collar and crouch down next to the upturned chick, a tiny ball of black fluff with almost comedy-sized webbed talons that are stuck straight in the air. I will it back to life. One raised foot flicks in response, and it begins to shuffle on its back in the long grass. I gently nudge it upright. It takes a couple of tottery steps before the determined dog comes from behind me and snaps her soggy jowls around its tiny body, the head of the bird lolling out of the side of her mouth. I scream. I put my hand on Margot's snout and squeeze it to release, as I do when she is carrying a sock or one of our slippers. She refuses to let go.

I try again and again, and finally she drops the chick.

Usually, I am squeamish about picking up birds, but this time I have no choice. It is like holding air. I check over the chick. There does not seem to be any blood, or anything broken, and its miniature wings begin to flap indignantly, so I put my hand through the bar of the gate and carefully place the chick on the bank of the pond. It stutters, falls and roly-polies down the bank, landing with a soft plop in the water, right side up. On land, it was pathetic and stumbly, but in the water it glides away and disappears into the safe haven of the reeds.

I jump, literally jump, for joy, and tell Margot that I will not be speaking to her for the rest of the morning. She is in disgrace. She shows no remorse, pretending to follow me before doubling back, vaulting the stone wall and searching the area where she last saw her defenceless prey, as I shout unanswered commands. Thankfully, the

SEPTEMBER

chick has outsmarted the dog, and Margot doesn't get my toast crust at breakfast either.

*

I miss Raff sitting at the kitchen table in the morning, bleary-eyed, chatting as he watches me go through our daily coffee routine, filling the bottom of the stove pot with water, measuring coffee into the filter, screwing the top on tightly. The hiss of gas on the hob, setting out two of potter Alice's beakers, and heating the milk in a small yellow enamel pan. A tiny caffeine anchor in each busy day, where we cradle the ritual with both hands wrapped around our mugs and talk about the nothings and the somethings. When he returns home, I know this is the first thing we will do together. I send him a photo of my coffee, and a couple of hours later he sends a picture of his, made in his soulless student kitchen.

Friends and family check in on me as the jagged edge of Raff's absence smooths to something I can rub my thumb over. Hebe and Jesse stretch out, physically and emotionally, spending time in Raff's room where the desktop computer is, filling his empty space with noise, discarded school shoes and dirty plates. They eat the extra food I make, because I am still in the habit of cooking for five, and there is no fight over who is sitting where in the back of the car. We start watching a TV series together – one that Raff wasn't interested in. These are some of the positives to soothe the occasional pangs of sorrow.

On the best-friend WhatsApp, we share the melancholy as offspring start or return to university, and the dynamic at home changes. I say I can't wait for Raff to come back for reading week, but please tell me that saying goodbye to him gets easier?! Cath's a few years ahead of me and sends a defining message.

It's simple.

1. *Excitedly greet their return*
2. *Enjoy/get irritated by them*
3. *Kinda ready for them to return*
4. *Feel sick at the prospect*
5. *Grieve when they leave*
6. *Turns out to be OK*
7. *Repeat for three or four years.*

Good to know.

*

Despite many books, social media accounts, podcasts and articles popping up on the subject, there is still some scepticism and ignorance around neurodivergence. Attitudes have definitely changed for the better in recent years, but there is a lot from 'this doesn't exist' ranging to 'well, aren't we all on the spectrum?' Steve has been subject to disbelief, misunderstanding and, in a couple of cases, mild derision. None more so than from himself and me, when after fifty-plus years of thinking he was one sort of person, he finds out he is another entirely.

When we talk about a particular situation, a difficult moment or a confusing social exchange, he now thinks it is because he is AutiHD. I unravel each thing and explain which parts of it may just be human nature. He is unable to separate these, and sometimes he gets cross with me for trying to help him make sense of it, even though he asked me to. He has to navigate a neurotypical world, which must feel like continually bumping into the furniture.

His issues with social events still fox him, and he can't understand how I can go into a room of people and move around it confidently.

'I can't,' I say. 'And I can.'

It entirely depends on my mood, the atmosphere in the room, the energy I sense from others, or whether I have the right shoes on. These things either help or hinder me, and I call that being human. I don't want him to think that neurotypical people have the golden ticket, all the answers and the ability to live an easy life. But I am very aware that I can access my feelings and often work out what makes me comfortable, or not, while Steve can't.

'Sometimes I feel sad about all the time I wasted before my diagnosis.' He sounds wistful. 'Imagine if I had known then what I know now. So many things would have been different.'

October

I wake up, and for a moment I am not sure where I am. The bed is hard, the thin sheet and blanket wrinkled down by my feet after the heat of the night. I get up and open the shutters. The sky is a velvety ink blue, and the birds are silent. As usual these days, I have woken up before dawn.

It is still too dark to go for a walk around the village, and definitely too soon to fill the kettle and risk the clanking pipes waking everyone in the palazzo. I prop up my pillows and get back in to bed, watching the sky gradually lighten until I hear the thrum of pigeon wings as they leave their overnight roost in the eaves of the castello opposite.

I am in Italy. I can hardly believe it. I have been invited as research for a cookbook, so technically I am working, but it is the sort of employment that requires me to do things I would happily pay to do. Like hang out in a fifteenth-century manor house, swim in a pool reflecting negroni sunsets, eat four-course dinners under the bright stars, and join creative workshops with smart, funny women from around the globe. I am the first to admit that I am not labouring.

Some things here remind me of home, albeit in an unfamiliar setting. The red tractor in the distance, buzzing through an ancient landscape of olive groves, chestnut forests and vineyards. The weekend vintage market in nearby Arezzo with a street lunch of piadina – an unsalted flatbread stuffed with salami, scamorza, tomato and chicory. My morning walk, from the palazzo where I am sleeping, to Villa Pia, the hotel hub of the action. A dog at my heels, although he is much smaller than my own. Lampo lives in the village but has adopted Villa Pia, where the staff and guests make a big fuss of him. I think Margot would approve. She would certainly respect the way he stretches out full length on the sofa in the breakfast room and sits on my feet under the dinner table, while I pass him shreds of chicken before he moves on to the next sucker.

And some things are blissfully different from home. Like the light: subtle and soft in the early morning, overexposed in the midday heat, and then as ruby-coloured as the Campari we pour for aperitivo. There are the hours happily lost in creative activities: bookbinding, collage, foraged foliage arranging, calligraphy, flower crown weaving. Also, I am not cooking. Dinner lasts for hours, eaten at a long communal table of raucous laughter and careful confession, which gets looser, funnier and more emotional as the week wears on.

It is not a deliberate choice to avoid speaking about the year I have been living, but I don't, and I feel free of it, in this beautiful foreign land surrounded by glorious strangers. It is an utter relief not to be defined by my recent experience, to find a place of respite beyond my marriage and shrug loose from parenting responsibilities. My spirit, worn thin and then stretched to translucent by Raff leaving home, is luxuriating in heat, anonymity and laughter.

I do tell everyone about my honesty box though, inspired by the fresh produce on the table every day, and the rural environment that surrounds us. The majority of the group know what I am talking about, although there are a few who have never encountered this sort of roadside stall. Louisa, a young artist from Charleston, USA, tells me that every summer growing up she would stay with her grandparents in Louisiana, along with her sisters and cousins. They called it 'Cousins Camp'. I am already envious, and we haven't got to the good bit.

Her grandmother would organise lots of activities, and one of them was jelly making. They would head to the local Pick Your Own blueberry farm. Louisa would strap a leather belt around her middle with a five-gallon bucket attached and pick as many berries as she could before she got bored, as well as sick from all those that made it to her mouth instead. Then the bucket would be weighed, the money deposited in the unmanned cash box. Off they would all go with their haul, teeth gritty from blueberry skins. She hadn't thought about this for a long time until our conversation brought the summer memory flooding back.

While I am here, I visit Monica, a local smallholder who offers to show me what she grows and how she manages her plot of land, which is on a scale far bigger than mine could ever hope to be. Monica reminds me of my grandmother, Doff, with similarities in height and open kind faces. These two remarkable women – the one standing in front of me, and the one surrounded by tiny hearts in my memory – represent a simple life, growing vegetables, caring for their families, happy with their unremarkable lot. Just like my grandmother, I imagine Monica also has a thread of steel running through her core. If anyone upset us, Doff would satisfyingly say that she would spit in their eye.

Monica's big industrial-looking barn is all things to all people. A section for garden tools and machinery, a comfy three-piece suite, baskets of fresh, folded laundry, and a fully functioning kitchen that runs along half of one wall before it turns into floor-to-almost-ceiling shelving. This isn't where she lives, but she loves being here more than anywhere else, she tells me. I settle in immediately. Lined up on these shelves are an army of preserves, including passata, bottled fruits, fig jam, peach compote, pickled vegetables and three different types of honey. There are crates of recently picked tomatoes of all sizes and variations of red, yellow and green, stacked up alongside gnarled bulbous peppers, shiny squat aubergines and unshelled walnuts.

Monica demonstrates the plastic contraption she uses to transform cooked tomatoes into sauce by extracting the skins: a simple piece of equipment that she has had for thirty-five years. At some point, her engineer husband made a metal dowel to replace the tired plastic one, and the machine continues. Her grown-up son says the clicking sound of the handle turning reminds him of his childhood. I am amazed that something so basic can do such an intricate job. Monica slices bread, lays chopped tomatoes on top and pours over a good glug of her own peppery olive oil. All the fine dining in the world can't compete.

Just as we have encountered at home, the Tuscan chestnut harvest has suffered terribly from the heavy rain earlier in the season. Monica describes opening their spiky jackets to find the nuts thick with worms, making the jars of last year's chestnuts in syrup (which she insists on opening for me to try) highly prized. We talk about the effect that climate change is having on her crops.

'The plants are struggling to understand what is going on,' she says with a sad shrug.

I am giddy on the generosity that Monica shows me in the hour I spend with her. It isn't just the glass of ten-year-old Vin Santo she pours me, made from the grapes she hangs in her attic to dry out, before a process that takes a decade to come to fruition. She also shares her frustrations in the veg patch, her unstinting passion for her own produce and the effortless way she transforms her harvests, giving me tips and ideas that transcend the language barrier and the very different weathers we both toil in. I concentrate on taking small sips of the vintage nectar, aware of the depth and maturity in each mouthful.

A jar of squat, speckled raw sausages immersed in sunflower oil are put in front of me, looking alarmingly like pickled, fat pinky fingers. Monica makes the sausages before leaving them to dry out, hanging on canes in the cellar during the day and moving to the warmth of the kitchen overnight. After ten days or so, she can tell by eye and touch if they are ready. If they feel a little sticky, they need to hang somewhere cooler; if they are crispy, they need more warmth. Or it may be the other way around. I can't remember because I have drained my Vin Santo at this point and am grateful for the gut-punching espresso that Monica makes.

Monica's husband comes back for lunch and, on seeing me, wheels out a large urn and proceeds to decant honey from it into a jar for me to taste. A small spoon dipped into the meadow honey first, followed by the *castagna* (chestnut) honey, a darker, smokier, almost savoury, version of the traditional. Every year, Monica says, they are excited to see the honey. They have eight hives, but only two produced honey this season because the bees were also thwarted by the rain ruining the blossom, so they feasted on their own honey instead.

Monica's friends and neighbours sometimes ask her why she bothers to fight the elements, jar sausages, tend geese and spend backbreaking hours in her vegetable plot planting things such as onions, carrots, spinach and Swiss Chard.

'It's simple,' she says. 'It gives me pleasure, I know what my family are eating, it reduces food bills, and it makes a difference to my spirit.'

She doesn't see it as a chore. For her, this is what she is good at, so why stop? She now focuses on produce that survives the meteorological vagaries, gives her a high yield and lends itself to preserving. This reminds me of my early decision-making around my veg patch and honesty box.

I ask if there are any honesty boxes in her area. This takes a lot of communicating, not just because of my non-existent Italian, but because she can't believe this sort of system exists. Firstly, she uses everything she grows, so there is rarely anything left over – it all gets eaten or preserved within days of being picked. Secondly, if there is ever too much of something, she may barter with a neighbour. She uses her harvest as a local currency and a gift, but she absolutely would not leave it on the roadside for thieves to run off with. She is horrified by the very idea. It is the only time she looks at me as if I am a stranger from another land.

I head back to Villa Pia through Monica's olive groves and the swaying yellow flowers of Jerusalem artichokes.

Past a wild pear tree, imposing oaks with acorns in froufrou jackets and a stretch of wild flowering mint on the lane from which a cloud of tiny, white butterflies rise. It reminds me of the meadow at home. As a parting gift, I have been given a large bag of tiny, candy-sweet tomatoes that explode in my mouth, and a pot of honey that feels more precious than gold.

*

The first frost. The radiator in Raff's room is leaking. We also have an unsolved drainage issue, the car insurance renewal, my overdue tax bill (the one you pay in advance for money you have not yet earned, which is why freelancers like me are always screwed), and Hebe's birthday coming up. Low-level anxiety buzzes in the early hours of the morning. I decide not to dismiss this as menopausal. Real shit is real shit.

I listen to a podcast about how to be a successful CEO. I think this will be a better approach to life rather than my current stance of an exhausted middle-aged working mother with high cholesterol and a thickly buttered toast obsession.

Steve has blocked out the house issues and their financial implications. He heads to the office to sort out other people's building problems instead. I can see why he doesn't want to do the same at home too, but I am useless at DIY. He at least has a toolbox. Although right now, he has something more pressing to worry about.

There have been reports about the shortage of ADHD medication due to production issues and an increase in demand. The problem is likely to continue until the end of the year, which includes Christmas, and could mean enjoying the festive season with a husband who is going cold turkey. I know that is a terrible pun. Anyway, the pharmacy can't confirm they will have his next prescription so he, and we, are dangling over a cliff, holding on by our chewed fingernails.

While I call the plumber about the heating, and chase the drainage company for an engineer, Steve leaves a message for his psychiatrist and then contacts two friends who he discovered were both recently diagnosed with ADHD. They were also prescribed the same amphetamine drug but, for different reasons, neither of them continued taking it. As luck would have it, both men have some pills left and are happy to donate them to Steve if he gets to that point. This may be an illegal manoeuvre, but he needs something that can act as a buffer in this worst case of scenarios.

He tells me this over breakfast, as he is splitting his medication capsule and microdosing to stretch supplies. He has the digital kitchen scales out and is carefully creating two thin lines of white powder. All he needs is a credit card, a rolled-up twenty quid note and a large martini with a curl of lemon rind, and I will have woken up in the noughties.

Maddie and a few other friends are coming over for dinner, so that afternoon I stop work and sugar-soap the walls in the downstairs loo to get rid of the worst of the mould. Later, everyone arrives, blown into the kitchen by a rainstorm, which means the glowing log burner and hedgerow cordial in cheap Cava go down well. Maddie has brought me a big bunch of last-of-the-season flowers from her perfect garden, and I make a note to plant the same heavy, froth-headed merlot-coloured dahlias next year. Even better, Maddie has left two bags of horse manure on the front path. She knows how to spoil a girl.

This is the first time we have had people over for ages. We have not felt sociable while we have been navigating a mental-health crisis, unsure how to manage what we each need from the situation and how to be with others. I am trying not to be both host and manager of Steve's emotions in social situations, yet I can't help but watch him out of the corner of my eye, even though I have sworn to myself that I will no longer get involved.

At first, the stress of the evening causes him to launch into a monologue, which everyone politely listens to. He forgets to pour drinks, he helps himself to the snacks without offering them around, and generally behaves like a guest while I juggle roasting trays and boiling pans with both hands and a foot, like a cack-handed audition for the circus. By the time we sit down to eat, he is calmer and relaxes.

With the inspiration taken from my recent Italian trip, I have tried my hand at rolling a piece of pork, stuffing it and hoping it's porchetta. We eat it with a side dollop of salsa verde made from a big handful of herbs from the garden. Steve went behind my back and planted the potatoes I didn't want, and I am glad he did, as I roast them with the pork fat and downy sage leaves.

In our early Dorset life, we rented a cottage on the edge of a farm with a very large potato field. Once the machinery had done its job of harvesting, there were always missed potatoes scattered along the edges of the furrows, left to rot where they lay, so we would scoop some up and carry them back in a coat repurposed as a hammock. Consequently, the children ate a lot of jacket potatoes when they were little and now see it as the worst of meals, even if I bury them under a grated-cheese mountain.

I have made the tricky torta della nonna in honour of Monica – a ricotta-and-lemon custard-style tart with a pastry that is almost all icing sugar. It takes several attempts to roll out. When I put the tart in the oven, some of the filling leaches through the cracks and sizzles on the oven's base. Assuming failure, I knock up a batch of meringues from the leftover egg whites, and compote the last of the damsons to add to whipped cream. Everybody eats everything, helped by the large glasses of Chianti. After the guests have gone, Steve and I talk about the evening as we clear the table.

I mention his frenetic beginning.

'I know,' he says, blowing out the candles. 'When people arrive, this stress bubbles up and I can't control it, but I just kept going and after a while it calmed down and then I really enjoyed myself.'

This matched my own emotions, which began with frustration that Steve wasn't the consummate host, moving to annoyance with myself for putting him in the position in the first place. I had subjected him to his own friends.

With the diagnosis comes the long list of characteristics with social communication issues close to the top. Steve is always going to be compromised or uncomfortable in certain situations, and we need to flag these before they happen. I read that some neurodivergent people have stopped putting themselves in social positions that they know will trigger their emotions. They may be fine in a professional environment, but at a party they fall apart. Or they may be happy having people around to their home, but can't relax in other people's houses. They understand this about themselves and are able to manage everyone's expectations accordingly. As for their neurotypical partners, some are content to lead independent social lives, while others cling on to the hope that their partner will occasionally accompany them. Then there are the ones who walk away entirely.

Now I know this, I can't believe I fought it for so long and dragged us both through years of pointless frustration. I am beginning to accept this part of who Steve is, along with an understanding of what these events mean to him as he walks into a gathering with buttoned-up anxiety, silent panic or over-exuberance. This new information will benefit us both.

Steve sends me off to bed, and he does all the washing up.

*

At the weekend, I lug the horse poo bags up the steps and past the shed to the raised beds at the back of the garden. This takes some time because they are heavy and in the process of carrying and dragging, one of the bags splits so I shovel the spill into the wheelbarrow and hoick the rest of the bag in after it. If there is an easy way to do these things, I never find it.

I cover the first raised bed and don't dig in the manure, as Maddie has instructed. It is like tucking soil up for the long winter ahead. One down, three more to go, but there are still carrots, beetroot and leeks to harvest, and the perpetual consistency of the kale and chard, so I don't want to disturb them yet. There aren't enough root vegetables to share, but I pick some of the rainbow chard and tie the leaves in bunches to put out for passers-by. We are coming to the end of the honesty box season, and I am plotting one last hurrah of the year.

*

Several spotlights have given up in the kitchen ceiling. Steve has fixed a small but powerful lamp above the cooker to shed some light when we are cooking dinner. He is pleased with his proactiveness, but all I can think is that this means we will never get the ceiling fixed. It is like patching massive holes in a wall with newspaper and old pieces of chewing gum.

Jesse agrees and has taken it upon himself to rearrange the larder after cleaning out the cutlery drawer. He lines up tins and satisfyingly pats the neatly stacked rows with his hand.

'This is how I want my whole house to be when I'm an adult,' Jesse says.

I have a flash-forward to a white box of a home with wall-to-ceiling storage, and him explaining to visitors how his parents' chaotic, hopeless Miss Havisham-style existence drove him to it.

*

This month marks seventeen years since we left London and I began working for Hugh and River Cottage. Before then, I had only ever lived in the city or on the suburban outskirts of it, but I was convinced that I was a country girl at heart. There was no reason for this assumption.

On the first night in our little rental cottage, opposite the manor house of a sprawling farm estate, in the middle of actual nowhere without pavements, billboards or streetlights, I realised my mistake. The rain was torrential then too. Luckily, I had no idea that it would continue like this for a fortnight. It soaked the cardboard boxes containing our belongings, which soggy removal men in cowpat-encrusted boots lugged across the pale carpets.

The house was only heated by wood burners, which took the skill of an experienced hand to light. How romantic, I thought, when reading about it from my sofa in centrally heated Hammersmith. I felt differently when I was there with damp kindling and a squalling baby under one armpit. I had only ever lived in houses with full facilities, so I didn't yet know that mains drainage wasn't compulsory and that heating could be powered by oil that ran out at the worst times and had to be delivered in a huge tanker blocking the lane.

On our first night, surrounded by our belongings, which seemed as out of place as we were, and a trusting toddler who wouldn't chastise us for leaving London for at least another fourteen years, I felt a new sort of desolation. I had only ever moved within a five-minute to half-hour radius of Acton. Most times, I didn't even need to change my tube line. Here, we were in an alien place, with speckles of charcoal damp in the corners of the bedrooms and with only basic provisions. Had we still been in the seething metropolis, we would have at least cheered ourselves up with a takeaway, or popped around to the local deli for a wedge of gooey brie and a baguette. But we weren't, and I knew we had made a terrible mistake.

Just then, there was a knock at the door. We weren't expecting anyone because we knew nobody, and the manor house was in darkness. On the doorstep stood an old man. He didn't seem to notice the rain as it dripped off the peak of his flat cap and ran in fast rivulets down his waxy coat. He was missing a few teeth and several fingers, the remaining ones curled around a plastic tray that he thrust at me. Under a tattered tea towel there were big mushrooms, neatly lined up, clumps of earth still clinging to them. I had never seen mushrooms like it.

He spoke in a heavy, reassuring Dorset accent and explained he had picked the mushrooms for our neighbours in The Big House. They were out, or couldn't hear the bell because they were the other side of a couple of bottles of wine, so did we want them? He refused an offer of money, saying he didn't want to see them go to waste. Trusting a stranger who came knocking with a tray of foraged fungi was a gamble. But wasn't that what being in the country was all about, we reasoned, as we sliced and fried the mushrooms in a little butter and garlic and piled them on top of toast. We had wished for a takeaway, and we got one.

So, there we were, living on a farm as winter set in, and I was driving through more farms to get to River Cottage, which was also a farm. The only colours available during those months were the sludgy ones, and I wore jeans, thermals and wellies until March. I had swapped my chic glass-fronted Covent Garden office with its sofa and telly for half a desk in a hastily built uninsulated shed. Lunches were not eaten in swanky restaurants and private members clubs. Instead, they were leftovers from the River Cottage kitchen, which on good days with nice chefs might be crunchy strips of pork crackling, sourdough loaves and creamy risottos full of veg from the walled garden. We always knew when someone resented cooking staff lunch because we would get a beetroot-coloured stew with undiscernible meat scraps and strange vegetable combinations.

Even the lavatory was a stark reminder of what I had let myself in for. No longer marble-sinked, warm and clean, I was peeing in a breezy lean-to with the odd chicken wandering in. I would have cried in there if I hadn't been so desperate to get out. Every morning,

I woke up with the certainty that today would be the day I was going to call my old boss, Maureen, and beg her for my job back.

Several months previously, I had been to lunch with Maureen, one of the directors of the prestigious talent agency and the woman who had hired me over twelve years earlier. Under her principled, hawk-like gaze, I had established myself as a reputable agent with a strong future in the company. Maureen, who erred on the side of caution with the odd slip into negativity, was my North Star in an industry not always known for good behaviour. She had excellent catchphrases that I borrowed, such as telling a client that a job wasn't financially rewarding by saying the offer would barely cover 'two toffee apples and a packet of ciggies'. She was the most diligent of us all, attending industry meetings and warning of the havoc that something called the World Wide Web would wreak on our contractual deals.

We thought she was exaggerating.

'Mark my words,' she said ominously, 'the reign of linear television is over, and we will soon be watching things "on demand".'

I thought that maybe Maureen needed a little holiday, but she was right. She had seen it all and was about to see it all again.

On the odd occasion I may have been approached by a rival agency or considered jumping ship, I knew I couldn't walk away from my colleagues, particularly Thea, Ruth, Dallas and Maureen. They were my work family, and I was lucky to have them. Until I had my own family and had that realisation that I was seeing one lot way more than the other.

OCTOBER

I was planning to resign over lunch, but just the thought of telling Maureen I was leaving made me want to throw up my breakfast. It took all my resolve to walk down the street with her to our usual place, swallow food that lodged in my throat, and share the general chat before I could summon my courage from my boots (Jimmy Choo, never to be worn again).

Maureen listened intently. She said she understood, even though she wasn't a mother, and she could see how little time I spent with my son. Then she did something I was not expecting: she tried to persuade me to stay, throwing offers of help and support at me. Anything I needed, I just had to say, and the company would be there for me, and so would she. Maybe I should have taken her up on it. Yes, probably I should have, but I had a unique opportunity to take what was possibly the only media job to exist in the countryside at that time, and I had seen too many other agents nursing difficult relationships with their children. I didn't want to be the sort of mother the job would turn me into. She understood that too.

Once everyone knew I was leaving, the agency asked me if I wanted a goodbye party: a big do with all my colleagues, clients and casting directors to celebrate my career and see me off into the – everyone shuddered – real world. I couldn't think of anything worse, and just wanted to mark it with the team of peers I had grown up with, got drunk with, fought with and loved wholeheartedly.

We went out for dinner. I was showered with gifts and a card I couldn't read in public for fear of ugly crying. There were speeches. I don't exactly remember, but I think Maureen said something, and I am sure Dallas did too. Then it was my turn. I thanked everyone, said some emotional stuff, and then finished with a joke.

   Me: 'Knock, knock!'
   Everyone (shouting): 'Who's there?!'
   Me: 'Lucy.'
   Everyone (chorusing in unison): 'Lucy who?!'
   Me: 'That's showbiz folks!'

Already forgotten. Except I wasn't quite. Over the years, Maureen, Dallas and Ruth have kept in touch. Ruth and her husband have been to stay with us, arriving with a cellar's worth of wine, and we pick up where we left off. We were all together at Thea's leaving party in Soho last year. Maureen was standing at the bar with a large glass of Chardonnay and several cocktail sausages harpooned on a stick. I hugged her and was immediately enveloped in plush, green velvet and a perfume that rolled me back twenty years. I had to force myself to let go of her.

   'Drink?' she said, grabbing a glass from a passing tray and sloshing it at me.

   'I need to take it steady,' I replied, taking a large swig. 'If I get drunk, I'll ask you for my old job back. It will get embarrassing for both of us.'

   She barked a laugh. 'Love, trust me, you made the right decision. This industry never sleeps. You got out at the right time, and you have your family to show for it, so don't ever look back. You do not want to return to this now. It's no fun any more.'

   From where I was standing, in the middle of a raucous party of old colleagues, I wasn't sure I believed her, but

I appreciated the sentiment. Ruth sidled up next to me and put her arm around my waist.

'Besides, everything is so corporate now,' Maureen continued. 'I mean, what does a line manager even do?' She looked at me expectantly.

'Actually, *you're* a line manager, Maureen.' Ruth grinned.

'No, I am fucking not!' Maureen looked from one to the other of us. 'Am I?!'

November

You know when you agree to do something, and a feeling of impending and weighty doom rises from the sugary pit of your stomach? And your instinct is to cancel but, against your better judgement, you ignore it because it is good to be open to new things and you aren't great at that as you get older? And so, you do The Thing you were unreasonably dreading, which then turns out to be anything from low-key fun to amazingly life-changing, and you are surprised and happy that you pushed yourself out of your comfort zone?

Well, this is not one of those times.

We are driving to Cornwall again, our car loaded down with what appears to be most of the camping equipment I expressly said I did not want to see until next summer and, even then, only in a heatwave, not in November. It is the back end of half term, which coincides with the start of Raff's reading week, so we are picking him up on the way home. The windscreen wipers are on frenzy mode, making it hard to see the edges of the A30, although I have spotted a large, spanking new M&S. My consumer senses are tuned to any retail mecca after living in the middle of nowhere for so long. I even get excited at the sight of Pets at Home.

The rain stops as we turn off the main road and head down sodden lanes, brushing against dripping hedgerows and winding through tiny villages of stone and slate cottages. I yell 'Honesty box!' several times and hit the dashboard, which I know is annoying, but I haven't come up with a better alert. They are all empty. This does not help my mood.

The track narrows and we drive under an arch of entwined branches, their leaves on the autumnal turn, before we are out in the light again with slivers of blue sky above us and the estuary ahead. There is not much wiggle room between the road and the water, and the wheels skid in the silt as Steve brakes.

Steve yelps with delight. 'It's exactly like the photographs!' He is looking at a small yacht that is tied to a bigger wooden boat moored close to the riverbank. 'And there's the tender to get to the boat.'

The tender is a tiny wooden rowing boat that ominously lists, half-full of water, its oars floating dangerously close to escape.

I make my first snide comment of the trip. 'I don't know anything about boats, but I know they shouldn't be full of water. And how do we even get into that leaky boat to take us to the big boat? Which is not that much bigger...'

'It's just collected a bit of rainwater,' Steve is undaunted, 'and we climb down here.'

He points to a rickety wooden ladder leaning against a protruding tree trunk. Its feet are submerged in water so I can't see what it is resting on. It is going to take a certain type of foolhardiness to attempt this, let alone the rest of the manoeuvre.

I don't say a word, but I can't relax my raised eyebrows. We unload the car of all the things we don't need while the kids wholeheartedly embrace the adventure. They climb down into the rowing boat, and Hebe takes Jesse to the bow of the boat where he effortlessly pulls himself aboard, and then she begins to ferry our stuff to him. I don't want to spoil their fun with my sour face, so I take Margot for a walk.

There are big, handwritten signs that warn of swans nesting along the bank of the estuary and to keep dogs on leads, so we stay on the top path. The light is fading fast, not helped by the menacing black clouds that hover overhead. By the time I turn around to go back, it is raining, and I arrive at the boat to see my bag sitting on the grass getting wet. Steve's earlier positivity has been stretched by the weather, the gathering darkness and the tide going out. This means we have minutes to get us both in the tender before we run aground.

Emboldened by my children, who have leapt from ladder to small boat to big boat and back again, I clamber down as Hebe rows over to me. The rain is coming in sideways. I can't see clearly as I dangle my leg trying to catch the edge of the tender. I am not worried about falling in the water – it is barely even a foot deep by this point. I just don't think my body can do the things I ask of it. I feel inflexible and ancient.

Getting in turns out to be the easy part. The issue is the transfer from the tiny wobbly boat to the bigger boat. I get one foot up and cling to the rail, while my other foot begins to do the comedy splits as the tiny rowing boat is dragged out with the swell. With all her might, Hebe pushes the oar against the water, and I try not to cry.

I can see how this looks: a paunchy, bedraggled middle-aged woman wearing a puffa jacket that makes her look like an overstuffed sofa. I feel incredibly vulnerable in front of my children, dangling off the stern of the boat in an almost grotesque, humiliating way. Hebe below me, Jesse above, both encouraging me as if I am the child. One small hand is pushing me up, and another small hand reaches down to pull me.

From the bank, Steve begins to scream commands. He is panicking. The children shout back that he is not helping matters and not to get angry with me. I know he thinks I am weak in these sort of physically demanding situations. I muster every ounce of might and heave-ho myself onto the deck, sprawling like an undone sack of potatoes. The relief is palpable amongst us all, and Hebe rows back for Steve and Margot.

Oh, bloody hell – the dog. How the hell do we get her up here?

Jesse wants to show me around. He uses an encouraging tone, the same I use with him when I am coaxing him to do homework or tidy his room. He has found the solar-powered lights that illuminate the small cabin and bounce off the water sloshing around on the floor. The rain has leaked through and created a big puddle. By the time we have manhandled the dog aboard, we are all soaked to the skin. We take it in turns to cram into the bow of the boat and change into dry clothes, standing on the flat side of a welly to avoid the sodden floor.

As kind as it is of Steve's mate to lend us his boat – and it truly is very generous of him – I wish I was in the cosy cottage I had been eyeing up on Airbnb before this watery option became a reality. I know we have limited funds and therefore should never look a gift horse in the mouth, but on this occasion, I wish we had. Borrowing things never seems to work out for us. It reminds me of a friend who lent her pony to another friend in what appeared to be a mutually beneficial arrangement, until things got tricky and the lender had to rustle the horse from the borrower's field by the dead of night. I am too old and knackered for these sorts of shenanigans.

No part of this experience is adventurous; it just feels a bit depressing and stupid. Steve keeps up a running commentary of delight as he discovers a logbook! A tiny oven! A mystery cupboard! Oh, hang on, that's where the teeny loo is! Even bailing the boat out with the dustpan does not defeat him. He brandishes the wine bottle at me in a last-ditch attempt to cheer me up, but I need a scalding mug of tea and to go to bed, even if that bed is damp and squidged into the pointy end of the boat. He puts the kettle on, and the cabin immediately fills with the alarming smell of gas, so we open the hatch and let the rain in again. There are no mugs. Steve begins to flag with the realisation we can't have a hot drink.

I surreptitiously text Raff to say: *Your father isn't ready to hear this yet, but we won't be doing a second night. We will pick you up tomorrow.*

Then I WhatsApp my girl group to let them know that I am in the middle of an unmitigated disaster. Nicki has just checked into Malmaison in Leeds and is in the bar with a glass of Chablis and a bowl of those olives with jalapenos stuffed inside them. My favourites. Cath is on her way home from a few days in sun-drenched Seville. Elaine is on her sofa in front of the fire and tells me what telly I am missing. I turn my phone off, and we get into our makeshift beds to begin an uncomfortable night.

I sleep for a couple of hours before Margot starts a low-level moan, indicating that she wants to go out. Added to her whine is the drip, drip, drip of the condensation from the ceiling less than a foot above me, landing directly on my pillow or in my eye if I move my head. Steve is snoring with gusto next to me. There are other sounds beyond the boat: the clanging of the rigging, an owl so loud that it sounds like it is perched on the boom, the relentless pounding of the rain, and then water lapping at the side of the boat. The tide is coming in.

By 3 a.m., my disposition to claustrophobia is overwhelming, and I tell myself it could be worse, so I think of all the things that could be worse. Like being trapped in an elevator, having an MRI scan or being on a caving activity. I have flashbacks to other times when I was stuck on a boat and couldn't get off. Like going to France on a ferry with Elaine and trying to sleep in a cabin that was nothing more than a diesel-reeking cupboard buried in the bowels of the boat. We were both so seasick that she spent the night in the tiny loo throwing up, and I sat on deck in the absolute darkness, begging for a big wave to wash me away.

Then there was the Thames river cruise in my talent-agent years. We hired a party boat and invited all the casting directors to join us. It was supposed to be a jolly networking opportunity, but once you were on that vessel there was no chance of getting off. I was dead set against it and wanted to go to the Groucho, but there wasn't the budget for it.

'It will be fun,' my colleagues said, which usually means the exact opposite.

I found it incredibly stressful, and as a lucky consequence, I didn't eat much, and I certainly didn't tuck into the fluorescent-pink prawn curry. By the following morning, half the guest list had terrible food poisoning. One casting director, after a long bout of having her head down the loo, tried to stand up, knocked herself out on the bathroom sink and had to be taken to hospital for concussion. You can imagine how much enjoyment rival agencies took from this turn of events.

There was also my job interview with Hugh, and we all know how that ended, OK, yes, with a job, but minus a cashmere scarf. Let's not forget that. I have never felt more incapable than when I am on a boat.

I doze as Steve gets up and takes his sleeping bag and Margot out on deck. The rain has stopped, and he says the stars are amazing, but then it begins to rain again so he comes back in. At some point, the dog climbs up and sleeps with me before freaking out and pacing. Around the edge of a tiny window, I can see the sky lightening, and I know the interminable night is finally coming to an end. Steve is snoring. Hebe is fast asleep, but I sense Jesse sitting up in the dark. He says he hasn't slept much either. We both go out on deck to wait for the sunrise across the estuary as swans and their cygnets glide about by the boat and the dog spies on them.

I hang off the boat backwards to do a wee, which is preferable to using the tiny pot inside. Jesse needs a poo and bravely heads to the toilet with the loo roll. After several attempts to flush, it is clear this isn't working. Steve has to go in with a bin bag, which I gain some gratification from after his snorefest. It begins to rain again, but I don't care because there is such peace to being on deck and I can't face the cramped cabin again.

I switch my phone back on, and a WhatsApp message from Cath pings up: *Just checking in with the shipmates.*

I respond: *Let's just say, I am not ready to laugh about this yet. Very little sleep, too much water inside and out, dog whined, Steve snored. It is beautiful here though ... if I was looking at it from a kitchen window.*

Nicki replies: *You made it through! It's like Celebrity SAS.*

Elaine isn't an early riser so it will be a while before she joins in.

I type: *We have realised we are not one of those families who leaves everything to sail around the world for a year. Well, I've realised that.*

The tide is out again. We are surrounded by slate-grey sludgy mud that shimmers in the sunrise and drizzle. Steve has not yet admitted defeat and has put the potentially explosive gas on to boil the kettle for our porridge pots. He comes out on deck and sees me standing, unable to sit anywhere because of the puddles on the bench.

'Shall we pack up?' he asks, in a tone that hopes I will say no.

I burst into tears. I don't expect to, and it takes me by surprise.

'For God's sake,' he is shouting at me, 'just pull yourself together. Get things in perspective. This is a massive overreaction, and you need to try and be a grown-up.'

He is exasperated by me, confused by my response to something that really isn't that bad. It makes me feel like I am a princess moaning about her tiara being too tight. Our attitudes to this situation are so opposite. He finds enjoyment in the adventure and wants me to love it too; he wants us to be in this together. I want to be in a hotel with a breakfast buffet.

For a split second, I worry about ruining the experience for him and everyone else, but this year has worn me out so I think fuck that and shout back: 'Pull yourself together?! Be a grown-up?? That is *all I ever am*! I'm always the one who keeps the perspective, stays strong and doesn't fall apart. Just for once, let me freak out. You've been freaking out for the last twenty years and *now it is my turn*!'

I know that I am screaming this, and I don't care. 'I am wet, cold, hungry, have had no sleep, am a bit scared and this is supposed to be a holiday! I'm aware this may sound selfish because the four of us are literally in the same boat, but this is not my thing. This is not my dream. I have no idea how I'm going to get off this bloody thing! I'm allowed to say how I feel and right now, I am not happy. *I am very unhappy*! And I can't think of a single friend who would swap places with me.'

That feels better. Amazing in fact. Letting it all out. It is great to be completely honest and not pretend for the sake of the children or to get a job or be in the boating gang, of which there is one in Lyme Regis, but they are sort of the same as the Christmas party gang. Mainly, it is liberating to say how I feel to Steve without doing a sensitivity edit before I speak. There is no way I can do another night, and by the look of the kids, neither can they. As for Margot, she is already ahead of me. She takes a flying leap off the boat and lands squarely on all four paws, then starts slowly sinking up to her neck in the mud. We all hang over the side of the boat, coaxing her towards us, but she is stuck fast and begins to whimper.

Steve says he is going to rescue her but needs to figure out the best way.

Something snaps. Maybe it is the fear of what might happen to the dog, the lack of sleep muddling my brain or the dread of being left on the boat without Steve and having to be in charge of practical things, but I have a compulsion to go over the side. My body moves without my brain agreeing. I swing my leg over the railing and find my footing on the fabric ladder that we spotted in daylight hanging from the stern. It is like climbing down a badly crocheted scarf, flimsy and sagging, barely taking my weight, so I can't let go of the rope. I am halfway down and stuck, a rung of the ladder hooked under my knee. Steve looks shocked that I have outmanoeuvred him in the impulsiveness stakes and that it could end in serious injury.

Everyone is shouting at me to come back up, and trying to grasp my hand or the hood of my jacket, but it seems easier to keep going down. Besides, I do not want to be on that boat a moment longer. I hang suspended for a minute.

'Let me go,' I beg them dramatically, before I do indeed let go, eyes tightly shut, fearing the worst.

It turns out that I am less than a foot from the ground with a soft mud landing. I still have one leg caught in the ladder, but I am upright. If I can just get my other leg back then I will be fine, except I am not fine because I twist free to find both wellied feet are suckered into the mud. It seeps over the top of my boots, making it impossible to move. Now I am as stuck as Margot, I think, as I watch her drag her back legs through the swamp and past me to safer ground.

Steve has hurdled over the other end of the boat where the mud is shallow and shimmied down the rope in pants, wellies and orange bobble hat, so he can deal with the dog. I decide to leave my wellies for the fish and climb out of them, taking my trousers and socks off as I do. Barefoot, I sink into the mud, pulling my legs out slowly and laboriously towards the riverbank. Wading through the treacle of all my bad decisions.

With a chain of children on deck and trouserless parents in the mud, we manage to get all our stuff off the boat, interrupted by the odd puzzled hello from a dog walker or a driver slowing down to gawp at us. One man stops to ask if this is our boat and would we consider selling it.

'No, it's not our boat,' I say, 'but if it was, you could have it with absolute pleasure.'

I don't have the energy to be embarrassed by the state of us. We aren't going to risk waiting for the tide to come back in. Enough is enough. There is a gushing outlet further along the bank (another sound that had kept me awake). I hobble to it and wash as much of the mud off as I can before dressing in the last set of damp clothes I have. Then with the few per cent of battery life on my phone, I look up how close we are to the Potager Garden café in Constantine and book a table.

Sitting in the greenhouse restaurant an hour later, clutching my coffee, warmed by the log burner and the sun streaming through the glass, Steve is deeply apologetic.

'Breakfast is on me. I am so sorry. I really didn't think this through. It was a really stupid thing to do. Although the one I feel most terrible about is the poor dog.'

I graciously accept his apology and also his decision never to organise another trip away again. Steve's stamina fascinates me. He can cope with leaky boats, collapsing tents and cars careering on ice. During various medical emergencies over the years, usually involving the kids, he takes control while I put my hands over my eyes and peer through my fingers. When I was pulling my eyebrows out, hair by hair by the second pandemic lockdown, he was unruffled by the whole thing, saying he lived every day with a lack of certainty, so now everyone else was in the same position. For once, he said, he didn't feel like the odd one out and he revelled in the social ban. He can keep it together during all the big stuff of life, and yet he completely collapses in the face of the mundane. Maybe we do make a good team.

The porridge comes with stewed Kea plums, apple compote, nut brittle and winged cape gooseberries that look like they have parachuted onto the plate. It is so substantial that I eat it with a fork. Steve has the same, Jesse has pancakes, and Hebe orders the poached eggs and mushrooms on toast. I have never eaten a breakfast quite like it, all the more special because we have damn well earned it.

We conduct a full post-mortem on the past twenty-four hours, which instantly becomes one of those family stories that will be twisted and embellished further in future years. I will always admit to losing my cool. That part can continue to be retold in gloriously awful detail because I am proud of my unfettered behaviour and wear it like a badge of honour for the rest of the day. As for ever getting back on a boat – highly unlikely.

*

We collect Raff on the way back for reading week. He is exhausted, nocturnal, sports rare pimples on his forehead, has no clean pants, and can't remember the last time he ate broccoli. He is also ecstatic. University life is everything he hoped it would be so far. Seeing him full of joy makes me feel inordinately happy. When he comes into the house, he eyes up the new back door mat, the mended gutter and the hospital-bright bulbs that Steve has fixed in the kitchen ceiling.

'Have you come into some money?' he asks suspiciously.

*

There have been a lot of storms over the last few weeks. Each one with a different name, handing the baton on to the next so there is barely a day without bad weather. My morning walk is a muddy plod, hopping over broken branches and pocketing the last of the unbruised windfall apples. The track from the field has turned into a small insistent stream with a hexagon of frogspawn nesting in the widest part. I am not sure this is the wisest place to nurture young tadpoles, but a quick internet check tells me I shouldn't move them to the village pond for fear of spreading amphibian disease. Let nature take its course, the advice tells me. I won't touch it, but I will make regular welfare checks.

I am very bored of hosing down a grubby dog every morning, so after one humdinger of a stormy night, I get in the car and take Margot down to the beach at first light. I used to do this a lot, but since the discovery of the village walk, I like not having to drive or worry about the parking attendant, who once accused me of being two minutes over and claimed he would put me down as 'a defaulter'. I still don't know what the punishment for that is.

As we get out of the car, the dog's ears fly straight up, making her look like a concerned husky. I keep close to the row of beach huts for protection from the worst of the buffeting. The wind is screeching through the rigging of the boats in the yard and making the gulls work as they attempt to hover over the waves. It is as rough as old boots out, and thrilling to see. Each storm changes the landscape of the beach, tossing more tree trunks on to the shoreline, encouraging landslips and ploughing furrows in the shingle.

The sleeping town, which tumbles into the bay, is shrouded in grey mist, punctuated by the occasional twinkly light. I know The Kiosk won't be open yet, but I walk the dog to the end of the esplanade, just in case some kind soul is firing up the coffee machine. The last storm sent a wave of pebbles onto the path. These piled up to their serving hatch and shifted their van several feet, but they were back in business the following day after council effort and a lot of local support. We are a community of shoreline coffee drinkers.

On my walk back to the car, soaked to my pants with a soggy Margot trotting beside me, I spot a lone swimmer striding into the waves. It makes me feel uncomfortable as I know the lifeboat is out of action for a day or so while an engineer tries to get hold of the right part. I mention this to Steve when I get home in his capacity as RNLI volunteer. He is currently on duty, but all pagers are off while the problem is fixed. It is a brief respite after a weekend of action, including a shout in the dark early hours of Sunday morning. This combined with his heavy workload means Steve is ricocheting between the office and the lifeboat station, and not at home very much, which is not helping our flailing marriage or his mental health.

If I drew a graph of our relationship this year, rather than a diagonal line that starts low and soars by autumn, it looks like a series of jagged slashes on a heart monitor.

I sense he is out of control again, and I say this. We are taking two steps forward and then one step back.

He agrees. 'I feel like I am in a speeding car and watching you all through the window. I can't make the car stop. I can't get out. It just goes faster and faster until…' He shakes his head.

I am struck by how these conversations used to be hard-won milestones, and now they are almost incidental moments where we can both immediately access how we feel and speak it. This is progress of sorts. I know Steve confides in my brother, Rob, and he also talks to Adam on a regular basis, which has really helped Steve connect with and accept his diagnosis. The two of them sense-check things for each other, as Thea and I do. It is so much easier to see into someone else's life and point at out-of-place things than it is to do it in your own life.

We talk about the changes he can make by coming back earlier, staying off his phone in the evening, picking up his darning again, and reading when he gets into bed. All the usual intentions. He won't agree to my suggestion of taking a break from the RNLI – it makes him feel useful and part of a team – but he knows he needs boundaries around his availability. Him volunteering makes the rest of us volunteers by default. Like the middle of the night call-outs that wake me up too. The beach walk, and promise of breakfast with Jesse who is then abandoned with the dog when the pager goes off. Those countless times when we are in the middle of a family meal.

It is clear to me that while he likes the dopamine hit of a call out, this sort of commitment is not good for someone who doesn't like surprises or spontaneous change, but there are only so many times I can say this to him. These are the things Steve is still clinging on to despite the advice from neurodivergent quarters.

'Look, it's really about learning how far you can push yourself, and at the moment you're way beyond what is sensible. If you can't consider the impact on you, then think about me. The time you're missing with the kids. The state of the house. We have these conversations, and then nothing changes. You want me to help you structure your day and organise work. Then yesterday, when I tried to suggest a way to deal with a client, you told me to fuck off and stormed out, even though you had asked me to help.'

'I was angry with myself,' he says. 'It's not personal. Just remember, it's not you I am cross with, it's me. While the ADHD medication helps, the autism can still catch me out. Particularly when I'm really busy. I seem to revert to old patterns of behaviour.'

'I get that but it doesn't make it OK to shout at me. You can control that. I'm happy to help, but not if I'm going to be shouted at.'

'I know, I know, I know.' He sighs, defeated. 'I feel so much shame when I behave like that.'

I used to work with someone who regularly communicated through shouting. It was an uncomfortable abuse of power. His saving grace was that I think he hated himself more than some of the people who worked with him did. On one occasion, after an episode of roaring and throwing things, I waited for the usual feeling of fear and panic and found it had been replaced with boredom. I was over it. No matter how famous or important you may be, it does not give you the right to crush those around you.

What I wanted to say was, 'Shut up and get on with your very well-paid job, which we are all here to support you through.'

Instead, I calmly went to make him a cup of tea to his exacting standards. He was subdued and a bit sheepish by the time I returned. I set the mug down in front of him, and he peered over the rim, asking if I had left the teabag in for exactly three and a half minutes? I considered pouring it over his head.

There are no excuses for behaving badly, no matter what you are going through. There is still accountability. This is a sketchy line that we continue to redefine. When Steve and I first started dating, he met a friend of mine and they did not hit it off for reasons they were both responsible for, not least because they were confrontingly honest with each other. Sometime later, she and I were at dinner with a larger group of friends, who mentioned how much they were looking forward to meeting Steve, and what was he like?

Before I had the opportunity to respond, the friend who had met him already yelled down the table, 'He's an arrogant cunt!'

At the time, this felt incredibly unfair. Our friendship, which had been strained for a long while, fractured irrevocably, but there was also the spectre of something else. A nagging fear that she was right.

Over the years, after a difficult period of mood disregulation, Steve will say to me despairingly, 'What if she's right and I am just an arrogant cunt?'

I watch *At Home with the Furys*, and listen to Paris Fury, the heavyweight champ Tyson's wife, talk about his battle with anxiety and addiction and how he deals with his dual diagnosis of ADHD and bipolar. Tyson's biggest fight is with himself. Paris speaks so supportively about it as the cameras follow them both, catching his impulsive, challenging behaviour disrupting family life and enraging her. She never stops loving him. It is one thing to understand what someone is going through, but it doesn't always make it easier to live with, or their behaviour acceptable.

I feel the same watching the musician Matt Willis's documentary about being in recovery from drugs and alcohol. His wife, Emma, was a client of mine. My heart goes out to her as she tries not to cry over a diary she had kept chronicling his substance abuse. Matt has made Herculean efforts to pull himself from the ever-present jaws of addiction and to face his recent ADHD diagnosis head on. Emma says simply that she loves him as she folds the laundry. These women stop me feeling so alone.

*

Two deer cross the full beam of my car headlights, and I slam on the brakes. This is one of the perils of catching the early train to London during the winter months before the sun rises. I always drive slowly along the edge of the woods, aware that one could bound out at any time. I have never hit anything bigger than a pheasant and can't bear the thought of being responsible for the death of an animal under the wheels of my motor.

Deer aren't the only thing to scupper a dash in pitch darkness for the first train. There is always the possibility the car won't start, the expectation of a train delay, or heaven forbid, a cancellation. It can make me feel very far away from things. I usually try to go up the night before, because of these pitfalls, but this time I am taking the risk and attempting the trip in a oner. Thanking the God of Rail Networks for my punctual arrival at Waterloo, I feel the usual rush of emotion and nostalgia as I step on to the platform and back into familiar territory.

Crossing the bridge, the whistling wind sticks strands of my hair to my hastily applied lipstick. I stop, like a tourist, to take photos of the skyline and send them to the family WhatsApp. The Millenium Wheel, Big Ben, St Paul's Cathedral and the Shard are interspersed with cranes topped with red warning lights, masses of them rising above the city looking like a mechanical alien invasion. How many more new buildings can this poor city take before it slides down the mudbank and into the unforgiving River Thames?

I march on, trusting my Londoner's inbuilt sense of direction, and immediately lose my bearings. New walkways seem to have sprung up, landmark shops have disappeared, and I go the long way round to Bloomsbury, except the café in the bookshop where I usually sit to prep for my meetings no longer opens before midday. This is news to me, although clearly not their fault. I head to Lambs Conduit Street, to find the Italian café I also love isn't there any more, or maybe it was never on this street.

With a sense of being off-kilter, I sit outside another café with coffee and an almond croissant the size of a gerbil, brushing icing sugar off my research notes.

My first meeting is for a writing project that could push me out of my comfort zone in an exciting way. A high-profiler, so opposite to me that I am surprised when I find connections and similarities between us in our conversation. In the middle of the meeting, I look down at the coat I am wearing and see threadbare patches under the strip-lighting of the conference room. I am in my one good coat, which hasn't been good for several years. I should have taken it off, but my arm is caught in the ripped lining, so I am stuck in it unless I make a big fuss and a large tearing sound. It is easier to let them think that my red cheeks are the result of a menopausal hot flush.

After the meeting, I tramp through Soho for an injection of Christmas and am underwhelmed by the general festive decorations. It feels very much like January with huge dark posters in shop windows proclaiming Black Friday offers. This is not the vibe I am looking for. I want twinkly lights, wafts of mulled spices, laden garlands around doorways, and those cleverly designed window displays that make you want everything.

The break before my next meeting is interrupted by Steve calling to say he has picked Hebe up from school because she is poorly, a friend updating me on her divorce, and Raff asking how to tell if the chicken he has bought has gone off. I have gone nose blind and headache-y in Liberty's perfume department and can't think straight, but I try to answer everyone. I also fervently wish for just one hour all to myself.

On the way to my next meeting, I pass my early career stomping ground of the BBC. What was originally two buildings either side of a narrow street is now one massive broadcasting corporation monolith, and the road has been consumed by it. I loiter on the circular steps of All Souls Church opposite, and take a photo to send to Cath, Nicki and Elaine with a caption about the good old times.

I draw a line at picking up one of the caramel-brown plane tree leaves plastered to the pavements and carrying it around in my pocket as I do in the country. I notice how many people are walking around seemingly talking to themselves, shouting into thin air about important situations, an earphone in one ear.

In a huge, noisy brasserie-style restaurant, the gender-neutral lavatories are so dark that my phone torch shows me where the flush is. I used to come to this café years ago, but it has been whipped into something unrecognisable. My colleague orders a Golden Milk and before I can stop myself, I ask her, wide-eyed and out of touch, what it is. Turmeric, milk, maybe some honey, a shake of cinnamon perhaps, a grind of pepper, and don't forget the ginger. I make a mental note to google a recipe later as a glass of luminous custard is put before her, the sort of colour that only comes in cashmere. My Americano with hot milk is a searing disappointment.

The Regent Street angels are sparkling from on high as I cut through to Carnaby Street on my way back to the station, walking under solar systems of globe lights and tinsel clouds. This road has changed so much since I had a Saturday job here when I was fifteen. I worked in one of those shops that was hoping you were off on a stag or hen do and in the market for phallic- or bosom-shaped pasta, candles, homewares and cards. I would stand outside with a big bunch of helium balloons and was instructed to hand them out sparingly. After a few shifts (when I would go and stroke the scarves in Liberty's on my lunch break), I resigned by giving the balloon bouquet to a thrilled child and disappearing into the weekend shoppers.

NOVEMBER

Waterloo Bridge is busy with commuters heading towards the railway station as the sun begins to set behind Big Ben. The jaunty festoon lighting, strung along the South Bank following the curve of the river, reflects in the murky depths of the Thames. These are the best sort of festive lights. I am halfway across and between two worlds, trailing reminders of my old life into the realities of my actual existence – a liminal state where I only have to sink into the bowels of the underground train system, and a portal will appear to whisk me back to before. To my little flat in Shepherds Bush, with pots and pans piled high in the tiny kitchen, my bedroom with inky blue walls and a large, creaky sash window onto the sunny courtyard garden full of herbs and roses. Before children. Before Steve.

I am too early for the train I have paid to travel on, so I stop off at the Royal National Theatre, returning to it like the pigeons who stalk its brutalist ramparts. It is my way-marker, where the sixteen-year-old me, on a school trip to watch *The Threepenny Opera*, was struck down with a mystery illness that I tried to sleep off in the circular corridor, outside the auditorium, catching the final twenty minutes of the show. The next day, my skin erupted in an army of angry chicken pox.

Then there was twenty-year-old me, queuing for cheap tickets and the hope of a career in the business. Followed by agent's assistant me, tasked with the job of repeatedly returning to the bar, balancing plastic glasses of warm white wine through crowds of people who liked air kissing. Then agent me, legging it round to the green-room bar after the show to congratulate a client and joyfully lose myself in the raucous melee of cast and crew.

And now just me, sitting at a table against the back wall of the enormous foyer, under a pool of light, watching people wander to the café, the bookshop or the box office. All the previous versions of myself would not have imagined this place would become a sentry for my arrivals into and departures from my home city. If I don't know where to go, this is where I come.

In the station, I get a limited-edition Christmas sandwich for the long train journey back from my home to my now-home, and I feel mildly festive for the first time.

*

Steve has been rationing his medication while he waits for his new prescription. His energy and attention have begun to wane, and he has removed himself from the daily bustle. He slips through the house in a dream-like state, leaving the fridge door open, the key in the car, and a pile of his clean and dirty laundry tangled together. His usual late-night flapjack baking and early rising is replaced with deep sleeping.

Again, I question how sensible it is to be this reliant on medication, because when you run out, life is ten times worse than it was before the drugs. Or it is at least for Steve – he knows other people on the medication who don't have the same issue. He says he couldn't work as much or be as present without it, and the occasional awful withdrawal is still preferable to the continual dance between brain fog and anxiety.

One of my answers to his mood and a post-London anti-climax is to get into the sea. The fossil-shaped streetlamps still shine as my mermaid friend Ros and I walk to the beach before daybreak. The sky contains streaks of dark grey with a sliver of apricot to herald the rising sun, and there is a finality about the chill in the air. Autumn has taken a definite turn, and winter impatiently drums its fingers. The shifting light feels like it might lead to snow and, for the first time in months, I am in thermals and double socks.

Ros is in her Prada coat and an extra-padded jacket, because she doesn't take any chances. She tells me about the MRI scan she had earlier in the week in the quest to understand her terrible migraines, and the absolute awfulness of taking her new nose piercing out and then having to try and get it back in again. After several attempts, including with hospital staff assistance, she ended up in a tattoo parlour in Taunton, where a new piercing was prised in with the addition of a butterfly.

'Now I feel like I have a massive bogey, all the time,' she says mournfully.

This was not what we were imagining for our middle-aged boundary breaking.

We wade into the sea, general chatter running out by the time we are waist deep. The wind whips across the surface of the water. I am not sure which is colder, air or ocean, but we are too far in to turn around so lower our shoulders under and kick forward. I take ostentatious breaths, and my groggy bed-head clears instantly. We talk in snatches of sentences: 'so cold,' 'the sky,' 'look,' 'seaweed, urgh,' 'sun is up,' 'turn back?'

As we swim to shore, we pass two women in chunky-knit bobble hats, and we all agree that it is so much colder than last week. 'You need hats,' they say, and their fluffy bobbles wobble in agreement.

Afterwards, we sit on the decking of a beach hut with a flask of hot chocolate (Ros's turn to make it and she has added a shake of cinnamon), and talk about the pros and cons of HRT, at which point a man walks past with his dog just as Ros is saying that at least we aren't suffering with vaginal atrophy.

When I get back, I put the kettle on and sit on the windowsill, my legs dangling over the radiator while I wait for it to boil. Hebe and Jesse have caught the school bus, and Steve is on the phone. I don't like the desperate tone of his voice and realise he is talking to the pharmacist, who I quickly ascertain doesn't have the right medication for him. Steve apologises for his earlier outburst, which I missed, and it sounds like there is some placating from the other end and a possible plan. He puts the phone down and bursts into tears.

Steve has been without medication for two days and was relying on this morning's prescription. He is also angry with himself because they had the tablets on Wednesday, and he forgot to collect them, so they have been given to someone else. This is news to us, but this is the way it works and we are learning as we go. Medication is delivered, but it isn't assigned, so if someone else asks for it before he does, they get it. The pharmacist tells him that people have been ringing from further afield as everyone races around grabbing whatever is available. The realities of a shortage – just at the point where the psychiatrist has approved an increased dose for him.

Steve cancels a planned meeting and gets into bed. He curls up under the duvet, dozing while he waits for the GP to issue a new prescription and the pharmacy to call him to confirm he can collect it. Outside, our neighbour with the manicured lawn noisily mows stripes in his grass and then fires up his strimmer to attack the hedge under our bedroom window.

NOVEMBER

I used to fight these times when Steve checked out, fearful of him missing work and therefore money, worried that this would be the beginning of a prolonged mental-health dive and wishing I had a husband who just got on with things. Now, with the safety net of a diagnosis, I am beginning to truly understand what Steve deals with and study the impact it has on me, in the hope that I can give different responses. It now feels less like being trapped in the rip-tide, and more like bobbing around in the ripple. Somewhere I read that 85 per cent of marriages with a neurodivergent partner end in divorce, and that this is double the statistics of a neurotypical couple. We are still in the 15 per cent.

*

On the last day of November, I am wearing thermals, a hat, gloves, scarf and thick socks. The dog walk starts in the dark before we get caught in the glare of the head torch belonging to fellow villager Harry. We talk about the forecast for snow, and he thinks it will affect the highest points of Dartmoor but it won't settle here. I wouldn't mind if it did because I am pretty much housebound anyway. Hebe is recovering from pneumonia, so I am on hand to feed her penicillin capsules, refresh her hot water bottle and make lots of hot lemon and ginger. She was born sixteen Novembers ago, arriving into a world that smelt of woodsmoke, surrounded by the golden blur of leaves and tucked up in hand knits. Reminiscent of this time, I stoke the fire in the sitting room. Hebe moves from her bed to the sofa – thin and pale, swaddled in a blanket like a consumptive Dickensian child.

The sky is blank over the fields. Stark skeleton trees spike the brow of the hill. At what point did they lose all of their leaves? I was watching so closely and still I missed this. In her voice note, Thea lists her winter prep – new waterproof walking boots, painting the bedroom pink – and a rundown of her Netflix viewing. She asks if I have any good vegetarian recipes, preferably without cheese. This follows a recent flurry of voice notes where we list things we love about Marks & Spencer.

It reminded me of London friends who had waved us off when we moved, saying, 'Mark our words, you will be back in six months,' and then when we weren't, they thought we might have a point. So they organised some house viewings in a neighbouring village and were halfway down the A303 when they rang to ask us where our nearest M&S was. 'Turn back,' I said. 'You are not ready.'

I need to pick through a recent discussion I had with Steve, so I get my phone out again to message Thea. He has acquired his medication. As he begins to climb out of his recent slump, he is self-reflective, talking about repeating the same emotional patterns again and again. I hit record, give the briefest of hellos, explain the background and dive in.

'So he describes it as running into a concrete wall, which he knows is coming up but he can't swerve it because he hasn't worked out how to. He has nowhere else to go other than smack straight into a large unforgiving object, so that is what he does. It is relentless and dangerous, and I don't want to stay and watch him hit it again and again. But he isn't choosing this; he is beholden to it. He's tried so hard this year in acknowledging the dual diagnosis, in embracing this being part of him and yet every time I think we … OK, he … is getting somewhere, there is a setback. He seems to forget he is neurodivergent, and beats himself up over mishandling a situation. And when I suggest that his actions are in line with his autism, he seems genuinely surprised, as if he's hearing it for the first time. I used the analogy that he's trying to run a hurdle race with a broken leg, while pretending it isn't damaged. It'll never get him over the hurdles, so it's pointless trying – he has to accept his leg's broken and find another way to get around them, to move forward. He listens, I think he has understood, and then a few days later we are back to discussing the same thing and his frustration at himself. Anyway, this voice note is now long enough to get you to Wigan, never mind Wandsworth Common, so sorry! Oh, and I forgot to get back to you about vegetarian meals without cheese. I can recommend a Mexican bean stew. I'll send you the recipe when I get home…'

Margot has sped up, no doubt powered by the thoughts of breakfast, but I stop by the pond as the first tiny flakes of snow catch on my scarf. It feels utterly magical. I can't see the moorhens and hope they are tucked up on the far bank or cosy amongst the reed thickets. I feel better after a good walk and a chance to air my thoughts. Further up the lane, the viburnum bush is covered in tiny pink berry-like buds that shine vividly against the backdrop of heavy, white skies. I snap a couple of stalks off to take home for the kitchen table. Outside the house, the magnolia tree holds on to its mass of tight buds as the snow gets heavier, whirling through its branches and dusting the top of the hedgerow. I can't imagine the buds becoming flowers, but in a few months this tree will be laden with blush-edged blooms again.

*

The military band play their unique take on a Meatloaf song, complete with big drums, clashing cymbals and a flautist. They are mesmerising, in their polished black caps and tailored red jackets with gold embellishments of tassels and epaulettes, arranged in smart concert formation in Bucky Doo Square in Bridport. One of the stallholders is watching them as he dips a knife into a jar of mustard and smears it on the edge of a sausage roll, his foot jigging along to the beat. There is often a musical feature on a Saturday morning during the market. It might be a lone musician playing banjo and tap dancing, or a pianist with one or two accompanying singers. They always draw a crowd, but none as big as the gathering for the marching band. I catch snippets of the live music as I pop into the bookshop, the hardware store and the butcher, and it plucks at my heart, drawing me close to the group.

I see an old River Cottage friend, Andy, in the throng. We decide to grab takeaway coffees, managing to find some space on one of the benches in the surprisingly warm late autumn sun. He is his usual jolly self, and we are laughing about a shared memory, so I have no idea how the mood suddenly shifts – it leads to a conversation about neurodivergence, and I tell him about Steve. I give the brief and upbeat press-release version of things. As I am waving my arms around annoyingly, because I can't seem to speak without my hands miming the words, I notice his eyes are watering. I think he may have a cold or be allergic to something, so I continue until a single tear slips down his cheek and I stop mid-gesticulation.

'This is me,' he says. 'I think I have ADHD. I am on the NHS waiting list, and they say it's going to take two years, probably more.'

I wasn't expecting this, but now that he says it, I can see the signs from the years we worked together. I am also having this conversation regularly, whether it is with someone who thinks they are neurodivergent, or with a partner or parent of someone who may be. By being honest about Steve's diagnosis and my response to it, it opens up a communication with others who may be standing where we are. I don't search this out, but I don't push it away either. I don't want us to be the local poster couple for this late-in-life diagnosis, but I do want to share our experience in case it helps.

Andy is waiting expectantly for my response, his eyes now properly full of tears. He thinks I can help. I think that I have a ticket for a local event which, if I don't leave soon, I will miss the start of, and this was a treat to myself. And I also think, I do have some answers – not many, but enough – and I know from Steve's experience that just talking about it without judgement and fear is powerful. I grasp Andy's hand and he begins to talk.

In the evening, I message Andy. I hope he is not regretting talking to me or feels silly or stupid for sharing. I want him to know that he is brave and brilliant. I also want him to tell his wife that she is too, and if she ever needs to chat, I am here. His response is reassuringly him, and funny, and he suggests meeting Steve for a coffee or beer soon.

As luck would have it, Steve and I bump into Andy in the street a couple of weeks later. The conversation quickly turns to their shared ground, and Andy describes how his thought process is like bonfire night.

'My ideas are bright, beautiful fireworks, soaring into the darkness and lighting the sky with multi-coloured explosions. In that moment, I know I can do anything, and it fills me with immense energy, a dopamine high and I have the answer. And then the following day, the firework is extinguished, damp on the ground, abandoned and trodden into the mud, and it is impossible to relight it. Even if it was possible, I don't want to, because it won't be the same. It's ruined, and I wonder why I ever believed in it, so I walk away and wait for the next one.'

Steve is nodding his head in fierce agreement. 'The firework!' he says in awe, 'and then its death. I recognise this. I relate to this!'

I stand back, watching them speak, and I am very glad that we have bumped into Andy. It is great for Steve to speak openly with people who really get it: those who are living these experiences, rather than those of us who are outside looking in. He doesn't seek this out, go on forums or buy books on the subject, but now, when he is faced with it, he doesn't shy away.

*

There is a forthcoming event with parents and other family members. These events are rare and important as nobody is getting any younger, so the six cousins get ready to assemble like the Avengers. This is exactly the sort of gathering that would have stressed me in the past, with Steve trying to be invisible, or worse, becoming mischievous and looking for trouble. So with this looming, we have a conversation about whether he will come or if this will be too much for him to take on. Maybe he should try coming at the beginning and then taking a break. We look at the event objectively and discuss all the possible permutations. This is our new approach, and it helps us both express what we want from the situation.

'Well, I don't want to miss it so I would like to try,' he says, 'but how do you feel? Would you enjoy it better if I wasn't there?'

This is something I have been asking myself.

'The thing is...' *Be honest*, I think, '... I would really like a husband by my side. I'm just not sure I want my own husband.'

There is a beat of silence and then Steve laughs, and I laugh too, although I am not entirely joking.

'That has really tickled me,' he grins, 'and I know you mean it. I completely understand. Do you think it is too late to find you an alternative husband for the day?!'

'I reckon so,' I say. 'Stanley Tucci is bound to be with his real wife, and Bill Nighy is probably filming on location somewhere so...'

'It may have to be me after all, then.' He shrugs.

'Yep, but there will have to be a few rules. Like, you can only swear three times, don't make any gags or begin conversations with "come the revolution".'

'Dull, but OK – it's a deal.'

December

It's raining again. I look back through my diary, and all I see are the days when I wrote about rain. Why didn't I write about the sun more? I know there wasn't a whole lot of it, but surely that's more reason to capture it when it appears. This month so far, we have had one day of stubborn white frost and a beautiful orange sun that lit up the hills at the far end of the valley, before the clouds opened and flooding stopped trains, closed schools and dripped through a friend's ceiling while she was in the bath.

I should be planting tulip bulbs. I should be collecting more manure from Maddie and digging it into my raised beds. I should be pulling up the withered sweet pea stems and packing the hazel support sticks away in the shed. I should be shrouding the thick bristly stems of the gunnera with its own leaves to protect it from future frosts. It is just too grey and wet to do anything other than the absolute musts, such as walking the dog, and even she looks at me like she can't be bothered. I have never known a year to be so rainy.

I leave the house in what feels like deep night – the white fronds of Margot's tail glowing in the gloom, a proud furry flag leading the way. I can hear rushing water, loud and insistent. Part of the lane has turned into a stream again, swooshing around the corner, past a neighbour's front door and crashing into a storm drain that leads to the village pond. By the time I splash down there, I can see the water from the other end has overridden the system and is gushing out into the pond, parting the thick algae. Margot and I watch it, transfixed by its power, before wading through more puddles, haphazardly forming through the village.

When we reach the track, there is another temporary river, racing off the fields and collecting where the cart lane veers off down a narrow rubble path that is now a waterfall. This is the worst it has been all year, and that is saying something. A robin flits ahead of us, the red of its breast flashing from hedgerow to beech to oak as we slosh towards the meadow.

I wonder if we will have snow this winter. We don't tend to get much near the coast, although when we moved to this village thirteen years ago, it just happened to coincide with one of the snowiest Decembers on record, probably brought on by people saying how rare it was to get snow this close to the sea. We got it in truckloads.

We were camping in the cabin while we fumigated the house, after its previous inhabitants included several incontinent cats. Our beds were lined up, with us against one wall, one-year-old Jesse's cot in the middle, and bunk beds for six-year-old Raff and three-year-old Hebe against the other wall. We were so rammed in together – you couldn't get a sick bucket between the gaps – that we would be climbing across beds to reach poorly children in the night. The rest of the space was taken up with a cupboard for our very-capsule clothes collection, two camping chairs and a board we used to create a table. Jesse bathed in the sink in the tiny kitchen, while the rest of us used the makeshift shower.

When the snow came, it froze the water pipes, playing havoc with the old gas boiler and making the village roads impassable. We were living in a wooden structure with paper-thin walls and three small children who wanted to go out and play in the snow and then come back to a warm and cosy house. Parent fail.

I managed to make it into work one day, walking down the track to River Cottage, which was covered in a blanket of pure white and silence. My office was also in a shed, but we had plugged in fan heaters and ate a lot of cake to get through the winters. Jessamy was already there when I slumped into my twizzly chair and put my forehead on the desk. I told her our predicament and how bad I felt as a parent.

She listened carefully. I knew she would have some wise, supportive words for me.

'I don't know what you were thinking?' she said, shaking her head disappointedly.

That night, we ended up staying in the River Cottage farmhouse. It had water, but it didn't have heating, so we lit the open fire in the kitchen and the range in the dining room and alternated between the two, drinking apple brandy once the children had gone to bed. We were all sleeping in the same room, which was cold even in the height of summer, so we didn't get undressed. I could see my breath and felt a bone-chilling numbness that only comes from a haunted room or a life decision that has gone spectacularly tits up. In this case, it was likely to be both.

We went to Rob and Ali's for Christmas, then dragged our heels back to the cabin in January and promptly ran out of money once we had fumigated and tackled the lack of drainage in the house. It was only a call from an old client of mine offering me some consultancy work that pulled us off the cart heading to the debtors' prison. Otherwise, I am not sure what would have become of us.

The kids remember this time with great fondness, and talk about the cosiness of us all being together, the games we would play and the sense of adventure they felt. Thank God for that because, for us, it only conjures up desolation and dread and the closest Steve and I came to divorce before this year. We would lie awake at night whispering about putting the broken house straight back on the market and then going our separate ways.

Snow days got better once we were in the house. The pipes still froze, the gas bottle jammed causing a minor explosion that blew the kitchen cupboard doors off, and three years in a row we ran out of oil, but by this point we had a group of neighbour friends to hang out with. We all trudged up Otter Hill with sledges, an ill-advised plastic tabletop and cinnamon buns.

Now, when I think about bad weather, it is associated with piles of village children's boots lined up by the fire, mismatched mittens dripping on the radiators, shared excursions into town for provisions, rescue missions in an old Land Rover, and taking it in turns to cook big pots of stew. Communal living never looked as good as those snowed-in days.

*

Steve has a check-up with the psychiatrist to review his medication plan. He says he doesn't need me to go too, but if I wanted to get a coffee afterwards then I could. This is code for him wanting me to come and, if anything is going to distract me from work for a couple of hours, it's a flat white. As it turns out, I can't accompany him because Jesse has been up all night with an agonising earache, so he is off school, and I am in the telephone queuing system for a GP appointment. I ring Steve afterwards to find out how it went. After leaving the house in a sulk of anxiety, he is buoyant and babbling.

'I told him the meds really work, which is why it is so tough if I don't have them, even for just a couple of days. Apparently, my response to coming off them is pretty severe. We were both interested in what that means, because you know I love a chat about brain science, but his eyes flicked up to the clock, and he said he had other patients to see, but that was OK because we can talk about it next time. He asked how much difference the meds made, and I said I had asked family members if I should come off them and each gave an emphatic no, so I guess that says it all and so we are going to stick to the higher dose for now. I made him laugh. I made him laugh a couple of times, actually. And he told me the latest statistic is that 3 to 4 per cent of the adult population have ADHD. Don't you think that's a lot because I was so surprised about how many people that is, and the ratio works out at three males to one female although I don't know where nonbinary people sit in this so they really should be thinking about that. And that's not a true representation because men are more likely to be diagnosed than women apparently. Anyway, the point is that the number of diagnoses has escalated, and so has the demand for drugs, but as the psychiatrist said, and he is so right about this, how does one work out the medication threshold? How do you know if someone will benefit from it or not? He says I clearly do though, so not to worry about not getting meds because he can see how much it helps me. I said even a neurotypical person would struggle with the amount of work I have at the moment, and the drugs keep me level, professionally and emotionally. They are a lifeline. And I told him I have battled most of my life with regulating my mood, and how this has got me into some difficult situations, caused relationship breakups and ostracised me from social events. For the first time, in forever, I feel in control of this. Mostly. Although I still don't know what I think about the autism, and he said we really do have to wrap this up but we will chat again next time. So, anyway, yep, all good, but I can't chat because I have to get back to the office.'

A few days later, Steve gets a letter from the psychiatrist: a report based on this most recent meeting. Under the heading 'Mental State Examination', he writes that he is happy with Steve's progress and that he was *a little talkative in clinic today.*

*

Raff and his laundry are home! He arrives back with an air of being too grown-up for the house, the village, our family. A giant in a doll's house. I suppress my excitement at his return, not wanting to smother him while he settles in. It must be so strange, but he carries a tinge of arrogance that annoys me, a dismissiveness to the life we poor pathetic creatures are still leading out here in the middle of nowhere. Margot gets all his attention.

What he really needs is a decompression chamber to ease the transition. This is exactly how I feel when I get off the London train and want to delay the reintegration back into family life. This isn't what I expected for his first big homecoming, but I wait for the real him to return. He can't be far behind.

There is a late-night drama about Raff forgetting to cancel his website account and being hit by a bill of almost two hundred pounds that he doesn't have. He blames Steve for missing an email. Steve says he can't focus because his brain is only half-functioning while on a lower dosage, and Raff says he can't deal with it because he has to turn in his first big assignment in the morning.

I get out of bed and sit in my dressing gown, freewheeling on the website chat function with someone called Trowa, who is incredibly helpful and leads me through a system, which really isn't hard. Within fifteen minutes, we have a refund, and I consider inviting Trowa to join us for Christmas. Maybe instead of Raff and Steve.

The next morning, project submitted, a pile of clean washing on his bed, website money back in his account and the two of us at The Kiosk for coffee and bacon bagels, Raff transforms. The shoulder-tight stress of uni work and giving up his newfound independence for a month have dissipated, and he is back to being my boy again. Happy to be home, interested in what we have all been up to, and with a childlike thrill about Christmas plans.

*

Steve is still surfing on basic medication rations. This makes him scratchy, and I imagine someone playing a violin badly as a backing track to these days. The reduced amount or lack of them changes Steve's mood so severely, more than his neurodivergence does. It doesn't seem to affect others we know who are on the same pills. They can dip in and out, take weekends off, but Steve is reliant on them.

There is a complicated communication involving precision timing and drug availability between the GP surgery and the pharmacy, who are both being helpful (the latter particularly so). Steve tries to remain calm in phone calls and emails, but the system is defeating him and pushing all his neurodivergent buttons. In fact, it is playing fast and loose with the elements of organisation he struggles to get a handle on, and everyone agrees this is unfair, but what can they do about it they say. This is bound to push anyone to their limits, and the clock is counting down to Christmas in double-quick time. I am holding my breath, turning the expectation I have for this part of the year over and over in my hands, waiting to see if it will be the same as it has always been.

It is Jesse's birthday, and he wants to spend it with his cousins. We go over to Rob and Ali's for the night. I know Steve is teetering, but I don't want to draw attention to it or ask him how he is, fearing that he will fall and take Jesse's excitement with him.

There is one moment though. On the doorstep when we have returned with food for supper for everyone, me balancing a tower of supermarket profiteroles and a box of Quality Street, I say, 'OK?'

He says, 'No.'

And I say, 'I know, but this is Jesse's birthday so you're just going to have to get through it as best you can. Remember what you're responding to is the withdrawal symptoms of the medication.'

What I am really saying is, 'Pull yourself together.' I am annoyed with myself that I can't find a better way to be in this moment. I know his reaction is due to a lack of meds, and I summon my kind voice even though I have to dig deep to find it.

The next day, we go on our annual family trip with Rob and Ali and all the kids to a local garden centre that wins awards for its Christmas displays. We meander through themed areas of snow scenes, a million baubles, light displays, past a life-size talking camel, and loiter by a trio of supersize singing penguins. There are joke hats to try on: Jesse always goes for the turkey, and Kitty dresses Steve in glittery deely boppers. One room is filled with an enormous model train track with a steam engine that wheezes around relentlessly. In long-gone years, the children would press their small faces against the protective Perspex screen and watched it chug past small ceramic houses, cafés and shops with tiny lights twinkling from tiny windows.

At the end of the festive experience, pumped full of all that glitters, my eye is drawn to a candleholder. It is a ceramic beaker, with tiny holes punched out that etch the lines of a snowy village, with cottages and a church spire that comes alive with the flicker of a flame. I am mesmerised by it. It is the sort of pointless schmaltzy thing Steve hates, and I can see he is thinking of ways to be rude about it.

'Why do you like it?' He has taken a refreshingly different approach.

'I'm not sure. I think it makes me feel safe.'

It reminds me of our cottage and our village in an alternative universe where nothing goes wrong. I would like to step inside it for the rest of December.

'Don't you feel safe at the moment?' His question is leading us both somewhere.

DECEMBER

'This time of year ... can be really hard.' I am careful about what I say.

'Choose one. I want to buy it for you.'

As we stand in the queue for the till, Steve darts off promising he will only be a minute, drawn to the area full of houseplants and then distracted further to a point out of sight. He doesn't return in time, so I pay for the candleholder and wait for him in the car park.

*

I have decided to do a big Christmas countdown honesty box. I feel I should give myself the sort of appraisal I used to have when I worked for other people. One of those roundups of successes and failures, what I could learn from, pinpoint things to do better next year and consider my long-term goals. Maybe I should take myself out for a staff Christmas lunch and invite Steve too as a thank you for his role as head gardener. After all, there is no honesty box without his diligence in the veg patch. My haphazard, fairweather approach isn't enough on its own.

My local friend and occasional freelance colleague, Alex, comes to help me pull the honesty box together in a day, in return for a few used notes and a big lunch. She refuses payment but accepts the cheeseboard, and while I make her coffee, she updates me on her trip to Switzerland.

'The country runs on honesty boxes,' she says as she shoves moss into copper wreath rings. 'They are everywhere. I thought of you the entire way round. There was even homemade miso in one box. I took a photo of it for you.'

She swipes on her phone and shows me what looks like a wooden bird box with a lacy net curtain over the front of it. 'That's not all – scroll left to see a photograph of what they claim to be Europe's first unattended self-service village shop. At 1,364 metres, it is higher than Ben Nevis!'

It is a real shop, with shutters at the window, geraniums in window boxes and a big sign saying 'The Honesty Shop'. My mind is whirring with possibility and excitement. Every time I see another honesty business or box, I feel a kinship and validation.

Alex and I hang bunches of greenery from the rafters, tie posies of dried honesty (see what I did there) and make wreaths to sell. I have splashed out on a string of festoon bulbs that remind me of the South Bank. They transform the space, reflecting off the corrugated plastic and throwing the cobwebby corners into grateful shadow.

Maddie has cut me tall branches of twisted willow to sell. These elegantly frame the lean-to and can be strung from a rafter or propped up in a pot and strewn with decorations. I put bunches of chard together and rename them Christmas chard, because of the rainbow stems, the colours of the multicoloured fairy lights of my childhood. Alex has made Christmas Chutney, and I put out several jars of Wild Cherry Plum Jam that I made in the summer, and decant calendula seeds into envelopes. I have only just realised that most of the stock begins with a C, which I didn't set out to do but is rather pleasing, as if I have an actual plan.

Last, but best of all, there are ceramic coffee beakers from Alice, who has wrapped one for me as a generous gift. After her cancer treatment, she had been in happy remission, but it is back and has crept into her bones, so she is taking a sabbatical, returning to her family's Welsh roots and a bedroom with a sea view. I send her a book about wild swimming because she loves a sea swim as much as I do, and we both wonder why we have never gone in together. We agree to rectify that next spring.

The last honesty box of the year reflects the support and creativity of the people so committed to helping me with the endeavour. I am incredibly moved by the thought as Alex chalks up the sign and I light the candles.

Steve has been absent throughout the honesty box prep, partly because he is on a mission to get work done before Christmas, and also because he is trying not to let his under-medicated mood infiltrate the house. He is much more aware of the impact he has on us all, and I really appreciate this. It isn't easy for him or me, but it is infinitely better than this time last year.

The neighbours come over for an impromptu honesty box opening and have to walk through the lean-to to get to the booze and mince pies. I figure this is the perfect method of subliminal selling. Steve is home in time to ladle out the mulled cider. The adults sit around the kitchen table eating sausage rolls while all the children, aged from five to eighteen, head to the sitting room and squash onto the sofa or perch on the arms to watch a Christmas film. This is after some argument about what to watch, followed by a serious vote, an accusation of cheating, a bit of sulking, and me delivering several bowls of popcorn. Will they all still want to do this next year? Possibly not, so I capture the scene by stealth camera work and show the photo to all the parents in the kitchen, who are now on the egg nog.

On Instagram, I post about my last honesty box of the year and offer to do a little personal shopping for local people. Taking snaps of Alice's creations, sorting bank transfers and wrapping the purchases in masses of tissue paper ready for collection. I draw the line at delivery because that really isn't in the spirit of the honesty box, but I do take a few things with me when I meet friends for coffee or a dog walk, in case anyone wants to buy anything.

I am stretching the true meaning beyond what is really appropriate, but heck, it is nearly Christmas and I want to deposit some money in Alice's account. This isn't the sort of honesty box I envisaged when I started this experiment, but the process has filled me with purpose and hope and connected me to friends and neighbours in ways I had not expected. So too has it bound Steve and me together, albeit with our own clearly defined roles, making it less collaborative than I thought it would be, and yet this has been the right outcome. A shared commitment that has also managed to give us our own breathing space, planting us in our small patch of soil and the village community.

*

It is the Sunday before Christmas and the annual carol service at the village church. I change into a dress and slap on red lipstick, which is complete overkill, but I always enjoy this traditional evening as it marks the beginning of the main celebrations. One by one, the rest of the family come up with excuses not to go, until it is just me and Hebe left in the kitchen. She feels bad, and doesn't believe me when I say I am genuinely, honestly, seriously happy to go on my own. Then she thinks I really do want to go on my own, but now she would rather like to come too, but doesn't want to muscle in. So then I backtrack to convince her to join me. We link arms and walk down the lane towards the glow of light streaming through the church windows and the distant hubbub of an annual village event.

The church is very small and rarely full – unless there is a funeral – but the carols always pull in a crowd. We scoot into wooden pews, with lots of hellos, waving to neighbour mates amongst the village congregation, and I inhale a significant waft of mulled wine, warming in the temperamental tea urn. Before the traditional service begins, there is a prayer for peace, which talks of the conflicts raging around the world, and then a moment's silence.

Heads bowed, small children still, I feel tears welling, my emotions close to the surface. I distract myself by focusing on the swathes of greenery dressing the high windowsills, the flickering candles and the twinkling Christmas tree next to the piano. I imagine how many generations this church has witnessed, although I can't get my head around its thirteenth-century origins. A drawing of a ship in the nave is thought to date back to the fourteenth century, and two of the three bells that ring out before a Sunday service are amongst the oldest in Devon. As a tiny parish church, it is one of eight on a rota for visiting clergy and, like many others, it needs a new roof. I am hoping I will have a tiny honesty box profit to share between a local worthwhile cause such as this one and a global humanitarian charity next year.

Hebe is sniffing next to me. I whisper for her to use a tissue, and she whispers back 'Why? My sleeve is doing just fine.' We all sing heartily, safe in the knowledge that nobody cares how we sound; they just want us to raise our voices to the wooden rafters. Comfortingly, there are the same Bible readings as the year before and the year before that, with the story of the Nativity read out by different neighbours, a sermon by the vicar, and then the setting of the Nativity on the font. The lights go down and we sing 'Silent Night' by atmospheric candlelight. I think how lucky we all are, in our tiny church, in our tiny village, safe in this tiny moment.

Lukewarm mulled wine and a tin of flaky mince pies are handed around as people loiter in pews. I am in the middle of a chat with fellow dog walkers, which results in us promising to bring our hounds next year – and if anyone has a lamb, that would be doubly great. Or we could dress the dogs up as animals from the Nativity. We all agree Margot will have to come as the donkey, what with her being on the large side. There is a discussion about the village chimney sweep rota, which I am not on and look hopeful about, before being told that I will have to wait for someone to die or move before I can get a spot.

A neighbour from the top of the village talks about the time she saw the Beatles at Abergavenny Town Hall. John Lennon was flown in by helicopter, she says reverently. Everyone asks everyone else where they are for Christmas and how many they are cooking for, as the male elders look nonplussed about the catering arrangements. Dave the Piano Man, who used to live in the village, cycles over every year to accompany our bad singing, and I tell him it wouldn't be the same without him.

'You could put a CD on,' he says, and we all look horrified.

Hebe is thrilled to finally qualify for a glass of mulled wine, although I am aware that a few neighbours still think of her as the little girl in plaits when we moved to the village. We sip and talk and edge our way towards the large oak door. When we leave, shouting our goodbyes to those still lingering in the porch and chatting in the graveyard, I expect it to be snowing like it does in films. We stumble back up the lane in the deep darkness, Hebe ribbing me about my awful singing, and both of us hallelujahing home. To Steve happily hoovering out the fluff from the tumble dryer, Raff and Jesse putting the finishing touches to the Christmas tree, and Margot spatchcocked like a fluffy rug in front of the fire.

*

Ros and I time our final swim of the year to coincide with the winter solstice: the shortest, darkest day. The car won't start at first. When it does, I over-rev the engine, sounding like an angry motorbike, and bunny-hop out of the village, convinced I have woken all the neighbours. The car park is empty, other than Ros, who is waiting in her motor with the heater on full pelt. It is like winkling a little snail from its shell as she clambers out, and we both wonder why on earth we do this. At 7 a.m. In winter.

The RNLI station is decked out in Christmas lights, which sketch the edges of the building against the vast pitch-black of the sky, highlighting its comforting presence. We can hear the sea, but we can't see it. This is the moment before the days begin imperceptibly to lengthen, but we are seasoned all-year swimmers and know we won't really see the shift of light for another month or so.

Ros apologises for letting the side down as she snaps on neoprene gloves and boots. We never wear wetsuits, mainly because they are such a faff to get on and off, and also because I get colder trying to extricate myself from one than I do if I didn't bother at all. We only know where the sea is because it mumbles in the distance at low tide, clouds obscuring the moon with no definition between the water and the sky. We stay close to each other, wading into icy nothing with a faint hint of sewage. There is something special about a friendship built on a challenge, an extra closeness that comes from a shared fear. Ros and I facing the ocean. Thea and I facing the diagnosis. The countless trials that Nicki, Cath, Elaine and I have faced together over the last three decades. We shed a skin of triviality, each of us tasked with keeping an eye on the other one.

'Fuckety, fucking, fuck,' Ros and I say in unison, plunging in, eyes desperately on the horizon for any glimmer of sunrise.

Our swim is briefly illuminated by the wobbly light on a fishing boat, but the foggy gloom is almost too much to bear. We stay in for a quick shoulders under to welcome the solstice, before zipping straight back to shore to layer up and burn our mouths with scalding hot chocolate (my turn to make it, and I add ginger syrup). I have brought mince pies for breakfast.

These are not the mornings for big swims. They are for anxiety-kicking and important conversations about whether we would ever have plastic surgery (no, but then never say never) and, unrelated, what it must be like to be Adele. Not without its difficulties, we conclude.

We head back to our cars, past the historic Cobb wall where several sunrise paparazzi are lined up, waiting patiently, tripods and long lenses silhouetted against the lightening sky. As I drive out of town, I look in my rearview mirror. The most stunning pumpkin sunrise fills the sky, turning from burn to blaze.

*

For the first time in a very long time, I do not cry on 23 December.

*

Every year, Steve finds a complicated, time-consuming crafting project that results in Christmas presents for those he buys for, which now boils down to me. I do all the other gifts. What can I say? I am a Christmas control freak. I also hate leaving anything to Christmas Eve, which is when Steve bounds into action, meaning he either disappears for much of the day or he stays up into the wee small hours and then has to be shaken out of bed on Christmas morning.

I know that this year something is afoot. I am not allowed to take anything out of the boot of the car when we get to Rob and Ali's, although it is impossible for Steve to remain discreet because he needs the kitchen to create in and the room is open plan. Teenagers are leaning over a board game at the table, and adults have collapsed on the sofas in a state of surprise that we are finally able to stop. There are wafts of ginger and golden syrup, the ruler is out, there are detailed pieces of tracing paper cut to specific sizes, and the oven is blasting heat.

I am not supposed to know that Steve is making gingerbread. I am frustrated that he has taken over the kitchen and is not part of the day's events and, at the same time, am pleased that he has found something to occupy himself. Mostly, I feel the latter. This is a clear coping strategy for an emotionally heightened, socially draining day. These are the terms I now think in. Everyone around him understands this. Ali supports him in these endeavours, at the other end of the phone for the pre-planning and there in the execution of it, providing him with whatever he may have forgotten.

'Where are your scissors, Ali?' 'Can I borrow your tape measure?' 'Why do you buy that type of butter?' 'That's not a very logical place to keep your flour, is it?'

She is there as his wing woman and one of his best friends, but she is no pushover and is the first to pull him back into reality, delivering truths with a concrete stare. Sometimes, I forget that they aren't siblings too, and that it is Rob and I who connect our two families.

Steve's reassuring comforts are still there for him – his oat milk, crisps, lemons and beer – but I see how many things are there for me too and how we all provide things for each other, to make us happy. Fresh coffee, shortbread biscuits, Wotsits and Campari are also tucked in Rob and Ali's larder because I like them. This year, before Rob rings the Italian restaurant I tell Steve the mushroom risotto he eats every year is no longer on the menu. In fact, I say, it hasn't been for several years, and I explain how Rob asks them to make it specially. Steve absorbs this information with surprise.

'He did that for me?' He is holding back tears. 'That feels like an act of love.'

He orders a risotto which is on the menu.

When we get back from the restaurant on Christmas Eve, Steve wants to give me my gift. It is impossible to wrap so he covers it with a tea towel, and there is a grand unveiling as everyone stands around in anticipation. I had expected a little gingerbread house. Instead, Steve has made a box with precision measurements, elegant joints and a lid with a clear panel of 'glass' made from melted sweets. Piped carefully round the edge, he has inscribed *Break in Case of Emergency* in icing. Inside is a generous selection of my favourite chocolate and sweets. There is something so thoughtful about this endeavour. He has crafted me my own confectionery honesty box. It is a triumph.

Flushed with the success and exhaustion of it all, Steve finally relaxes into Christmas. We have a really great time. Six cousins entwined in games, food, beers and hilarity, while the adults cook, drink, dog walk and hang competitively over a jigsaw.

As we leave Rob and Ali's house and say goodbye to everyone after days of festivities, Steve hugs Ali.

'I didn't fuck it up this year, did I?' It's a funny statement, but also a hopeful question.

'No, you didn't!' she says in surprise, and they high-five.

In the car on the way home, each teenager plugged into earphones, we talk quietly about what a good time we had.

'I think I am getting the hang of this neurodivergence thing. I mean, it isn't easy, but I am facing it all. I just wish I knew where ADHD and ASD end and I begin.'

I don't think it works like that, I want to say. It isn't a line that you cross back and forth over: it is enmeshed in your being. Don't try to distance yourself from it, let it be part of you.

I go to tell him this, but I stop myself, because after all, what do I know? I am not in his head. I am not him. I am beginning to feel more like me again though.

January (again)

I am not sure what I think about this new fashion for leaving glittering Christmas trees up past Twelfth Night and, in some cases, until Candlemas on 2 February. It is bad enough that people are putting their trees up in November, without stretching it out at the other end. Maybe they can't face the dreaded melancholy that comes with the end of Christmas and need to soften the blow by delaying the deconstruction of the festive landscape. That would be understandable. My sadness operates in a different way and demands that Christmas is stripped from the house before the final hours of the old year. New year, clean slate.

We have just tipped into January, but I am not ready for the abrupt return to real life. I am woken by what sounds like several characters from a Beatrix Potter story reconfiguring the insulation in the attic, directly above my head. There is scratching and scampering, gnawing and then silence. It is usual to get something hibernating in the attic during a cold spell.

Some London friends are horrified by this. Those who have never been out of the city for more than a fortnight, that is. Surely, we need to get someone from pest control in, they ask worriedly. Or put humane traps down. Have we tried poisoning the fuckers, they want to know. People seem to get bloodthirsty at the thought of a small rodent chewing through a box of old photographs. And look, it isn't ideal. I wouldn't choose to have them in the house, but we are surrounded by fields, and mice come with the territory.

'Can you hear the mice in the attic?' I whisper to Steve.

He is swaddled in the duvet with just a tuft of hair poking up. He groans. 'That isn't mice,' he says. 'It's much bigger than that.'

Gulp. 'Rats?'

'No, squirrels.'

The vestiges of my city mind can't compute this.

I go downstairs to put the kettle on. While I am waiting, I have a quick blast of Instagram. Ben Branson, the founder of the non-alcoholic drink Seedlip, has posted with the headline 'Personal News'. I know before I scroll what this is. There have been significant reveals of high-profile people in different industries sharing the news of their neurodivergent diagnosis.

Here's a list, Ben types. *It's a list about me.*

In this list, several points stand out. Ben loves patterns (literally and figuratively) and punctuation. He is blunt, direct, has no friends and is anxious about basically everything. He has a very high IQ. He prefers animals and plants to humans. Ben says he can act 'normal', but it is really tiring. He is curious, and also gullible and naïve. These are just a few of the things on the list that sound familiar. I forward the post on to Steve.

Ben has recently been diagnosed with ADHD and autism, and finally things make sense. He takes it as a green light to be himself, and he has established a charity and a podcast called *The Hidden 20%* to reflect the one in five people who are neurodivergent, which equals 1.6 billion. In his post, he includes some shocking statistics.

> *Up to 40 per cent of neurodivergent (includes ADHD, ASD, Dyscalculia, Dyslexia, Dyspraxia, Tourettes) adults are unemployed.*
>
> *Up to 85 per cent of those in the UK prison system are ND.*
>
> *There's an up to ten-year assessment waiting time in the UK.*
>
> *There's an ADHD medication shortage.*

And this last one…

> *There are hundreds of thousands of people scared to share their diagnosis with employers, friends and family.*

'We are different, not deficient,' he says.

*

I get a message from Alice, the potter. She is living one day at a time, navigating the unbearable landscape of a terminal cancer diagnosis surrounded by love and radiating peace. She sends me a video of her on a windswept Welsh beach of stunning greys, facing a choppy winter sea.

She is in a wetsuit, and someone is supporting her as the waves threaten to knock her back. For a moment, they let go. She is free in the water, arms stretched, legs kicking out before her ravaged body begins to sink, too weak to withstand the swell. As she is helped out of the surf, her family rush towards her with towels and blankets. The camera zooms in on her beautiful, euphoric face.

I did it, she types underneath the film. *I got in for one final time.*

*

It has been a year since I discovered this walk through the village, along the uneven track and out into the meadows. It is still dark and raining hard, rendering my specs useless and waterlogging my phone as I try to record a voice note to Thea. I give up, and instead tuck the phone in my pocket and listen to a new podcast about the entertainment industry with Richard Osman and Marina Hyde, which has become my absolute favourite and is far too short. If they could make it a full hour, it would cover my walk. I am counting on the pair of them to get me through the winter.

The track has returned to a slow-running stream, with big pools of surprisingly deep water that catch me out and slop over the top of my wellies. Brambles drag against my coat, and my trousers are plastered to my legs. It is unseasonably warm, and I can't wait for the cold snap that has been forecast if it means no more rain. In the meadow, there is no view to speak of – just a muddling of fields and sky with the occasional twinkly light from the few houses on the opposite side of the valley.

Margot is despondent and hangs around my heels, her red glowstick collar reflecting in the puddles. She is waiting for me to about-turn because she wants her breakfast, but I won't give up until we have reached the entrance to the woods. I like to touch the gate for luck, before I retrace my steps. It will be light by then.

When I get home, everyone has left for school and work, and Raff is still in bed. It is another couple of weeks before he returns to uni. I unpeel my wet clothes and get into the shower, psyching myself up to return to my desk. I go through the routine of clearing up the kitchen, putting a load of washing on and sweeping the floor.

In each room, there is evidence of tasks that Steve started the day before, like a whirlwind in a wardrobe. He hosed down the patio and scraped all the gunk into a pile to be left for the wind to redistribute. The spice trays have been emptied, and the jars lined up randomly in the larder amongst tins and packets of dry food. My walking boots are without laces. The vacuum cleaner has been abandoned in the middle of the sitting room next to a half-excavated box of old toys. I accidentally kick a bucket of dirty water over in the hall.

I check my response to this. Angry? No. Frustrated? A little. Can I laugh about it? Yes.

I finally sit at my desk. Maybe I need a strong coffee. Or a nap. I start as I often do when I am warming up, by checking the news headlines, and find out that it is National Divorce Day again. The realisation that an entire year has gone stops me in my tracks. I see how I have been counting the time in sunrises, frosts, daffodils, wild garlic, lambs, elderflower, cricket matches, long sea swims, university visits, damsons, apple bobbing and 'Good King Wenceslas', not by arguments, psychiatrists, diagnoses, sadness, prescriptions, overdrafts and exhaustion.

Steve and I are still together, with neither of us sure how. This isn't a fairy tale, or a Hollywood movie, but it is a happy ending of sorts, or at least an ending of the

JANUARY (AGAIN)

part of our lives before the diagnosis, when we knew so little, moving in a smog of confusion and despair. Now we have a clarity that comes with knowledge, which has been both revelatory and life-changing. And yet, in many ways, much remains the same.

Steve is who he has always been. What started as a pact has become a quest we are still on, and who knows what will happen next. I can't be sure that this is where we will be next year or the year after, there is no certainty, but then isn't that the same for all of us? I don't think of marriage, or indeed life, in those terms any more. I just think about the immediate days ahead. Picking up Seville oranges for this year's marmalade, sorting through our seeds ready to make a plan for the veg patch, roasting a chicken for Sunday lunch, five of us dipping soldiers into runny eggs at the kitchen table as the days begin to get lighter. That's enough, isn't it?

Unable to settle at my desk, I message Steve to ask if he wants to meet me in town for elevenses, and then I grab the car keys and Margot's lead. She has just climbed back into her bed after her morning walk, but bounces up and is out the door in a flash.

It starts to rain as we head along the coast road. By the time we get to the deserted beach, the drizzle has turned into a downpour. Steve messages to ask if I want to cancel, but I am here now – and besides, I want to see him.

We both run from opposite directions in the rain along the esplanade, and I laugh out loud at how this must look. Two unwieldy fifty-something people in anoraks, one with a small pony on a lead and one in an orange bobble hat, jogging towards each other and colliding under the awning of the kiosk in a flurry of soggy coats. Steve orders coffees, and we shelter from the rain coming in sideways and watch the weighty waves rolling high into shore before smashing down on the pebbles.

'Here's to National Divorce Day,' I raise my takeaway cup to Steve.

'Oh, already? Well, I'll drink to that.' Steve raises his.

'Still together then.' I shake my head in wonder.

'Yep, how did we manage it?' He smiles at me.

'None more surprised than us,' I say.

'I know this doesn't mean we have resolved everything, but thank you for sticking around,' he says as I shrug away his gratitude. 'No, really, thank you.'

The rain slows, we finish our coffee and get ready to leg it in opposite directions, Steve back to his office and me to the car. He steps outside the awning, which is sagging with collected rainwater, just as a huge gust of wind lifts the canvas and tips the lot on his head. I want to hoot with laughter, but I watch his face for tell-tale signs of distress. There are other customers milling around who witness this and stop, also waiting for his reaction. We are all paused, holding our collective breath. This is the sort of moment that would have sent him into a tailspin a year ago.

Steve throws his hands up to his face in shock and then a big grin spreads across his face.

Steve's Afterword

Change of voice. I get to have the last few words, which is, perhaps, not something you expected to happen. If you are one of those people that on purchasing a book immediately turns to the back and reads the ending, well, you've fucked up this time. This would have been a nice surprise. OK, a surprise.

I have encouraged Lucy to write this book. I have egged her on every bit of the way. No holds barred, no punches pulled, tell it like it is. Raw. Unadulterated neurodivergent mayhem. Why would you want to dial it back, soft soap it or sand the edges smooth when the truth is way funnier and sometimes uglier.

I have spent fifty oblivious years living with two conditions. ASD and ADHD have made my life challenging. Difficult. Interesting. Now I know of them, I can't honestly say (and I must be honest, because this is the honesty box) that I consider them bad, but also, I can't say they are good things either. The situation is simultaneously good, and bad; Schrödinger's neurodivergence. For me, it is this dichotomy that can be the source of so much frustration: I can't have the advantages and not the disadvantages. And neither can those around me.

For the neurodivergent curious to know more, there is an ocean of information freely accessible on the web. Information on your condition ... on coping strategies you can deploy ... on medication. (It is good that there are such vast quantities of information because it gives you something to read whilst you wait 550 weeks for a diagnosis on the NHS.[1] In that time, you could study medicine, become a psychiatrist and diagnose yourself.) But what about information for those in a relationship with a neurodivergent person – what sort of information do they need? Whichever side of the coin you are on, NT or ND (obviously it is heads if you are ND), being knowledgeable about the medical facts does not make it that much easier to live with day to day.

While I would rather not be reminded of some of the events in this book, reading it gives me, and you, an insight into how they affected those closest to me, particularly Lucy. This is an honest account of our relationship and how it has survived – so far at least. The travails of life with neurodivergence.

Lucy is full of fortitude and tenacity, and has a supremely optimistic nature. She has stuck with me for over twenty years, and I count myself very lucky she has exercised those traits above so considerably when it came to our relationship. There are many neurodivergent people who are not supported and loved like I am but equally deserve to be.

Often, the most significant and immediate help for people with problems of any kind is knowing that others share the same struggles. From that knowledge comes community: a sense of belonging and safety. It took me a while to understand that but it is a great comfort knowing I am one of many. I hope that reading this book enables you to feel more positive about your own life and relationships with or alongside neurodivergence, or that you feel empowered to share your story. You are not alone.

1. ADHD UK (2023) *NHS ADHD assessments waiting lists report, ADHD UK*. Available at: https://adhduk.co.uk/nhs-adhd-assessments-waiting-lists-report/ (Accessed: 10 June 2024).

   Dorset Healthcare University NHS Foundation Trust: 12 weeks.

   Herefordshire and Worcestershire Health and Care Trust: 550 weeks.

ACKNOWLEDGEMENTS

This wasn't the book I set out to write. I know a lot of authors say this, and I used to wonder if that really was the case, but I can tell you it is. What I thought was going to be a journal of our fledgling honesty box and village life, took a very different turn when Steve was diagnosed with ADHD and ASD. I was depicting a fairy tale version of my year, with rabbits hopping at my heels and songbirds circling my head while squirrels did the washing up. I felt like a fraudulent Pollyanna who was peddling a country idyll while ignoring the battered Ford Cortina on bricks in the garden, on fire. I couldn't, in all good faith, continue to write about one part of my life without telling the truth about the rest of it. I figured it may even help someone else in our situation.

There are several incredible writers who inspired me to be brave. Diana Henry urged me to write for myself and gave me the impetus I needed. Mark Diacono encouraged me with humour, wise words and coffee summits. And Cathy Rentzenbrink unearthed my life-writing confidence in an online Curtis Brown Creative course.

My exceptional agent, Antony Topping, saw a glint of something in my idea, patiently counselled me through the twists and turns, and supported my change in direction. Without his notes, wit, clarity and frankness this book would not be what it is. I value his judgement above all else. I doubt it is easy to agent someone who used to be an agent and still thinks she knows stuff, so

ACKNOWLEDGEMENTS

additional credit to him for running that gauntlet and to his brilliant colleagues at Greene & Heaton.

I have worked with Bloomsbury on other people's books but didn't dare hope they would publish my own. It has felt like coming home. Here is a roll-call of deep appreciation for a few of the team; Faye Robinson, for expertly managing the schedule and me, Victoria Goldman and GiannaMarie Dobson for forensic edits which made the book better, Laura Cope for additional welcomed support, designer Mia Butcher and illustrator Holly Macdonald for a cover which captures the light and dark of the story, Youssef Khaireddine in Marketing, Ben Chisnall in Production and the wonder, Ellen Williams, who I trust to take this personal account and traverse the PR world with sensitivity and aplomb.

The biggest, most heartfelt gratitude is reserved for my dream of an editor, Katy Follain, who championed this book from the proposal stages and immediately understood how I wanted to tell our story. She has simultaneously held my hand and thrust me forward. Not only has she encapsulated the nurturing, challenging, protectiveness of an expert editor, she has been a luminescent pleasure to work with throughout the process.

To those who appear in these pages, either knowingly or not, I thank them for being an integral part, especially Matt Haig and Ben Branson, for sharing their stories at exactly the time we needed to hear them. And to Ros – who swam with me literally and emotionally through the writing of this – Alex, Maddie, Suzanne, Olivia, Cat, Jessamy, Andy, Lucy, Miranda, Tara and Susie. I am grateful to them for being themselves in the book and in my life.

ACKNOWLEDGEMENTS

To Anna Maxwell Martin, Richard and Rox Pink, and Veronica Henry, for being early readers and vocal advocates of the book.

Nobody was a bigger supporter of my honesty box endeavour than potter, Ali Herbert. Had she been here, she would have been one of the first to read this and have likely wondered if I needed to swear so much. I hope she would have been happy to be included. We continue to celebrate her in the beautiful ceramics we use daily, and her work is alive with her spirit.

Thea is a beating heart in this book and in my every day. Having her listening ear at the end of my interminable voice notes (so long I actually got cut off once) and receiving her insightful, thought-provoking responses, was key to navigating regular struggles. And to Adam for fulfilling the same role for Steve. Both she and Adam have displayed huge generosity in allowing me to include their story and this feels like the most precious gift of love.

Then there are the golden girls – Elaine, Nicki and Catherine – who have been steadfast and true through every one of our almost forty years together, ready with advice, irreverence and laughs. Their friendship has made me feel secure whatever else is happening in my life.

Talking of safe harbours, I am indebted to my brother Rob and sister-in-law Ali, and their children Jacob, Emilia and Kitty, who have lived our marriage, loved us unconditionally and kept us talking. Their patience, acceptance and family roasts are a constant, and the way we have grown within our individual relationships with each other and as a collective of ten, is one of the things I am most proud of.

ACKNOWLEDGEMENTS

I dedicate this book to four people. To our beloved children, Rafferty, Hebe and Jesse, for displaying an awesome level of maturity and understanding, and allowing me to dig around in our lives and show the stuff we kept hidden; they are the very best of everything.

Finally, and all importantly, to Steve, for letting me write about the parts of himself he didn't want to think about and plunder his privacy, knowing that many strangers and worse, friends and family, may read this. He is an exceptional person, who taught me what being honest really means, who propelled me onwards through my doubts and encouraged me to journal our experience, guts and all. Love endures.

Between me writing this book and you reading it, the length of waiting lists for a neurodivergent diagnosis will have increased significantly. There will be neurodivergent people who will have lost their jobs, their relationships and in some awful cases, their lives. And those close to them will be in turmoil. We face a mental health epidemic of unbelievable proportion and yet there still seems to be little urgency or understanding around it. Being able to talk about it openly, without fear or prejudice, is one of the things we can do to break taboos, educate people around us and shift this world into a more accepting place.

A NOTE ON THE AUTHOR

Lucy Brazier is a ghostwriter and author. She began her career at the BBC before becoming a talent agent at PFD (now United Agents) representing actors and presenters. After twenty years, she and her young family left London and moved to Dorset, where she worked with the broadcaster Hugh Fearnley-Whittingstall before becoming a full time ghostwriter six years ago. She has worked on many writing projects and written nine books on behalf of high-profile people across a range of subjects including lifestyle, food, interiors, education, money and memoir. Her first book in her own name was *Christmas at River Cottage* and she regularly contributes to *The Simple Things* magazine. She swims in the sea most mornings, but doesn't like to go on about it…